John van Tiggelen worked as a tour guide in the Daintree rainforest before becoming a writer for, in turn, the Great Barrier Reef Marine Park Authority, the *Townsville Bulletin* and *Good Weekend*, the Melbourne *Age* and *Sydney Morning Herald* magazine. He was born in Holland, grew up in Gippsland, studied in Melbourne and Cambridge and presently lives in Townsville, North Queensland.

MANGO
COUNTRY

A journey beyond the brochures of Tropical Queensland

JOHN VAN TIGGELEN

MACMILLAN
Pan Macmillan Australia

This project has been assisted by the Commonwealth Government through the Australia Council, its arts funding and advisory body, and the Queensland Government, through Arts Queensland.

First published 2003 in Macmillan by Pan Macmillan Australia Pty Limited
St Martins Tower, 31 Market Street, Sydney

National Library of Australia
cataloguing-in-publication data:

Van Tiggelen, John.
Mango country: A journey beyond the brochures of Tropical Queensland.

ISBN 0 7329 1193 1.

1. Van Tiggelen, John – Journey. 2. Queensland, Northern – Description and travel.
3. Queensland – Social life and customs. I. Title

919.43

Typeset in 13/16 Garamond by Post Pre-press Group
Printed in Australia by McPherson's Printing Group
Front cover photograph: Ray Cantrill in Urandangi. Photo: Ian Kenins
Back cover photograph: Main Street, Thursday Island. Photo: John van Tiggelen
Cover design: Deborah Parry Graphics
Cartographic art by Laurie Whiddon, Map Illustrations

For Dad

CONTENTS

FORETASTE

The Reef 'n' Beef Experience

THE TWO DISHES ARRIVED in all their dinkum glory. In the middle of each lay a slab of rump steak ridden by four orange prawns. Around it steamed vegetables and a baked potato lolled in a swill of cream sauce.

'What do you call this again?' my Melbourne friend asked.

'Reef 'n' Beef,' I said.

'It looks like a prawn rodeo.' Kegs poked a fork at the meat. 'At least it doesn't buck.' He picked up his steak knife, cautiously sawed off a corner and inspected the grey-brown interior. 'Hmm, it's dead all right. Very dead.'

'Yes, they like it well done here.' I was slightly peeved. At my invitation and expense, Kegs, who was photographing tropical Townsville at the expense of Tourism Queensland, had ordered the priciest dish on the menu. But all he could do was poke at it.

The young waiter, detecting Kegs's hesitation, or perhaps my chagrin, sidled by to ask us how our rumps were. I said fine. Kegs broke into a cackle. 'Actually, his is a little wobbly. But I'm not sure about this Surf 'n' Turf affair. Is the sum of the whole supposed to be greater than the sum of its parts?'

'Beg your pardon, sir?'

'Do you recommend I put bits of prawn and meat in my mouth at the same time?'

'I . . . well, to be honest, sir, I wouldn't know. I've not tried that dish.'

'Would you like to try some?'

'Umm, no thanks, sir. You have it.'

'I might. Why is it a piece of meat with prawns? Why not a fillet of fish with meatballs?'

The hapless waiter stood perplexed. 'I really wouldn't know. I can ask the chef if you like.'

'That would be good,' said Kegs.

I looked at my friend with fresh dread. Ostensibly we were scheming how we might twist his regular junketing at the government's expense to coincide with a four-month trip I was planning around North Queensland. To be sure, Kegs and I had worked together before on a number of magazine assignments, during which we'd discovered a shared fascination for small-town Australia. But our approaches to reportage were vastly different. I liked to blend in as much as possible, whereas Kegs tended to get louder still. These differences were exaggerated in, say, an outback pub. While I'd drink, drawl, slump, swear and wear jeans and boots even at the height of summer, Kegs (who earnt his nickname in just such a pub for being a two-pot screamer) couldn't be less subtle if he walked in naked.

I watched him gingerly pick up a prawn by the feelers and attempt to peel it. Was he really the man to take into the outback, I wondered. True, people no longer disappeared in North Queensland, at least not so often. But it would help if he knew how to eat a steak.

Suddenly Kegs yelped and stuck his forefinger in his mouth. 'Ow!' He began flinging his hand about as if it might detach from the wrist. 'It pricked me!' He was attracting attention from other diners. Not to mention the waiter.

'Everything all right, sir?'

Kegs shook his head. 'Could you peel these prawns for me?'

The waiter hesitated. His limited experience had not prepared him for the likes of Kegs.

'I'll do it,' I said quickly. Kegs paused midwhimper to stare at me. A smile began to play on his lips.

'I'm embarrassing you, aren't I?' He was smirking now. 'Could you cut my steak into little cubes as well?'

The waiter took a quick step back. 'By the way, the chef has agreed to join you later,' he said.

'Oh, good,' said Kegs. 'I was going to leave some for him anyway.'

That was the thing about Kegs. He was brazen to the point of self-harm. How he wangled his travel junkets out of various state tourism authorities was an utter mystery.

'I've been offered a car,' he told me abruptly. 'A whopping big 4WD bloke-mobile for three weeks. To promote tropical tourism.'

This was good news. There were places my car would struggle to get to. I passed him a prawn safely beheaded and peeled to its tail.

But Kegs was on to me. 'I know what you're thinking. But this is my trip, all right? I'm not going bush. I'm done with all that small-town stuff. No desert, no dust, no flies. I'm here to smell the frangipanis. I want to see the reef meeting the rainforest, not' – he eyeballed a prawn – 'sitting on top of some steak.'

'The reef's overrated,' I told him. 'It's just a big aquarium. Watching all those fish is like being stuck in a doctor's waiting room. Besides, it's a waste of a good car. I say we drive to Urandangi.'

'Urine-what?'

3

'Urandangi. You'll love it. It's a speck of a town near the Territory border. Its tourism potential is untapped.'

'What's it got going for it?'

'Absolutely nothing. That's the beauty of it.'

'Is there a brochure?'

'I wouldn't think so.'

'That settles it. I'm told if it's not in a brochure, then it's not tourism.'

I mulled this over. 'Who told you that?'

'A girl from Tourism Queensland. She gave me a stack of brochures and said she'd be happy as long as I covered a number of those. And I want to keep her happy.'

I was eager to argue the point, but Kegs wouldn't have it. 'Listen, I'm here to snorkel. I'm here to see big blue butterflies. I'm here to sip mango daiquiris on balmy verandahs while watching svelte Scandinavian backpackers rollerblade by in their bikinis, understand? I'm here to capture the "Tropical Lifestyle". That's what I've been sent here for.'

'That "Tropical Lifestyle" nonsense is just a marketing ploy,' I mumbled through a mouthful of meat. 'It's got nothing to do with the real ambience of the place. Life in the tropics is all about sweaty jocks and swatting mosquitos and sleepless nights spent listening to rum-driven domestic disputes during the build-up to the Wet.'

Kegs twiddled an empty prawn tail between thumb and forefinger. 'You know, that's not what Tourism Queensland said. And besides, they told me all that Mango Madness bizzo is a myth.'

'No way. It's a clinical fact. A researcher at the local university found that depression, violence and suicide peak here in summer just as they do in Scandinavian winters. Over there they call it SAD, or Seasonal Affective Disorder. Over here it's Going

Troppo. She reckons it's the same syndrome. Come November, the cops are flat out. It's raining in the rainforests, it's stinking hot in town, the house is full of bugs, the yard is full of toads, the trees are full of fruit bats and you can't swim in the ocean for the deadly jellyfish. No wonder the locals go loco. Their last resort is the airconditioned shopping centres.'

Kegs eyed me intently. 'You've been here too long, haven't you? Have you considered that maybe it's time you came back to Melbourne?'

I glared at him. 'You know the city makes me madder.'

'Yeah. But really, people go to *shopping centres* for relief? For their *sanity*?'

'Yes. That's how bad it is.'

'Christ.'

He resumed prodding his steak.

'So this trip of yours. What's it about again?'

I explained it to him one more time: that I wanted to rummage around the North, to stray beyond the brochures, to visit places that tourists were ill-advised, unable or simply disinclined to visit, to linger in slack-arsed hamlets and to loiter on forgotten islands. That I wished to explore life away from the bungy jumps and fusion cuisine of the presentable bits. That I felt the North's culture was special – not unique, perhaps, but larger than life – because if travel had taught me anything, it was that the further you ventured from a nation's capital, the likelier you were to encounter its culture in the raw. At the very least, I was sure, the Deep North was Australia in extremis.

Kegs stared at me for some time.

'Culture?' he said finally. 'Up here? That's a shocking notion. Culture is like light. The further you stray from the source, the fainter it gets. You're just going to be groping around in the dark.'

I didn't reply.

'You're not on the run again, are you?'

'From what?'

'From yourself.'

'You can start peeling your own prawns now, Sigmund.'

But Kegs was on a roll.

'You think you can live life as an outsider. That's how you see yourself, right? A Dutch dago clogwog, a resident but not a citizen, in this country but not of it. Always the bemused observer. But you can't go on clomping about the landscape and upsetting everyone you write about, you know. At some point you are going to have to settle somewhere and live with yourself and deal with your cynicism before it turns to bitterness. Why don't you find somewhere really nice and write about that?'

'I do like it here.'

'Really? You know what I reckon? I reckon that you like surrounding yourself with the weird, the uncouth and the ugly so you don't have to confront your own foibles.'

I looked at my weird friend. He had a point.

'You're okay, Kegs.'

'Am I? Be honest. Why do you want me to come? As a friend? Or as an offsider who can be the butt of your travelogue? Kegs, the two-pot screaming dandy from the city? Forget it. I know the genre. You'll make fun of my hairdryer, my impeccable hygiene, my longing for a latte. Take your dog instead.'

'Fine.'

We played with our food in silence for a while.

'So what do you recommend I do while I'm here? What cultural delights might I sample? Aside from Brawn 'n' Prawn, or whatever this is. What's hot and hip in Townsville?'

Somewhat spitefully I took him through his options. There were the usual weekend wet T-shirt competitions, Miss Beach

Girl contests and hoons-in-utes gatherings by the Strand. Unluckily he'd just missed the city's annual Bad Bitch Challenge, an open-air event at the showgrounds where women kick and slug each other senseless in front of hundreds of spectators. But he was in time for the World Bellyflop Diving Championships. These were traditionally staged in a seaside beer garden around an above-ground pool. Points were awarded for technique, style and water displacement, scored by how many tables of revellers got wet. Yet Kegs seemed unimpressed.

'I don't think it's quite what Tourism Queensland has in mind. Is there a brochure?'

'Maybe a flyer.'

'That's a pity.' Kegs grimaced and shook his head. 'You know what really bugs me about you? You say you want to lay bare North Queensland. But you're just homing in on the raw bits. You know, its soft white underbelly. Take this pile of Shrimp on Rump. Why couldn't we have had the coral trout? I mean, the North is way more sophisticated than you give it credit for, and you know it.'

He was right. In many respects the Deep North bears more similarities than differences to Byron Bay and Bondi. And he was also wrong. Reef 'n' Beef remains the dish of plenty on many of the city's menus, and variations on the theme are slight. At one riverfront restaurant they even do Reef and Chicken – for the ladies, presumably.

Besides, I've come to like Reef 'n' Beef. It's like two-in-one shampoo and conditioner – you get an entrée with your main, for half the hassle. Sure, it makes the choice of wine a challenge, but there's always beer.

'Tell you what, Kegs. We'll go and see King Billy Cokebottle's next gig.'

'Who's he?'

'A local comedian. Very popular up here, and with truckies everywhere.'

'We have zillions of comedians in Melbourne.'

'Not like this guy. He's white, paints himself black and tells Aboriginal jokes.'

'Cripes. Isn't that illegal?'

A burly, bearded man in clogs approached our table. It was the chef. 'You wanted to ask me something?' His manner was gruff. Perhaps he found Kegs's plate upsetting. The steak was nigh untouched and the potato now lay on top of it, sculpted into a mound bristling with carrot spikes and prawn tails.

'Do you do mango daiquiris?' asked Kegs.

The chef didn't reply. His eyes were still fixed on Kegs's plate.

'It's an echidna,' said Kegs.

The cook raised his eyes slowly.

'You're from Melbourne, am I right? We call them porcupines up here. And we squash them.'

MANGO COUNTRY

Thursday Island
Bamaga
Weipa
Coen
Laura
Cooktown
Cape Tribulation
Daintree River
Port Douglas
Cairns
Innisfail
Tully
Burketown
Normanton
Ingham
NORTH
Einasleigh
QUEENSLAND
Burdekin River
Townsville
Charters Towers
Ayr
Bowen
Mt Isa
Julia Ck
Richmond
Homestead
Pentland
Airlie Beach
Proserpine
Cloncurry
Hughenden
Prairie
Mackay

Travelling North I

I WAS THIRTEEN ON my first trip to North Queensland. Having driven up from Melbourne, my father got his family as far as the fabled Daintree River. It was our 'farewell Australia' trip – we were moving back to Holland within a month. Back then, in 1980, the Daintree was a final frontier, Australia's mini-Amazon. At the river ferry's ramp the cultivated east coast – cane fields, bitumen and mains power – abruptly terminated. We didn't take the tiny ferry across, or even board the river cruise. We just looked at the river in awe. Crocodiles were sure to throng beneath the surface, and the dense jungle on the other side seemed barely penetrable. As far as my father and our hulking orange station wagon were concerned, it was the end of the road.

Nine years later, on the run from my father's expectations, or possibly my own, I returned to the river's murky bank. This time I'd hitched north, and my ride – two stoned hippies in a clapped-out wagon without a windscreen – rolled forth onto the ferry. Two of us clambered onto the bonnet, where we stayed as the car tunnelled through the jungle. I spent the wet season in a Cape Tribulation hostel, cleaning for my keep. We swept and sweated in the morning, hit the beach and waterholes in the afternoon, the bar and pool in the evening and took backpackers croc-spotting at night. Around 2 am, well after the generators had fallen silent, the rain would come down in torrents. It was an intoxicating time. A year later, still running, having deferred my studies yet again, I returned in a Kombi van with hitchers of my own. I had a notion to write a book – in so far as I'd brought along a typewriter – but instead found myself washing dishes in Port Douglas until scoring a job as a tour guide. Five days a week I'd take a truckload of tourists, mostly from overseas, across the Daintree River to Cape Tribulation and back. My company's brochure described the trip as a 'wilderness safari', and indeed still does, although the road has since been entirely sealed.

The tour included a barbecue by a rainforest waterhole, a jungle walk, a beach stroll and a river cruise. On a good day – in winter, when the water was cool – we'd see a crocodile. Occasionally we'd spot a python, or maybe a forest dragon. But in summer, when the rainforest by day was still as a corpse, we'd be lucky to spot anything.

The trick was to raise tourists' expectations just so high that they might consider themselves unlucky not to have spotted a cassowary or a tree kangaroo. Truth was, I'd never seen these on tour either. If they missed out on seeing a crocodile, they'd usually settle for a photo opportunity behind a crocodile warning sign, with one leg tucked out of sight.

At lunch I'd play a didgeridoo, cook the steaks and swing the billy. I'd sample green ants and offer them around. And I told stories. Staple eco-tales such as how the scrub fowl builds its eggs an oven, how the strangler fig got its shape and how dinosaur plants survived the ice ages. The standard patter also featured a small cast of historical characters, such as Beryl Ruck, whose fatal dip in the Daintree sparked a crocodile killing frenzy, and Captain Cook, who must have been having a rotten time when he named Mount Sorrow, Cape Tribulation, Mount Misery and Weary Bay. And of course Christopher Skase, the late entrepreneur who transformed Port Douglas with other people's money.

At that time up to sixty tour buses were rolling off the ferry a day and I was one of maybe a hundred 'naturalist' guides on the

Cape Trib run. Naturally, dressed in our khaki safari outfits, we all exaggerated to some extent. Our charges were more attentive the more dangerous we painted the jungle out to be. Take the stinging tree. How bad was the pain if stung? Worse than childbirth, we liked to say. But really, what did we know? Most of us had experienced neither its sting nor parturition.

After a while, though, I tired of presenting the same postcard images of North Queensland, and of Australia. My so-called safari route, once a precipitous logging trail, was fast becoming an elongated theme park. Along its length sprouted an ice-creamery, luxury lodges, an entomology museum, a monstrous pub, a canopy tower, an eco-centre, and countless other gimmicky tourist traps. Natural attractions such as the Bouncing Stones, the big fig and various waterholes were blocked off from overuse. The Daintree itself bore twice as many crocodile-watching boats as it did crocodiles.

On days off, I began climbing the chain of rainforested mountains which hemmed in the Daintree coast: the Bluff, Devil's Thumb, Thornton's Peak, Mount Sorrow. Beyond them lay the 'back country', a bigger, browner place, a land I hardly knew.

At first it was the landscape that beckoned on long weekends: Lakefield National Park, the Quinkan rock art galleries, Undara's lava tubes. But gradually it became the people. Towns like Einasleigh, Cooktown and Laura were like Steinbeck novels – populated by likeable losers and dry-witted drunks. The further I went, the better the stories got.

I reduced my Cape Trib runs to three a week and began freelancing part-time. I found good stories close by, too, for the Daintree basin was as politically colourful as it was physically beautiful. Its two main towns, cane-farming Mossman and pseudo-green Port Douglas, were forever locked in a battle of wills.

Then, one steamy November day in 1993, the Daintree ferryman stopped my 4WD truck, a packed thirteen-seater, at the ferry ramp. 'You've been called back,' he said. 'Not sure what it's about, but another driver's coming up to relieve you.' I parked the truck by the river and chatted while we waited. Some fifteen minutes later, Graham, the company's popular Aboriginal guide, rattled up alongside in his diesel truck and threw me the keys. 'I'll take over now, mate. You'll want to head back and book a flight home. Your father's died.'

I gave up my Steve Irwin act not long after that. Crossing the Daintree had lost its appeal. I followed a girl to Townsville, where she'd study marine biology and I'd try my hand at free-lancing full-time.

On the map, Townsville had seemed an excellent base from which to write about the North. Up close, however, it came as a shock to live in a city this ugly. It didn't have its $30 million waterfront then, nor its restaurant strips. Water restrictions were in force and the garrison city was dry as toast. Soldiers, then aptly known as AJs (army jerks), plagued the nightclubs, or at least those they weren't banned from. Women were routinely groped and rape was reported weekly. Each weekend extra police were flown in from Brisbane to deal with the brawling.

Ugliest of all was the city's attitude to race. My girlfriend car-pooled to uni until her driver, a fellow student, gunned the car at a terrified Aboriginal woman walking along the road. 'Double points!' the driver screamed to the delight of her boyfriend, veering away at the last moment. In those first few months, we read about kerosene bombs being thrown at 'parkies' (black park dwellers) and gangs of drunken hoons beating them up. Club bouncers killed a black man by throwing him into the river, and a drunk driver was charged after speeding seven times at a group of Aborigines by the side of a city road, mounting the footpath and doing U-turn after U-turn until he finally ran over someone.

A year later, in June 1995, I covered the tombstone unveiling and accompanying celebrations in honour of Eddie Mabo, the indigenous land rights hero. It was a grand, national day, attended by a who's who of Aboriginal politics. The next morning, however, the nation awoke to the news that Mabo's tombstone had been defaced overnight. Red swastikas and the word 'ABO' had been spray-painted all over it, and Mabo's bust had been prised loose.

No less shocking was the city's reaction. In the face of nation-wide outrage, civic leaders denied that it was necessarily a racist act. 'We're treating it as a case of wilful damage,' said the police chief. 'People could have put the swastikas there to put us off the scent.' Police even sunk so low as to tell reporters they were questioning Aboriginal youths over the incident.

Over time, however, my sense of shock gave way to something else. Fascination, I guess. In its own working-class way, Townsville was much wilder than Cape Tribulation. Our neighbours fished, crabbed, and hunted pigs. The most rabid fan of Townsville's national rugby league side, the Cowboys, wore a dog collar, growled and went by the name of Mad Dog, yet he became a champion of the people. These days he's even got young fans of his own, who call themselves Mad Pups.

And Townsville did prove a good base for journalism. The North is an edgy place, fraught with natural tensions. It hosts both the country's hottest and wettest spots. People must live with droughts, cyclones, jellyfish, crocodiles, cranky cane farmers, hordes of hippies and not one but two indigenous cultures.

In the North, the race issue is real, it's in your face and it's complex. On the one hand there are the hundreds of colourfully dressed Islanders from the Torres Strait and the South Seas who festoon the Townsville foreshore each weekend, picnicking, laughing, playing football. On the other, people are equally attuned to the soul-destroying nature of the weekly indigenous welfare cycle. Just twenty minutes north of Townsville lies Queensland's largest Aboriginal community, Palm Island, one of the most socially debased societies in the western world. Runaway recidivism means rape is endemic, and barely a month goes by without a stabbing. (The time I visited, Alf Lacey, a convicted gang rapist, had just been elected island chairman, and the woman who ran the women's refuge had had her face smashed during a drunken domestic brawl.)

In Townsville itself, Aborigines occupy a muggy fringe camp called Happy Valley, literally and chronologically between the youth prison and the cemetery. Yet they don't wish to budge. Neither do those who drink and sleep in the city parks. For over a decade the mayor has huffed and puffed to move them on. With a spectacular lack of success, he has campaigned to disperse the parkies with threats, goons, dogs, lock-outs, buses, burn-offs and even night-time sprinkling regimes.

Their haunting presence seems to bring out the worst in a city that increasingly longs to be seen as sophisticated. Is it racism? I used to think so. For years my southern sensibility homed in on the parkies as tragic victims. There they sat each day, drinking and dying. But these days, having met some of them and, perhaps, having been here too long, I drive past and almost smile. Huddled in the shade, clutching their enamel mugs of plonk, they might be the men from *Tortilla Flat*. Seemingly impervious to their surroundings, they hold the city to ransom, soundlessly diminishing the chest-thumping efforts of the mayor and his coterie of backers – developers, real-estate types and media personalities – to sell the city.

For the city is terribly sensitive to criticism. Townsville loves itself – someone has to – and Townsville Enterprise, the city's marketing arm, makes it official. It busies itself with producing brochures but its main preoccupation, it would seem, is actually Cairns.

Of course, Townsville's nothing like Cairns. It has barracks but few backpackers, industrial wharves but no cruise-ship terminal, ore refineries but no luxury resorts. It has no Vietnamese restaurants, no department stores and only one internet café. And it is brown where Cairns is green. Its nickname is Mount Isa-by-the-Sea, or Brownsville.

It should come as no surprise, then, that its younger, brasher rival hogs the limelight. But evidently it does to Townsville Enterprise. For example, when a government brochure advertising a new train service to Cairns didn't mention Townsville, Townsville Enterprise demanded it be pulped. (And it was.) When a breakfast television weather map listed Cairns but not Townsville, there were protests of discrimination. And when an east coast guidebook poked fun at Townsville and described it as 'a place abandoned by God', Townsville Enterprise threatened legal action.

The local paper likes to get in on the act too. When it short-listed a number of slogans for use on North Queensland numberplates, the readers picked Paradise Central. Townsville may be pleasant enough in parts, but Paradise Central? Melanoma Central, more like it. The city boasts the world's highest rates of skin cancer. Or perhaps Mosquito World, given that Townsville's river has lent its name to Ross River Fever, and another mosquito-borne scourge, Dengue Fever, breaks out every few years. And what about Stinger HQ? Nowhere along the coast, say the experts, are lethal box jellyfish more concentrated than in the waters off Townsville.

Still, if it were up to me to pick a numberplate slogan for the

North, I'd settle for North Queensland Ay. No one's quite sure why North Queenslanders like to say 'ay' so much. But they do. A casual conversation might go like this:

'Ay mate.'

'Ay.'

'Sod ay.'

'Ay?'

'Said soddiday ay.' [I said it's hot today, isn't it.]

'Reckon. Binodder but ay.'

'Yeah. See ya later ay.'

'Ay mate.'

In his book *Glancing Blows: Life and Language in Australia*, Alex Buzo speculates that ay is used 'to signify the speaker has finished and now it's the listener's turn'. Others have suggested that the use of ay affords extra thinking time. Still others believe its origin is class-related, as in 'ay boss'. (Certainly Aborigines use ay more than whites, and doctors don't say it at all.) Yet the North's use of ay goes further, as demonstrated by the 'Stop Dengue Now Ay' anti-mosquito campaign of recent years. Many newcomers to the North found the slogan uncomfortably ocker. Perhaps, thought some, this was by design? Was it a declaration, of sorts, of cultural identity?

A visiting commentator, commencing a stint as the local university's inaugural professor of Australian literature, observed that North Queensland at times affected a 'cultural strut', which he described as 'the arrogant, aggressive, unreflective self-promotion of Australianness'. Then he hastened to add, 'But I don't feel there's a particular affliction here,' perhaps mindful of his five-year contract. 'People here are astute enough to know they're connected to everywhere else. Plenty have come from elsewhere. And their mangoes are going south.'

In many respects North Queensland is like the rest of

provincial Australia. People fish, hoon and hunt and say it's a wonderful place to raise kids. They cut down their forests yet emboss their pottery with gumleaves. They welcome tourists but are wary of newcomers. They abhor change but champion development. And they claim their resources are being pilfered by Canberra while farmers clamour year in, year out for drought relief, flood bailouts and industry rescue packages.

Yet North Queensland continues to yearn for separate statehood. North of Mackay there is hardly an editor, mayor or federal member of parliament who does not support the 'movement', at least in public. It would cost them readers and votes if they didn't, as survey after survey has shown.

The push for separation began in the late nineteenth century. North Queenslanders then, as now, felt the provision of services from Sydney and Brisbane didn't match the supposed wealth of resources they sent south in return. But a major impetus was racial. Following the demise of world slavery, the south (including Brisbane) and its British masters wanted to end the exploitation of indentured South Sea Islanders along the North Queensland coast. The North's squattocracy, however, favoured the plantation system and its reliance on coolie labour. They felt the tropics were unfit for white toil and argued the North's pearl beds and cane fields could not be harvested without the trade in South Sea Islanders. (Townsville itself is named after Robert Towns, the Sydney capitalist who pioneered the blackbirding trade.) But in the end, the nineteenth century separationists were overrun by the campaign for Federation.

These days, the case for separation makes up in symbolism for what it lacks in logic. There are three flags of North Queensland, for instance. One is occasionally flown by the mayor of Townsville outside the council offices. Another, on display on the website of the so-called North Queensland Party, features a marlin and appears to be Cairns-based. The third and most authentic is flown by Laurie Fabrellas, an octogenarian cane farmer and secretary of the North Queensland Self-Government League in Ayr. 'We're still smouldering away,' Fabrellas told me when I visited him. 'A new colony may not happen in my time but it has to happen. We don't need to change much. We don't even need a parliament, not at first. We could run the whole show from under a mango tree if we wanted to.'

Another moot point, however, is the capital. Townsville won't have Cairns, or vice versa. Bowen is keen on Bowen, but no one else is. Laurie Fabrellas likes Sellheim, a ghost town on the Burdekin River, while cowboy MP Bob Katter, the would-be premier of any new state, favours Rollingstone, a community of pineapple farmers north of Townsville.

There's also debate about where the North begins. The first time I drove north, the tropics blew in with a rush in Mackay, when the windscreen mysteriously imploded. The Kombi came to a halt in front of a billboard advertising Kev's Windscreen Repairs, and to this day I have an image of Kev holed up behind it, taking pot shots at passing windscreens with a slug gun.

Historically, the North starts with Bowen, its first settlement. But there are a number of other likely gateways to choose from along the Bruce Highway (a fine name for Australia's Highway One). Most separationists argue that the North commences at Sarina, home of the Big Cane Toad, thereby annexing the sugary riches of Mackay.

Backpackers, on the other hand, vote with their feet for Airlie Beach, the jumping-off point for the Whitsundays and party town extraordinaire. Certainly the case could be made that the North starts here with a bang. Its artificial lagoon is known as the Shagoon by locals, or the Sperm Bank, and its filters reportedly yielded eighty used condoms on New Year's Day, 2002.

Moving right along, another potential gateway is the North's biggest bridge, the Silver Link across the Burdekin. Supporters of this option like to point out that if a line is drawn from the tip of Cape York to the New South Wales border, the midpoint lies precisely at the river's mouth.

Until recently, however, the defining landmark, in my book, came a few kilometres north of the bridge, on the outskirts of Ayr. At Number 40 Bruce Highway lives Henry Petersen, perennial mayoral aspirant, mango farmer, owner of racehorses called Girls like Mangoes, Mangoes in June, and Henry the Fruitbat, and self-declared wife-hunter.

When Henry turned forty, he grabbed a phone book, started ringing Sydney girls at random and discovered that fifty per cent 'would give their right arm to live on a mango farm'. So he compiled a four-page brochure about himself and sent it to sixty up-market metropolitan hairdressing salons in order to bait 'a well-groomed woman'.

In anticipation of the deluge of mail that would surely follow, he constructed a forty-four-gallon brick receptacle in front of his house and painted it a matching green. Sadly, almost ten years on he remains single. But for many years, until it was supplanted as a border post by Bowen's Big Mango, I knew I was back in Mango Country when I passed Henry's giant gaping letterbox.

BOWEN

The Cult of the Big Mango

A DAY AHEAD OF the official opening of Bowen's Big Mango, I go looking for it. I cruise down the main street and idle by the harbour. I skirt Bowen's outer beaches. I drive north, I drive south. But it isn't in any of the spots you'd expect a signature tourist attraction to be. It isn't at the turn-off to town. It isn't in town. It isn't even within cooee of the Big Mango Motel, a good eight kilometres south of town along the Bruce Highway. I cover my tracks again, more slowly this time. Perhaps it's not so big. And mangoes *are* out of season. Yet I know it is around. The Big Mango has been big news all week. I've heard about it on national radio and have even read about it on the BBC website. The story that has everyone giggling – everyone but the people of Bowen – is that the Big Mango has been erected upside down.

The local paper and regional radio have been abuzz with debate and feedback. The Big Mango was completed at a cost of $90,000 – $60,000 over budget and two years over time. For some, the notion that it had been built upside down was the last straw. 'We've been made to look stupid,' fumed one resident. Another suggested it wasn't too late to build a Big Tomato instead, atop the local lookout, to be 'lit up at night in brilliant red'. Still another suggested that the Big Mango should be laid on its side. But many have latched with some relief onto the official, face-saving line that the Big Mango is indeed the right way up, because this is how mangoes are packed and presented to shoppers. Besides, goes the case for the defence, tourists wouldn't have a clue which way is up anyway.

As well as the Big Mango's orientation, there are other debates. There is consternation about the colour – way too bright, say some – and even official debate, in council, over the barbecue planned for its official opening. 'It's time to progress from the sausage sizzle,' the deputy mayor declared to her fellow councillors. 'It's bland and mundane.' Finally, there is alarm about its location. Apparently it has been built in a potential black spot. 'Someone's going to die for sure,' one caller tells a radio jock while I drive around in circles. Where on earth is this thing?

THE BIG MANGO IS an integral part of Bowen's tourism strategy. It says so in the *2002–2003 Free Holiday Guide and Reference to Bowen and Collinsville Districts*, which is an integral part of Bowen's tourism strategy too. 'By visiting us now you are about to witness Bowen's leap forward into the tourism and hospitality industry with the launch of our tourism strategy,' writes the mayor, whose picture looks like it was taken at the end of a very long buck's night. 'You have taken the first step by reading this magazine.'

Fifty-five thousand of these fifty-page brochures have been printed, and they are everywhere. I find them at the bakery, at the hairdresser's and at a café which uses them as placemats. Page 19 features a picture of 'the famous Big Mango which has become a talking point around the world', and I note that it is indeed installed sunny-side down. But its whereabouts remain undisclosed.

Reading on, I learn that Bowen is the Gem of the Coral Coast. It's also the Top of the Whitsundays, Winner of the Clean Beach Challenge, the Salad Bowl of the North and the Mural Capital of the World, no less. It is further a Retirement Paradise, a Divers' Paradise, a Fishing Paradise and a Birdwatchers' Mecca.

At the very least, the brochure confirms that the locals need little convincing of their home town's irresistibility. It's an impression I've already gleaned from a letter in this morning's *Bowen Independent*, in which a reader named Bruce called upon his civic leaders to mimic Hollywood's eponymous landmark. 'Would it not look great if the town of Bowen had "TROPICAL BOWEN" [written in giant letters] near the reservoirs on the hill overlooking the town? The impact would be vast for Bowen, the Climate Capital of Australia.'

Meanwhile, however, the reason tourists continue to bypass Bowen is because they can. The Bruce Highway hits a particularly flat patch after the green glamour of the Whitsundays, and nowhere is the scenery drabber than around Bowen. The turn-off to the town itself is marked by an expanse of tidal ponds which many travellers suspect is a sewage farm. It's actually the salt works. The sewage farm is close to the centre of town, behind the harbour, from where its stink mingles with that of the nearby coke works.

Still, when the winds are favourable, Bowen, as the Lonely Planet guidebook acknowledges, is an 'agreeable' town of wide streets and lovely buildings. As the North's first settlement, it was designed as a potential state capital. It is also well endowed with beaches, as hordes of wintering retirees have discovered. But these 'vannies' don't spend their money widely. Neither do the pickers who hit the town as the capsicums, melons and tomatoes ripen. What Bowen wants is *real* tourists; basically, Bowen wants what Airlie Beach is having. If only the freewheeling mobs bound for

Cairns could be made to stop and pick up a brochure. Which is where the Big Mango comes in.

In the past Big Things were little more than over-the-top promotional hoarding for highway businesses. Tropical Queensland built more than its share, including the Big Melon, Big Mud Crab, Big Cassowary, Big Marlin and Big Captain Cook, but by the late eighties Big Things, it seemed, had had their day in the sun. During the nineties no new giants emerged along the Bruce Highway. They were seen as tacky and American and, besides, the Big Banana already existed elsewhere.

But in the early years of the twenty-first century, Big Things are back and bigger than ever. The difference is that they carry not the hopes of some enterprising motel owner, but of entire towns. Tully's Big Gumboot, Babinda's Big Umbrella, Normanton's Big Croc, Proserpine's Big Barra (still in the planning stages at the time of writing) and Bowen's Big Mango are all community initiatives, spurred on as often as not by a government grant.

More and more struggling rural towns are seeing the light, and it's the glare of tourism. There's hardly a town in the country that has not called in a tourism consultant or 'future search facilitator' to guide its way out of troubled times. These consultants, sometimes dubbed 'small-town doctors', tour the nation's community halls to spruik reinvention and dazzle the desperate with inspiring examples. Big Thing or no, tourism strategies are fast becoming the cargo cult of small-town Australia, with the small-town revivalists standing in as its high priests. And in North Queensland, where once-wealthy sugar towns have looked on incredulously as tawdry, sandfly-ridden hamlets next door have attained star quality within a generation – think of Airlie Beach, Mission Beach, Port Douglas – the village chiefs are particularly vulnerable.

ON THE MORNING OF the Big Day of the Big Mango's official opening (though several months after its erection), Mayor Mike Brunker picks me up in downtown Bowen in a sleek council car bearing the numberplate MANGO 1. He's cheerily forsaken his Saturday brunch hour to take me on a tour of his precinct. In recent months Brunker has volunteered Bowen as a site for aquaculture expansion, a toxic waste dump, a new prison and a detention centre for illegal immigrants, and I'm curious to see how all this might fit in with his tourism strategy.

Mango Mike, as he's known these days, is dressed in board shorts, a polo shirt and loafers. His receding hairline has left a baby-lick of hair, and his moustache resembles a pair of raised eyebrows, but there's no hint of grey. At thirty-seven, Brunker is what's known as a can-do mayor, a man impatient to reinvent Bowen as swiftly as he has reinvented himself. Formerly known as Moscow Mike (for having attended a trade unions meet in Russia), he was a coalminer and self-confessed union thug from Collinsville, an hour's drive inland from Bowen.

He relates how he once met a contractor new to Collinsville for a drink. The contractor was nervous about standing on union toes. While he was in the toilet, someone else elected to settle a score with Brunker. 'This bloke got the first one on me and split my lip. I took care of him and went back to the bar with claret pouring out and my shirt ripped. When this con- tractor bloke came back from the dunny he said, "What happened?" "Oh, a bit of industrial relations, Collinsville style," I told him. This bloke's face just went white ay. We never got any trouble from him after that.'

Retrenched in 1997, Brunker threw his hat in the ring for the job as Bowen's first full-time mayor. At the time, the town, which has a hapless history of breaks going Townsville's way (including gold, copper, cattle and sugar), had lost a thousand jobs and two thousand residents in six years. 'The place was rooted,' reflects Brunker. 'Before that, the show was run by the usual old establishment grazier cockies in their spare time. Their focus was the three Rs: roads, rates and rubbish. Jobs weren't a priority. So I thought, "Why not go for a change of life and have a go at fixing Bowen?"'

Just weeks into Brunker's reign the meatworks closed, costing a further five hundred jobs. 'That's when "Cowabrunka" struck Bowen,' says Brunker. 'History will tell you that for any town to get off its arse, a disaster has to happen.' He lobbied hard and successfully for a rescue package, which he spent on training and employing people to 'do up the town'. The barren ugliness of the approach to town was smothered with billboards and plantings of bougainvillea and oleander. The beaches were cleaned up and the foreshore landscaped. Historic buildings were restored and the main street revamped. There were twenty-four new murals, a new town square and a new festival: the Bowen Mango Alcoholic Frolic. It worked. The business community rallied, population decline slowed, and Brunker was re-elected in 2000 with seventy per cent of the vote. He promptly awarded himself a $15,000 pay rise. 'That caused a bit of drama,' he admits with a chuckle, 'but they'll get over it.'

Nonetheless, he still calls himself a worker. Brunker pronounces Bowen as 'Boan', stars nude in the local football club's fundraising calendar, and says of Airlie Beach's lagoon: 'It's a bloody good perve on a sunny day.' Meanwhile Lady Mayoress works as a 'checkout chick' at the local supermarket.

We drive by the old meatworks, which Brunker recently tried to sell to the Commonwealth government as a detention centre for illegal immigrants. His argument was simple: Bowen was already a haven of illegal immigrants, forty having been arrested while picking tomatoes in the past two years. Yet the government turned him down.

Brunker appears immune to NIMBY (Not In My Back Yard) syndrome, having also lobbied for a prison, prawn farms and a massive regional dump. He tells me he wants North Queensland's garbage, all of it. 'Why not? There's money and jobs in rubbish.' He reckons such ventures needn't affect tourism: 'We'll just plant more bougainvilleas around them.' Likewise, when Mackay and Townsville tried to ban brothels, Brunker put up Bowen's hand. 'We're not queasy about stuff like that,' he says. 'I see brothels like I see churches: not everyone's religious; you only go if you want to.' He also promoted a scheme to fill Bowen's saltpans with sea-monkey, a form of brine shrimp popular in South-East Asia. Bowen would be the 'Sea-Monkey Capital of the World'. Like the other concepts, it bombed, but he maintains it was worth the publicity.

We motor up Flagstaff Hill, the local lookout, past another spray of bougainvillea and oleander. 'Behind it is our shit depot [sewage farm],' explains Brunker. Nearby is the site of an on-again, off-again marina development, which Brunker hopes will be on again soon. Heading north to Rose Bay, where Brunker lives, he shows me what will soon be Bowen's first up-market apartment-style resort. 'The council spent two years in court fighting [an irate neighbour] for this to go ahead. He pulled us up on every detail. Cost us about $80,000 in legals. Not to mention lost time, the prick. He would have made a good union official, actually.'

Around the headland is a picturesque little cove called Horseshoe Bay, by far the prettiest of Bowen's eight beaches. It's not yet eleven, but already scores of retirees have emerged from the fringing van parks to stake out their places. The mayor points to a number of elderly folk lolling in a sheltered stretch of seawater, like a scene from the movie *Cocoon*. 'They are there every day. I call it Had-A-Bypass Corner.'

The hordes stay for as long as four months, spoilt for choice by the town's three bowls clubs. Over a coffee at the seaside café, Brunker recounts the time his workers were laying a concrete footpath along the top of the beach. It had been roped off, but 'this big fat Victorian bloke came charging through. My foreman told him to use the walkway, so this Victorian said, "Why are you idiots doing this now? In peak season, when we all use the beach? Why not do it in summer?" My foreman looked at him long and hard, then said, "Because that's when we use the beach."'

Brunker spots a burly policeman in the beach car park. 'He's booked me twice for speeding. Would book his own grandmother, that bloke.' Brunker's not happy with the local constabulary. In recent years the town has been racked by violent crime. Elsewhere, vandals merely graffiti public toilets. In Bowen they grab a boulder and systematically smash each pedestal. Bowen also seethes with domestic violence, its courthouse issuing more protection orders per capita than any other town in the North. Just weeks after my visit, a woman was raped in the new town square, right behind a Reclaim the Night plaque dedicated to 'all Bowen women and children whose lives have been shattered by violence'. In addition, a handful of well-publicised recent murders remain unsolved.

Brunker blames slack policing for the crime wave. 'I've let off a roach bomb under the cop shop and things are going to change around here,' he says. 'Someone's got to run this town.' Yet I suspect Bowen's social problems run deeper than most. Just days later a local fruit picker is committed to stand trial for buggering a Brahman heifer.

COME LUNCHTIME THE MAYORAL tour is over. Brunker hasn't shown me the Big Mango because it's ten kilometres south of town and we need to be there midafternoon anyway, for the official opening. But at least I now know where it is. 'It's not in the best spot,' Brunker admits. 'Coming from the north you flash past it. Really, with all the trouble we've had, it's like it's jinxed. The first bloke building it went into liquidation, so we ended up with half a mango. Then the next bloke went broke, and we were still about three slices short.

'Then it's finally finished and they whack the thing in place upside down. At first people had the shits when I said that. They said, "I don't think you should advertise that because it makes us look dumb." But I said, "Turn it up." Any publicity's good ay. Who gives a fuck, as long as it puts us on the bloody map. And it sticks out all right, which is what you want.'

I while away the hour before the official opening at Bowen's cemetery, where the pioneers' stones stand tallest. Eventually I find the cairn I'm looking for. It's a modest obelisk of cemented rocks. The plaque reads:

In memory of James Morrill, aged 41 years, shipwrecked mariner who lived 17 years with Aborigines and thus is the first known white resident of North Queensland. Died in Bowen 30 October 1865.

That's it; the story of James Morrill, one of the great stories of Australian history, as Bowen sees fit to celebrate it. The story was first printed in 1863 under the title *Sketch of a Residence among the Aboriginals of North Queensland for Seventeen Years, being a Narrative of my Life, Shipwreck, landing on the Coast, Residence among Aboriginals, with an Account of their Manners and Customs and Mode of Living.* The tale tells the truth, from the other side of the frontier, about the murderous violence of the advancing settlers, and it's a tale worth recounting: in 1996 author David Malouf won the world's richest literary prize for a novel (*Remembering Babylon*) based on Morrill's life.

Shipwrecked in 1846, Morrill clung to a raft for six weeks before washing ashore east of Townsville, where an Aboriginal tribe claimed him as the ghost of a lost relative. Fourteen years later, in 1860, a surveying party landed nearby. Aboard was George Elphinstone Dalrymple, the founder of Bowen, who wrote:

Some blacks came down and we gave them biscuit and tobacco etc. being kind and civil to them, which they appeared to appreciate. They, however, began to feel us all over, and especially the botanist [believed to be John Dallachy, the man who introduced the mango to the North], *who was in good condition – smacking their lips and giving unmistakable evidences of a relish for human flesh, and a desire to gratify it. More blacks came down; they attacked us with stones and spears, when we were necessitated to fire upon them repulsing them with loss.*

But there was no Aboriginal attack. Neither were there cannibals. As Morrill was to relate later, the blacks had approached the whites on Morrill's instructions, to let them know he was there. But instead, 'a friend of mine was shot dead by someone in the boat, and another was wounded,' wrote Morrill.

Over the following months the frontier approached at a ferocious pace. Morrill learnt of the founding of Bowen (then Port Denison) by hearing that whites and native police on horseback were killing a tribe he'd spent time with in the south. Reports filtered from tribe to tribe that cattle were drinking the waterholes dry and clans were being run off their land. One day Morrill heard that fifteen Aboriginal men had been shot dead while fishing.

In early 1863 Morrill decided to approach a settler's hut near the Burdekin River. Deeply tanned and heavily bearded, he scrubbed himself to make himself as light-skinned as possible, for fear of being shot. Hearing voices inside the hut he called out, 'What cheer, shipmates!' The men rushed outside with their guns raised but Morrill added, 'Don't shoot, chaps! I'm a British object!'

Later, settling in Bowen, he remained friendly with his former tribal hosts. They asked him to ask the squatters to let them fish in the rivers, but the invaders gave no quarter. As one local station manager wrote: 'Life was never safe and the only wise thing to do on seeing a black was to shoot and shoot straight.'

The following year Morrill joined Dalrymple's maritime expedition to Rockingham Bay for the establishment of Cardwell, to try to avoid a repetition of the bloodshed that heralded Bowen's founding. However, the killing of Aborigines continued apace with the full condonation of the Bowen newspaper, which fervently backed the 'unhesitating recourse to powder and ball'. The advice of Morrill, who'd married a housemaid, was of little consequence to Bowen society. It was mostly left to Morrill's own class to celebrate his efforts: when he died the following year, in 1865, the shipping crews in the harbour all flew their flags at half-mast.

YET IF BOWEN TODAY has a hero to celebrate, a figure who might well intrigue tourists, it either doesn't know it or doesn't care. Instead, the townsfolk have chosen to erect an eight-metre tribute to a fruit. When I finally round a sharp bend of the Bruce Highway to catch sight of the thing, it strikes me that this may be the Big Mango's greatest folly. Not that it's upside down, or overbudget, or painted day-glo, or built in a dangerous spot. Or even that it's not a tomato. But that it is so utterly inanimate. There is no *story*.

Unlike, say, Normanton's Big Croc and Tully's Big Gumboot, the Big Mango is neither reverent nor irreverent. It's just there –

a vast fibreglass artless blob, which can be neither climbed nor entered. I park my car behind a fruit stall on the other side of the highway and join the crowd milling beneath a marquee. There's a mobile bar and a stand selling souvenir stubbie holders, T-shirts and caps. Waitresses buzz about with platters of crumbed prawns and fried chicken.

Shortly, the modern cargo cult ceremony commences. A choir of schoolkids, dressed in green and gold uniforms, arrange themselves in the shade of the Big Mango to sing the national anthem followed by several Big Mango tribute numbers, including one called '*Konichiwa* Big Mango'. They seem to have struggled for lyrics, but then who wouldn't.

Next the mayor and the 'Father of the Big Mango', a Dr Ingham, unveil a plaque. As well as being the secretary of the local Rotary club, Dr Ingham has been healing the townsfolk for forty-three years. He's Brunker's opposite, a clean-spoken establishment figure who pronounces Bowen as 'Beau-win' and has come dressed in a white shirt, white shorts, long white socks and white shoes. After the fanfare I ask him why he came up with the idea. 'We had to come up with something,' he says with a shrug. And would he do it all again? To my surprise, he utters a resolute 'no'. 'I fear the whole exercise has been rather wasteful. It's a nasty bit of road, this. Three service stations have gone broke here already.'

When I ask him about the reason for the mango's orientation, he introduces me to an octogenarian whose uncle bred the Kensington Pride, better known as the Bowen mango. She doesn't think the mango is upside down and says, 'It's lovely the way it is.' But a little later, with a little prodding, Dr Ingham comes clean. The mango *is* upside down. He reveals the Big Mango was judged to be too unstable if rested on its pointy end, whereas sunny-side down it can withstand a modest cyclone. After all, the town's not called Blowin' Bowen for nothing.

ALVA BEACH

The Coast of Lost Soles

ON THE NORTHERN LIP of the Burdekin delta, at a cane farmers' beach haunt called Alva Beach, a man comes charging towards me along the deserted foreshore on a four-wheel motorbike, a fishing rod held lance-like in one hand. For a second I fancy he's jousting, but instead he putters to a sandy halt in front of me and, grinning madly, gestures with his rod at the thongs I'm carrying. 'Sure you want those?' he asks.

Well, yes.

He looks disappointed. I notice his fishing rod really is a spear of some sort. By way of explanation he jerks his head at the basket on the back of his bike, which is full of washed-up thongs.

'Russell Doig,' he says, introducing himself. 'I'm a thong collector.'

Five minutes later, over a beer at his shack in Alva Beach, he explains that it all began innocently enough. 'I was away to the point a lot, travelling down the beach on the four-wheeler to go fishing or just booze-cruising with my mates, and I'd see all these thongs scattered on the beach. Then I read somewhere that someone had a collection of six hundred and thirty thongs. And I thought, well, look at all these thongs. I can beat that.'

35

Six years on, Doig has nailed over three thousand thongs to the back fence of what is now the most popular yard in town. 'When my mates do a thong, they'll come and look for one that fits and rip it off my fence. Half the town's getting about with mismatching thongs. Like me, look. I got two different ones on me feet.'

The thongs have also crept up the posts of his back patio, along the rafters and down the back wall. One corner of the yard is devoted to a 'thong-scape', an arty arrangement of driftwood and fish netting strewn with sun-bleached rubber soles. Another corner features a pot-bound 'thong-plant'. And still the thongs keep coming. 'I've got a special spike now, so I can just pick them up and toss them in a basket without having to hop off my four-wheeler.'

The fifty-one-year-old panel beater, who is single, has big plans. Last year he narrowly failed in a bid to buy at auction the glittering giant flip-flop which bore Kylie Minogue at the closing ceremony of the Sydney Olympics. 'I was gonna put that on me roof, see. I'm thinking of turning my place into a thong museum.'

As North Queensland tourism ventures go – the Floating Hotel, the Big Mango, Port Hinchinbrook – it's not the worst. Thongs are back in vogue. But among the coastal villages of tropical Queensland, thongs, known colloquially as Chinese riding boots, have long been a staple of barbecue conversation. At issue is not the sheer numbers washed up on remote North Queensland beaches, though this phenomenon never ceases to amaze visitors. No, what confounds locals is how hard it is to find a matching pair. In fact, legend has it that North Queensland's beaches are biased. From Mackay to the Torres Strait, left-footed thongs are said to outnumber right-footed ones by as much as two to one. Local beach dwellers have hatched ready explanations. Some believe a containerload of left-footed thongs must have toppled overboard at sea. Others speculate that most people, being right-footed, wear out their right-footed thong first and selectively pluck replacements from the beach. A few even suspect Asian thong manufacturers of deliberately mismatching supply (by creating more and/or tougher left-footed thongs) in order to increase demand. But most are simply left scratching their heads.

Enter science. In a breakthrough study entitled 'The Case of the Left-Footed Islands: Accumulation and Distribution of Lost and Discarded Thongs in the Marine Environment', Gary Carlos, a kite-surfing marine biologist with a penchant for oceanography, not only claims to have confirmed that northern beaches are left-footed, but he claims to know why.

Carlos's theory is a highly elaborate one – some might say alarmingly elaborate. (Indeed, the university's head of media relations is keen to stress that the Townsville scientist's thong research is not taxpayer funded. 'If you really have to write about this,' she pleaded, 'can you please not name the university?') As Carlos points out, rubber thongs are the most popular footwear in tropical countries. They are also long-lived and unsinkable. As a result, up to six million thongs are bobbing on the world's oceans, including one hundred thousand from a single container spill in 1996.

Once flushed, washed, tossed or swept into the ocean, Carlos proposes that right-footed thongs will separate from left-footed thongs as they ride the ocean currents. The key, he says, is that their innate asymmetry produces both hydro- and aerodynamic drag. Whether the thong floats upside down or not is irrelevant, as long as it still has a strap. If upside down, the strap acts as a rudder-keel; if right side up, the strap becomes a minisail and the thong reverses direction.

Either way, a left-footed thong will veer to the right, a right-footed one to the left. Observations in his pool have confirmed this. The upshot is that, in the anticlockwise swirl of the South

Pacific, 'left-footed thongs will be pushed to the outside while right-footed ones will accrue in the centre. Thus Samoan beaches will be right-footed, while Peruvian beaches, like North Queensland's, will be left-footed.' He has even come up with a thong separation equation to predict the degree of bias.

So far Carlos has only sampled a number of outer barrier reef islands to test his theory, with initial field counts confirming a 3:2 left-footed bias for thongs with straps. However, in keeping with an unwritten doctrine of postgraduate biologists – never study in your own backyard what could be studied in a remote exotic location – Carlos is more interested in discovering the whereabouts of the right-footed thongs than sampling the left-footed ones. 'Determining just which beautiful palm-fringed beach these right-footers end up on could be the key,' he says. 'I mean, the whole topic is just crying out for a pilot study in the South Pacific.'

More realistically, however, his theory sinks or swims in a pokey backyard in dowdy Alva Beach. Although Doig is not the only beachcomber nailing up thongs. Weeks later I come upon the 'thong tree' of Cowley Beach, near Innisfail, a beach she-oak shingled with over a thousand thongs. It's not so strange: its creator tells me he used to have an almond tree with five hundred teapots hanging in it. And even further north, in the Torres Strait, there is a 'thong pole' sprouting on a coral cay called Masig. Its owner tells me he wants to turn it into an archway, or possibly a 'beach thongbrella'.

But Doig's collection remains by far the most authoritative sample. Asked whether he has noticed a left-footed bias among his 3000-plus thongs, he shrugs: 'Maybe. I've never looked at it that way. I just pick 'em up and put 'em up. My worry is what will happen to them when I'm gone. I just hope my grandkids will go on with it ay.'

INTO THE OUTBACK

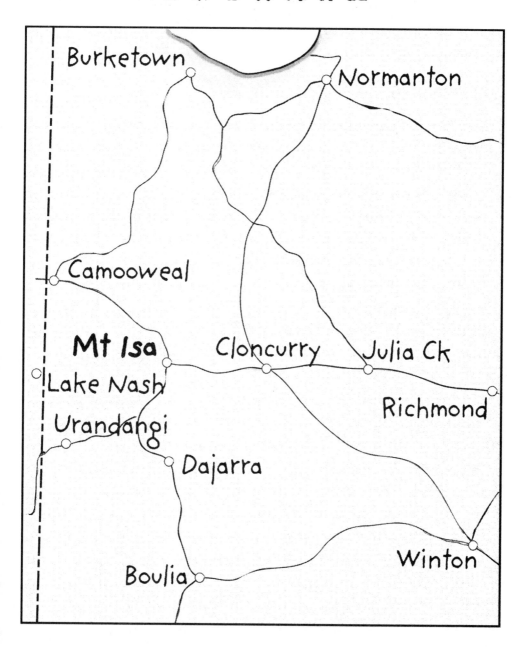

Travelling North II

IN 1990 I WAS hitching home to Melbourne via Alice Springs after my hippie holiday at Cape Tribulation. Tragically, I had beads in my hair. After a string of short rides skirting around Townsville, an elderly grazier in a decrepit ute dropped me off at Woodstock, which he'd assured me was both a town and a major intersection. It was neither. The place consisted solely of a dingy shop where no one stopped. A few cattle trucks charged past at a hundred and forty kilometres an hour, reeking of dung. Black kites circled overhead. Crows regarded me from dead trees. I was only forty kilometres inland but already it felt like a thousand.

After several hours in the February heat, with my thumb eliciting just a raised middle finger in return, a tradesman's van screeched to a halt in the gravel. Music – Jimmy Barnes – boomed from within. I ran for the slide-door, half expecting the van to take off at the last moment. It wouldn't have been the first time.

'We're headed for Richmond,' announced the driver, a short, skinny Kiwi with a handlebar moustache. I nodded and clambered into the back. There were no seats. Just dozens of drums of chemicals, a roll of carpet, a toolbox and two eskies within arm's length of the men in front.

'Help yourself to green or blue,' said the Kiwi. I noticed he had a can in his hand. So did his mate, an enormous bullet-headed brute in a singlet top. They reminded me of Asterix and Obelix. I looked in the right esky. It was filled with Fosters. I looked in the left. It was filled with VB. I grabbed a green can and sat on a tin drum. The cabin reeked of smoke and beer.

The two men were roaring drunk, though Asterix showed it less. He was a carpet layer, due to start work at a remote cattle station the next day. All morning and most of the afternoon he'd sat in Townsville's Seaview Hotel, where he'd met Obelix, who was twenty, out of work and of no fixed address. The two had drunk for six hours straight, at the end of which Asterix had offered Obelix a job as his offsider. After settling that Obelix would be paid all the beer he could drink 'and not a beer more', they'd bought two slabs (forty-eight cans) for the road and took off.

'That's when we saw you. Jack' – Obelix – 'here wanted to run you over, but we were going too fast.'

Three cans later the van rolled into Charters Towers with Obelix hanging out the window barking vulgarities at women. We ducked into a pub, ordered a beer but were ordered out almost immediately after the barmaid objected to Obelix reaching across to twang her bra strap.

I'd had nicer rides, but this was a cultural experience in the making. It was soon dark and as we left the 'Towers' Asterix and Obelix appeared to be on a quest to punctuate – and prolong – the trip with as many pit stops and piss stops as possible before the highway pubs closed. We drank at Balfes Creek, at Homestead and at Pentland. At Torrens Creek, the publican declared last drinks at the prospect of a brawl between Obelix and several station hands. Apparently a request for oral sex had not been well received by one of their girlfriends. To make matters uglier, Asterix seemed to have disappeared. Suddenly a car horn tooted right outside. It was Asterix. He'd snuck out via the toilets to start the van. I dashed outside and Obelix lumbered after me. Flinging gravel, we sped away into the night.

The cans kept coming as we rolled through the blackness. There was no moon, the road dead straight. I briefly dozed until I woke to a cold can shoved in my crotch and Obelix's fat face leering at me: 'Ya piker!' He was getting bored and began haranguing Asterix to let him drive. 'Later,' said Asterix, to my relief, but just before midnight, hurtling along at a hundred and thirty kilometres an hour, he abruptly told his mate to take over. With that, Asterix clambered out through his window and vanished. For a while I could hear him clawing for grip on the roof. Then nothing.

Obelix, having wedged his bulk behind the wheel, suddenly swung it hard. The van careened into the opposite lane, then back just as sharply. In the back of the van I crashed around with the rest of its contents. But Obelix wouldn't desist. As we lurched from side to side across the highway, he whooped and guffawed like the evil lunatic I finally realised he really was. Eventually he straightened the van. I listened for the faintest sound from above. Deathly silence.

We drove like this for ten, maybe fifteen minutes. Not a word was said. Obelix crushed another can. I stayed in the back. Perhaps I was in shock.

'Do you think we should turn back?' I finally suggested.

'What's the fucking point?' said Obelix.

'He might have fallen off.'

'We didn't put the fucker up there.'

No.

But still.

'WAAAAHHH!' We both reeled. Plastered like road kill against the windscreen was Asterix's face, upside down. Steadily it broke into a grin.

'You fuck!' roared Obelix, punching the windscreen.

Asterix dropped back through the passenger window and both began hooting hysterically.

'You dumb fuck!'

'You murderous cunt!'

'Whooohooo!'

It was too late to get out now. There was nothing, but nothing out there. And then it started to rain. Not rain. Pelt. Distant electrical flashes had been igniting the northern horizon for some time, but suddenly the storm was upon the little white van. Amid devastating peals of thunder, shards of lightning stabbed manically all around us. The plains showed up treeless in the flickering half-light. Water sheeted across the highway.

Yet Obelix refused to slow down. If anything, he seemed to want to take on the bolts of lightning and the flooded stretches of tarmac, hollering each time the van went into a skid. I was scared witless. Even the Kiwi seemed subdued. I gripped the door handle tight and closed my eyes, no longer able to watch the storm or the road. But shortly a new glow shone dully through my eyelids. I opened them and was dazzled by the high beam of a road train fast approaching. The driving rain and reflections in the wet road, which was too narrow for both vehicles even in fine conditions, reduced visibility to a blur. Yet we weren't slowing down. Obelix, I realised, was intent on a game of chicken. Last one to budge wins.

I felt sick with fear. Road trains never budge and never lose. Their sheer size and momentum – most carry three trailers – give them utter right of way. I think I screamed. I think we all screamed. A moment before impact, Obelix swung away sharply. With left wheels spinning in the soft verge and right wheels skidding on the tar, the van slew viciously back towards the centre of the road and the monster truck. In horror I watched us slide side-on towards the first trailer, then the second, the third . . . until suddenly we'd come to a halt in the bog on the wrong side of the road, having missed the back of the truck by inches in a violent streak of tail-lights.

One by one we stumbled out of the van. Our boots immediately sank shin-deep in the black mire, which had already swallowed the van to the axles. Doubtless the softness of the soil had saved us from rolling.

'You can drive now, boss,' said Obelix, the rain spilling off his gut. But we weren't going anywhere, at least not for a while. Asterix pulled clear an esky and made for the tarmac, caked in sludge.

Half an hour later we waved down the first vehicle to breach the horizon. It was a Greyhound bus on the night run to Townsville. The driver obligingly dragged the van out of the bog, and around 4 am we finally rumbled into Richmond. I doubt I said another word. As the men drove off to lay carpet, I found shelter from the wind and rain at a shut roadhouse, where I curled up on the concrete, soaked and shivering, but grateful. Grateful to have survived, and grateful because, having survived it, that was quite a ride.

The next morning, after the proprietor had served me a breakfast of eggs, sausages, steak, bacon and chips, I warmed myself by the road until a nurse heading for Mount Isa picked me up. As I threw my pack in the boot, I noticed a bunch of stickers on the back of the car: 'Wrangler butts drive me nuts', 'Bulldoggers make me horny', 'I'm a barrel racer, cowboy chaser'. I didn't quite know what it all meant, but clearly she was in her element out here. And I wasn't.

'Are you gay?' she asked me somewhere around Julia Creek.

'No, why?'

'Because you look gay.'

I couldn't believe it. I'd just spent three months in the jungle, cheated death on the ride from hell and spent the night with a petrol bowser. Frankly, I felt as rugged as I'd ever be.

'It's the beads, isn't it?'

'No, it's not the beads.'

She dropped me off in Mount Isa, her home town. The town

had all the charm of a road workers' donga and was direly in need of a woman's touch. As if the priapic smokestacks, sulphurous air and unwashed streetscape weren't enough, each morning the town awoke to a round of belching, courtesy of a daily regimen of explosions at the adjacent mine. As for the people . . . Suffice it to say I stayed two days because that's how long it took to get out. Twice I toted my backpack from the hostel to the city limits. Twice I trudged back at dusk, luckless. On the third morning I took the Greyhound bus to Alice Springs. I guess I owed the company a favour anyway.

I vowed never to return, but it's funny how things turn out. Years later, when I was stuck for a freelance photographer, a colleague mentioned someone living in Mount Isa. It seemed unlikely, and even less likely when I heard he was named after the singer of 'Rhinestone Cowboy'. We exchanged folios and met on the coast. There was a swagger to Glenn and I remember imagining the challenges of growing up in the Isa with artistic leanings. Having given up his job in the lead smelter to pursue his passion for photographing the outback, he cleaned buses part-time to make ends meet. On weekends he followed the rodeo circuit, photographing each rider with a hired tele-lens while his girlfriend staffed a stall at the ground taking orders. They'd stay up all night developing the black and white prints in a makeshift dark room, in time for the next day's rides.

But Glenn knew the north-west and roped me into joining him for a three-week trip around his beat. Bouncing around in his twenty-year-old Land Rover we garnered stories from Boulia to Borroloola about camel hunting, Aboriginal boxers and tribal law.

It was Glenn who taught me the art of outback driving: a carton of cheap cigarettes on the dash, a cold six-pack for the road, Johnny Cash on cassette and a pantry stocked with tinned corned beef, canned stews and rum. Not to mention his camp-anywhere ethos. One morning we woke to the snorts of a scrub bull, another we were roused by machine-gun fire and overrun by soldiers, having unwittingly pitched our swags in the midst of a major army exercise. I also learnt the code of bush hygiene. A 'bush toothbrush' was a piece of chewing gum, a 'ringer's shower' a change of shirt, and a 'Pommie shower' a dab of deodorant under the arms. Also, to go for a 'bogey' had nothing to do with picking one's nose. It meant to take a dip. This was not to be confused with a 'grogan'. Once, keen to cool off in a creek already brimming with Aboriginal kids, I announced I was going in for a grogan. They couldn't get out fast enough – I'd announced I was about to defecate.

There were many more trips out west after that. I liked the terrain (if not Mount Isa itself) and the wide open skies that gave up their heat at night. The vastness of the outback lent its towns and characters added definition. You didn't need to look for stories, you simply ran into them in the pub. But its rodeo culture seemed a closed shop. I just couldn't crack it. For one thing, I found as a journalist there was nothing quite so frus-trating as getting a decent quote out of a cowboy. Time and again I walked away thinking I'd have done as well to interview the horse, or possibly the bull.

True, the game dictates that actions speak louder than words. It is a hard man's culture, after all. Silence rules. No one complains, no one brags, no one cries and no one wears a helmet. No one even yells 'Yee-hah!', unless they're very drunk. Perhaps the walk back to the chutes sums it up best. Whether a rider has ridden 'time' without a blemish or copped a hoof in the head on the way down, he will pick himself up, retrieve his hat and walk back in his chaps, tassels aflutter, with precisely the same stoic limp.

I'm not the only one who feels excluded by the culture. Many

Mount Isa miners stay well away as ringers flock into town for the biggest and richest rodeo in the land. 'I live by the three C's,' is a line I've heard more than once in the Isa. 'I hate coons, country (music) and cowboys.' At night the pubs bill tag teams of strippers, the streets pile up with cans, and those who fail to arrange a street brawl can have it out in Fred Brophy's travelling boxing tent.

Yet I've come to enjoy the odd rodeo. Never mind the cowboys, at the end of the day it's all about colour and movement, albeit with a distinct American twang. Competitors' hats, boots, jeans and shirts are imported from the US (forget Akubra and RM Williams), while their kids answer to names like Maverick, Harley, Clint and Riley. My favourite spectacles include the bareback bronc event, known as the 'suicide ride', and the chaotic lunacy of 'wild horse racing', where all the chutes open at once to release wild broncos dragging ringers who must try and mount them. And of course there was the farewell appearance of Chainsaw, the legendary bucking bull, at Mount Isa in 1995. Never again do I expect to witness an entire stadium of people perform a Mexican wave for a beast. That was special.

I've even come to appreciate the Isa. Last time, for the first time, I went just for the weekend. I'd even bought a pair of Wranglers. The rodeo was on, and Glenn was up from Sydney, where he works these days. We stayed at his sister and brother-in-law's place, among the spinifex hills and ghost-gum-lined gullies on the outskirts of town, in a suburb called Breakaway Estate. Theirs is a generous pad much like any other, except that instead of, say, a pool or a garden, the house overlooks a private rodeo ring.

At one end of the arena, Paddy, the brother-in-law, and Col, a mate who runs a saddlery and has a son called Colt, had penned half-a-dozen Brahman steers. The men were competing in the weekend's steer-wrestling event, or 'bull-dogging' as the Americans call it. While their families hung out on the porch, the men took turns at chasing a steer out of the chute on horseback, sliding off to tackle it by the horns and twisting it to the ground. As soon as they let it go, the steer would stumble to its feet, shake its floppy ears and look around as if thinking, 'What the hell was that for?' Six steers later, down it would go again.

The weekend before, at Cloncurry's Merry Muster Rodeo, Paddy had impaled himself on a horn when a steer had pulled up short. He was lucky: any lower and it would have broken a rib, any higher and it might have pierced a lung. As it was, the wound looked bad enough, but Paddy wasn't worried. Equally unfazed was his four-year-old boy, who, kitted out in cowboy garb, seemed to have caught the bull-dogging craze. Evidently he likes nothing better than to ride up to the family dog on his tricycle, slide off sideways and wrestle it to the ground. He's going to go far, Glenn reckons.

As well as introducing me to rodeos, the Isa and the lingo, Glenn helped me understand something else about the outback. In his words, it's a place where a bloke can lose himself, bed down under a big sky, let himself be swallowed up by the landscape. The city is no place to feel lonely. But out west, it's okay, even natural. It's a place where nothing happens, except you.

DRINKASTUBBIE DOWNS

Boys' Weekend

THONGS ARE THE SPORTS shoes of choice for what is reputedly the world's biggest cricket carnival. The Goldfield Ashes are held in the mining town of Charters Towers every Australia Day long weekend, and with over a hundred and forty sides from all over Queensland slogging seventy-five thousand runs over three insanely hot days, uniforms are the least of the organisers' worries.

This particular year, over forty-seven fields – three more than the previous year – have been found, mown and mapped. Nine mine shafts below the main venues have been capped to protect fielders. A 207-match draw has been published in the local paper's souvenir lift-out. Chinee apple trees, on the run from CSIRO ecologists for decades, have been trimmed to provide tidy clumps of shade. And in a welcome improvement on past years, most ovals show signs of grass.

As in previous Goldfield Ashes, the committee has vowed to crack down on on-field drinking, particularly by umpires. No success is expected, however. The Goldfield Ashes remain, first and foremost, a social event. If a few teams are serious, the vast majority, bearing names like the Laid Back XI, the Bumgrubs, the Guatemala Hog Herders and the Mexican Jumping Shrubs, are anything but. Donning a dress remains mandatory in many a side for a dropped catch. So is a strict no-water (beer only) policy during drinks breaks. Others share one bat, will appeal against the light (too bright) or refuse to run singles and twos. The Hughenden Mutts field with nine slips, the Bloody Huge XI's twelfth man serves beer and sausages from a ride-on mower, and the Wallabies have been known to employ fresh road kill as a mascot.

All quaint enough, in a fly-blown, outback kind of way. Though spare a thought for the young Melbourne-educated reporter who, still struggling to come to terms with her cadet-ship at the local paper, the *Northern Miner*, was told to quit asking about cricket: 'Mate, I'm telling ya, we're not a cricket side with a drinking problem,' remonstrated Captain Aub of McAubo's Inebriated XI, which takes to the field in fetching kilts. 'We're a drinking side with a cricket problem.'

OFFICIALLY KNOWN AS FIELD 43, Drinkastubbie Downs is the only privately owned ground in the tournament. It's not easy to find. You head north out of town, past the aerodrome, across Sheepstation Creek, then turn down a red-dirt road through drought-stunted scrub en route to the weir. The property's former name, Lawn View, clings to a rusty gate like a tired joke. Beyond, a short track gives way to a large clearing, reasonably flat and roughly oblong, ringed with bleached tree skeletons and splashed with regrowth after recent downpours.

This is the home ground of Chad's Champs, a clan of mostly coalminers from Dysart, some five hours drive to the south. The Champs made their first appearance in the Ashes' lowly but legendarily friendly B2 division ten years ago — losing each of their three games. Their record since suggests they may have peaked that year.

Yet they're not the worst. In an attempt to restore some competitiveness to bloated B2 ranks, organisers decided last year to create an offshoot division, the B2 Social, for the demonstrably less focused. Chad's Champs applauded the move and asked to be demoted. 'You get teams in B2 who won't drink ay. Breaks your heart,' says the Champs' chain-smoking captain, Chad Hutchings.

Curiously, their request was turned down. It's possible organisers took into account that Chad's Champs were the only XI to play all its games at home. However, the team remains winless at Drinkastubbie Downs. As Hutchings points out, the side's sole home ground advantage is that it no longer gets lost looking for the ground. 'There are nine grounds at the airport, three at the gun club. Before we had Drinkastubbie Downs, we'd be driving around the backblocks of town full of grog and forever ending up at the wrong place,' explains Hutchings. 'One day I said to the old man, I'm sick of this. You're a miner, you need a block of land [to retire to].' His father, Al, duly obliged. The pair bulldozed a clearing, laid down a slab of cement and christened it the Sam Hutchings Oval, in honour of Chad's grandfather, a gold prospector who earnt his twilight dollars making beer-can sculptures for Cape York pubs.

CHAD HUTCHINGS WAS A rabble-rousing labourer in a coalmine the first time I met him. Two years on, he runs a hotel an hour's drive south of Longreach, in Isisford, a two-pub town barely big enough for one. In the forsaken main street one of a dozen shops still trades and, at either end, the shire's pitch to travellers is 'Isisford, Yellow Belly Country'. The tag refers to the sweet-fleshed fish of the coolibah-lined Barcoo River, but even anglers barely give the place a second glance, preferring to pursue barramundi further north.

It's a scorching forty-two degrees when I arrive at the Golden West Hotel to find Hutchings cajoling a silver-bearded local into going the full monty, evidently to raise money for the local school. Hutchings notes wryly that Australia's richest man, Kerry Packer, who owns a vast pastoral spread nearby and appears to employ half the pub's patrons as shearers, won't answer the call.

Hutchings is thirty-four. Distinguishing features include a big gut, big laugh, shapeless shorts, skinny legs and a beard like a boogie board. When he doffs his battered Akubra, he's as bald as a melon, and the beard looks stuck on. He might as well have stepped out of a cartoon. The Ettamogah Pub, perhaps. Not that the Golden West need yield much ground there. A string of motley undergarments hangs above the bar, souvenired from those eight-balled at pool, and although yellow belly is not on the menu – its sale is illegal – a raid last year did net several counter meals' worth in Hutchings's freezer. 'Never even knew it was there,' he reckons. 'I was set up.'

Early next morning, a Friday, Hutchings raids his own cool-room in preparation for the six hundred kilometre trip north to Charters Towers for the cricket. Meanwhile his wife roars off in the family 4WD without so much as a kiss goodbye. She has taken their three daughters, Phoenix, Madison and Jacobie, to spend the weekend on the coast. 'It's not the drinking she dislikes,' shrugs Hutchings. 'She'll drink any bloke under the table. But she can't see the point of playing cricket to do it.'

He slings the esky into the back of the 'F1', a hulking Ford utility, along with a guitar, a bag of uniforms, a pile of girlie calendars (courtesy of a rum representative), two shearers' beds (scavenged from the local tip) and a bagful of metal seagull cut-outs (to evoke some big-ground grandeur at Drinkastubbie Downs). 'We'll have to manage without Willie [Nelson],' says

Hutchings, clambering behind the wheel in blue overalls, hat and bare feet. He means the tape deck is broken. As is the aircon.

Not far out of town Hutchings brakes for a couple of emus and tells me to keep my eyes peeled for a white one. 'I've seen the bugger four or five times now,' he says, reaching for his first beer of the day. 'I'm a bit worried about him because a lot of the local lads like to blow 'em away.'

Hutchings is no yahoo. If he were given his day in Canberra, he'd ban individual worker's contracts, jettison the GST, jail John Laws, listen to 'blackfellas' and raise a flag for the republic. And he's a happy drunk. There are worse men to go driving with.

The five-can (two hundred and fifty kilometres) stretch of dirt between Aramac and Torrens Creek is cratered with bulldust, but Hutchings skids and slews with apparent skill to negotiate road trains, sheep, roos and a plains turkey. A bearded dragon and several galahs are not so lucky. Still, says Hutchings, 'Not bad going for a bloke with one eye.'

Eh? The F1 bucks across another cattle grid, and Hutchings laughs. 'I'm blind in one eye ay. Can't see a cracker. Lost it in the mine when a rope snapped while changing rollers for a drag line. BHP offered me $5000 to start with. When they came back with $50,000, I nearly fell off the phone. That's how I got my deposit for the pub.'

After a quiet minute I ask him how his batting's been since then. Hutchings's eyes dance. 'Got better ay,' he says.

FOR ALL THE BEERY talk en route, the atmosphere is rather subdued at Drinkastubbie Downs when the dust settles. It's not just the heat. There's a young woman present among the men clustered about the front porch. From a distance she appears to be breastfeeding, but in fact she's bottle-feeding a joey.

Jodie Hutchings is married to John, Chad's younger brother, a bull-riding car-racing pig hunter who owns a racehorse called Easily Excited and opens the batting for the Champs. The pair are living at Drinkastubbie Downs until Al and his wife Vi retire. In the meantime Jodie looks after two children, three pigs, ten sheep, five horses, six cows, three dogs, three cats, two ducks, seven chickens, a goat and the joey. To the Champs' chagrin, none is intended for eating. Jodie's one concession in recent years was to release Missy, a goat, for twelfth man duty. The side trained her to pull a cart but during the game Missy bolted to up-end both cart and esky deep in the scrub. The men wanted Missy put on the spit, but Jodie, whose use of expletives is peerless, soon put them in their place. Nevertheless, throughout the long weekend the animals seem to sense they are under siege and remain quiet as mice.

Many of the Champs have not seen each other since the last Ashes and it's noted that several are looking somewhat long in the moustache. The two who were unable to avoid bringing their families are staying in motels. The rest are camping under the stars. Says Chris Dibdin: 'Every year I come here and it gets more ridiculous – the heat, the cricket, us – and I wonder why the hell I am here.'

Of the three senior Hutchings brothers (Chad's father and uncles), Al is fifty-seven, Glenn is fifty and Sid is forty-four. Like most of the Champs, the trio works in the Norwich Park open-cut mine at Dysart. Al Hutchings looks and moves like he's fallen down one shaft too many. 'Things are crook,' he says. He has three years left in the mine to pay off his mortgage on Drinkastubbie Downs and wonders if he'll see them out. If his heart doesn't pack it in, he says, the mine might. Norwich Park's open-cut days are numbered, and there is talk of the men being sent underground. 'Thing is, we have no say in the matter,' says Harry Townsend.

'That's why we come here,' thumps Chad, their former union delegate. 'Come rain, hail or childbirth, for half a week in the year we get to feel like we're millionaires, do what we want, forget our problems.

'Between us we've got divorces, dying mums, fuck all money and kids with problems. One kid's got a brain tumour. Ringo's has got cerebral palsy. A few years ago I stopped over at his place and found the bloke bawling his eyes out. You know why? Because his kid had managed to wipe his arse for the first time.'

Sheet lightning flares beyond the horizon. The storm appears to be coming our way. 'It never rains on a full moon,' predicts Townsend. 'Not when you can see it,' says Hutchings. Townsend's offer of a wager is met with guffaws. For four Ashes running, Townsend collected cash from team-mates to be put on a horse called Harry's Game. Then the side heard the horse had died three years previously. Late at night it buckets down, but the verandah is wide and dry and the thunderclaps provide welcome relief from the drunken snores, croaking toads and the generator of the mobile coolroom.

THE OVERNIGHT STORM HAS settled the dust but left a fearsome humidity. A tin toilet on wheels, supplied by tournament organisers, swelters like a sauna at 7 am. Glenn Hutchings is giving the 'Sam Hutchings Oval' sign a fresh coat of paint. 'Dad was one of those old bushies who found nuggets where they said there were none. Mind you, he was deaf as a beetle,' says Glenn. And a cricket fan? 'Never saw a game in his life.'

A team of battles past, Finn's XI, drops by after breakfast to drink beer and trade Troy Dann jokes. Having smeared his bat with resin until it gleams like a sword, Billy Black produces a banjo. Two team-mates join in on their guitars and the pile of gold cans in the middle continues to grow. Only when Glenn threatens to fetch his drum machine does the gathering disband for lunch.

The day's opposition arrives in big hats and a convoy of utes. Slim Dusty wails from a car stereo. The extended Hutchings clan stare from the shade of the porch as a dozen rangy types, some black, some white, unload their gear by the oval. The Carneys (slang for big lizards) are a team of ringers from the Gulf of Carpentaria – young, lean and hardly drunk. Big Billy Black swears in disgust. The Carneys don't look like opposition, he says. They look like opposites.

Chad rouses his side by handing out the girlie calendars, along with a commemorative wrap-up of the Champs' ten years of Ashes glory. The latter is rather brief. Sid Hutchings, wearing a cap with a yellow duck on it (being the last to score no runs), is declared twelfth man. It's an unenviable task. Not only must he cart beer to thirsty team-mates in the field, but the opposing side gets five runs plus a beer if they hit the cart. He's a running duck, so to speak.

While Sid props the imitation seagulls on the field, his brother Al, the dishevelled curator, has a poke at the ground. 'It's come good this year,' he says, 'but you've got to watch this bloody prickly purple stuff. I've had the sheep on it, the goats, and finally had to whack it with a heap of poison.' The 'grand-stand' is also a concern. 'Each year the women and kids sitting under the tarp get sunburnt to buggery. We reckon it must be the reflection off the cars.'

The Carneys, batting first, are off to a merciless start. Shortly, two utes pull up, brimming with women. It seems the Carney Ladies won their morning game in the women's grade, for they are on a spree and are keen for some lusty hitting.

'What's wrong with ya, Carl, slog the cunt to the shithouse!' bellows one.

Harry Townsend's loopy off-spin eventually nets a wicket. One cowboy down, nine to go. Catches spill for sixes, twos trickle into fours. Ball after ball is lost in the scrub. 'Gotta get the goat onto that stuff,' mutters Al. By the time the ringers have blazed to 274 raucous runs off their allotted 35 overs, the square leg umpire has keeled over, fast asleep.

In reply, the miners last an hour. 'They shouldn't be in this grade,' mutters Townsend, after swinging and missing at ten balls in succession before one hits the stumps. 'These blokes are playing to win.' The wickets fall faster than the men can pad up. But when Colin Dibdin goes for a duck there is a whoop of joy from a team-mate. It's Sid Hutchings. 'Here you go, son,' he shouts, running across with his duck hat. The one-eyed captain saunters to the wicket wearing only one leg pad. He is clean bowled for one. Balls likewise skim by big Billy Black's gleaming bat, until suddenly he swats a ball over mid-on for six. His feet haven't moved an inch. He clips another, then another, and is caught. All out for 75.

'There's always next year,' grins Vi Hutchings. She is handing out slips of paper for the men to nominate their best contributors. The votes are returned to her ice-cream container to decide the player's player award at the end of the carnival. Sweat-drenched Billy Black fingers his bit of paper, shakes his head as if to clear it, and looks around in the vain hope a name might come to him. 'I'm stuffed if I know,' he gasps, leaning heavily on a ute tray. 'I shouldn't have run that single.'

Upon seeing his mother's scoresheet the captain declares himself a proud man. 'Three got double figures, that's an improvement. And there was no middle order collapse, no late order collapse. It was a nice and steady collapse all the way. I mean, look at 'em,' he urges, a note of earnestness creeping into his voice. His men are falling about, sweating, laughing, pouring beer down their throats. 'Have you ever seen a better bunch? We get a hiding every year and just look at the spirit of these blokes. They really couldn't care a stuff.'

The men seize an esky, pile into a car and careen down the road for a wash in the river. Four pelicans below the weir slowly take wing as the Champs, cans held aloft with one arm, slide into the hot brown Burdekin like sinking Statues of Liberty. Several make for the spillway to shelter behind the falling water, but the current is strong.

Only the captain disdains to move. By now stoned as well as drunk, he reclines in a rock pool and watches his men over his floating beard, like a rebel mullah savouring the day's battle. No one seems to have noticed the sign warning for the presence of estuarine crocodiles. But then, no one seems to have noticed they lost.

Later that night, Glenn and Sid hold court on the verandah. Backed by the drone of his drum machine, Glenn plays guitar, mouth organ and sings. Sid rattles the lagerphone, a stick bedecked with beer bottle caps. A handful of women and children are linedancing, while the men squat well away from the light and the swarming bugs. Some of the younger men head into town. There's a night rodeo on, as well as the usual run of strip shows.

Meanwhile the captain is found passed out behind the water tank. 'You reckon he's all right?' his mother Vi asks. 'The mossies will have him alive out there.' 'Nah, his blood alcohol should kill 'em,' someone answers. Vi Hutchings grimaces and throws a sheet over him. 'They might be grown boys, but you still worry ay,' she says to no one in particular, before rejoining the linedancers.

Postscript: Chad's Champs finished fifty-third out of fifty-four teams in the Goldfield Ashes B2 grade.

CHARTERS
TOWERS

Advance Xenophobia Fair, by Jingo

THERE'S SOMETHING SLIGHTLY UNSETTLING about jingoism, something cloying, and the air is thick with it when I walk into the glum, low-ceilinged hall of the Charters Towers RSL for the Fourth Festival of Australian Bush Poetry.

On stage a crimson-cheeked fat man is bellowing an upbeat version of 'Waltzing Matilda'. He's wearing an Akubra hat, RM Williams riding boots and a waistcoat made from the Australian flag. The Union Jack's on the front, the Southern Cross on the back. About fifty people are being urged to clap along, which some do, though not very well. Some seem too frail to clap.

I take a seat alongside one of the nonclappers, Henry Weare. Weare's an old acquaintance. He's wearing a moth-eaten jacket with a frayed collar and his fine hair is white as a cloud. In front of him, beneath a trembling hand, lies a plastic folder of carefully typed poems, one or two of which he'd hoped to read out on stage. But he's already been told not to put his hand up. As the festival convenor tells me later: 'Henry's past it, everyone can see that.'

Instead we watch a middle-aged woman carry on like an old one, wielding a walking stick in one hand and waving a handbag in the other. Her poem is about an outdoor toilet. She gets

61

a good laugh and is followed by a man who flaps his arms and has a cut-out cockatoo strapped to his back. His poem involves a backyard dunny too.

It's enough to make Weare tug at his holey jacket sleeves in irritation. 'What on earth are people doing here?' he says to me. 'Poetry is literature, not vaudeville.' But his is a lone, tremulous voice. Weare, who is ninety-three, is a bush poet of the old school. He writes his own verse and he'll happily read it out, but he won't *perform* it. Unfortunately, bush poetry festivals, which have been sprouting fiercely all over the country of late, prefer poems to be performances. It's all in the delivery, organisers say. In fact, there are professional bush poets who only recite the work of others.

The MC is a tubby figure who calls himself Wally the Bear. His real name's Wally Finch. He, too, wears an Akubra and waistcoat. The vest has a small koala bear embroidered on it. Above it is the word 'AUSTRALIA', and above that is a map-of-Australia pin, the kind you find at airport souvenir shops. Perhaps that is where these men buy their clothes. They look so Australian, they could be tourists.

'Bush poetry is all about patriotism!' roars Wally the Bear to the fusty audience. Henry Weare drums his bony fingers on his folder. 'I enjoy writing poetry particularly in order to remember my friends, thank you very much,' he mutters. The poets, most of whom tote Akubras, are competing against each other for trophies. The poems have titles like 'That Special Drovers Stew', 'The Power of Cooee' and 'The Pie With No Sauce'. They are long and packed with cliches. Dingoes howl, sheilas nag and billies boil.

After each performance contestants are given a report card by the three judges, one of whom is the fat bald man in the flag-vest. The others are a woman who insists on smiling like she's in a 1960s toothpaste commercial, and a festival regular who doesn't write his own material but whose CV boasts that he can recite the work of others for two and a half hours nonstop, if required.

Jotting notes behind a desk at the back of the hall, the judges appear to award extra points for the degree of drawl and the use of Aussie slang. The judge in the flag-vest, in particular, chuckles appreciatively at the well-timed use of words like 'bloody', 'thunderbox' and even 'arse'. (The word 'fuck', however, means automatic disqualification.) When I approach him during a break, he explains that what he's looking for in a performance is 'Aussie larrikinism' and the ability to 'spin a yarn'. The poems must also rhyme.

He hands me his card. It reads: 'Bob Burgess, Entertainer, Have mouth – will travel'. He's a former radio announcer and city councillor from Cairns. As a federal political candidate in 1996, he famously referred to citizenship ceremonies as 'dewogging'. He chuckles at the memory of the outrage that ensued, and how the Prime Minister, an arch conservative by most standards, refused to shake his hand at a subsequent gathering. Interestingly, Burgess was not born in Australia. 'I'm a Pomorigine,' he says. 'I'm as passionate about this land as anyone, black or white.'

Burgess attributes the revival of bush poetry to what he asserts is the parlous state of the nation. It's a national paradox: those who claim to love Australia the most are the ones who think the place has gone to buggery. Burgess feels that globalisation, restrictive gun laws, homosexuality, Aboriginal land rights and Asian immigration have laid siege to the 'real' Australia. 'The bush has been marginalised by the city, but this country was built on bush values. Bush poetry gives real Australians a chance to express themselves, to say what they believe in.'

Such as outdoor toilets, no doubt. On my way to the bar I browse through the merchandise by the door. As well as a magazine called *The Patriot*, there are books by Wally the Bear with titles like *A Fun-Burnt Country* and *Australian by Choice*. There's also a stack of Bob Burgess's CD: *Australiana Volume 1*. Henry Weare's self-published collection, *Goldfield Gleanings*, is nowhere to be seen. I return to my seat with a copy of the local newspaper, the *Northern Miner*.

Wally the Bear clambers back on stage to introduce the 'Barramundi Bard'. The bard's actually not bad, but the week's Letter to the Editor is better. It's written by a man called Smiley Burnett from Wild River Station. Though his abode sounds apt, Smiley he certainly isn't. In Burnett's opinion, the troubles besetting North Queensland's banana, tobacco, sugar, fishing and beef industries are being intentionally wrought by a conspiracy of state, federal and international governments. Globalisation and free trade are just a smokescreen, he writes. The real agenda is to 'close down the bush north of Townsville' in readiness 'for the United Nations-inspired intentions to turn the top of Australia into a resettlement zone for overpopulated Asian countries preferably of Muslim persuasion'. Burnett winds up with what sounds like a call to arms: 'She's all over, fellow Aussies, unless you are prepared to stand up and be counted. A revolution sounds more like our only chance.'

I push the page over to Weare, who nods. 'I've read Smiley's merry ramble,' he says. 'I'm not big on it. But a lot of people here are. It's a worry.' I ask Weare for one of his poems to read. From his plastic folder he pulls a sheaf entitled 'The Old Stamp Mill'. Weare is a former gold miner who still lives in the house where he was born, a rambling, festering den he shares with a clutch of semiferal cats. Nurses keep coaxing him to move, the council keeps knocking off his cats and he's been robbed too many times to count. But he likes the desert air.

At eve when shadows gently fall
Darkness descends indoors, in palls
Whilst cooling shrinking iron skin
Contracts and creeps on nails worn thin

But the air is getting hotter in the hall. On stage, Wally the Bear introduces the local member of parliament, Bob Katter, another who likes to warn of an impending Indonesian invasion. But then Katter, like most of his fans here, has never left the country. 'A true patriot,' announces Wally the Bear. 'And the dark horse in the competition.' I bid Weare goodbye and steal outside into the cool of night.

RICHMOND

The Professor Comes to Dinosaur Town

RICHMOND LIKES TO CALL itself a Dinosaur Town. Each year it stages a Fossil Festival in the main street. The signature event is something called the Moon Rock Throwing World Championships. About a hundred locals turn up, including competitors and a few curious travellers en route from Townsville to the Territory and beyond. Other highlights include the Outback Billy Boiling Challenge and the Caterpillar Loader Pull, as well as the Fossil Festival Race Meeting at the racecourse. The race card is tiny. To make up the numbers, horses may race more than once and it's not unknown for the same man to train every starter in a race. Even then he'll only admit to being 'hopeful' of a win.

The dirt racetrack forms part of the black-soil plains, which stretch for at least a hundred kilometres in every direction. One hundred million years ago the plains were an inland sea, teeming with marine dinosaurs. Even now, when it rains, the hard-baked soil turns to a glug that will bog a tank, let alone a horse. The mire later blooms into a carpet of Mitchell grass and booming mice populations sustain feral cats the size of dingoes. The cats rule the plains, along with feral pigs. Native bilbies are extinct and cattle graze just one to the ten hectares. But that's still too many for this friable country. Some years, days turn to dusk as the desiccating north-westerlies simply lift the topsoil and dump it as far away as the Great Barrier Reef.

Little wonder Richmond looks, well, a little clapped-out. And its prognosis is poor – its population is dropping, its young have fled and its vital shops are shutting down one by one. Its main industry, grazing, seems to be on a semipermanent drip of drought relief. And the decline is painful to watch, with the town feverishly clinging to delusions of a rural revival on the back of fossil tourism. But euthanasia? Would anyone dare suggest such a thing? That Richmond be *helped* to die? That the government should fund the good folk of Richmond to quit their ailing town, rather than fan false hope by propping it up? Who on earth would dare say that?

Well, Professor Rob Stimson did. Or at least that was what Stimson, the director of Brisbane's Centre for Research into Sustainable Urban and Regional Futures, was reported to have said. He didn't actually single out Richmond, or any other town for that matter. In fact, it was an enterprising regional journalist who made sure that someone took it personally. After all, John Wharton, the Wrangler-wearing Mayor of Richmond, was always good for a quote. All it took was a phone call: 'Hello, Mayor, this professor in Brisbane reckons that small towns like Richmond should be put out of their misery. Do you have anything to say about that?'

Wharton snatched the bait. 'He wha-at?! Tell that bastard to come up here and say that! We'll sort him out!' The next day other journalists followed up the story. The mayor did not disappoint: 'Stimson should be sacked! His salary would probably keep us in clover!' And, 'The professor should get out of his cosy office. Has he ever been out of Brisbane? If any government ever takes advice from this man, they will lose power immediately.

We live here because we love our town and he bloody well better get that into his thick skull. I'd like to see him come here and see things for himself.'

It was an invitation of sorts. Surprisingly, Professor Stimson accepted. After all, he'd never been to Richmond; that much was true. So Mayor Wharton decided to make a day of it. He arranged a public showdown. The professor would be allowed to put his case to the people of the district. After that, it would be the people's turn. 'We'll be ready for him,' the mayor told one journalist. 'We do still shoot people out here when they cause trouble.'

IT'S MOST UNLIKELY PROFESSOR Stimson would have had his views on the unsustainability of small towns challenged en route to Richmond. Driving west from Charters Towers along the Flinders Highway (to be renamed the Dinosaur Highway if the 'inland sea' shires have their way), most towns are in various stages of extinction. Balfes Creek, Homestead, Pentland, Torrens Creek, Prairie and Nelia are all ghost towns in the making. Maxwelton, or 'Maxy', sixty kilometres west of Richmond, is the furthest gone: it has no store, no school, no post office and, crucially, no pub. A home in Maxy costs $5000. One day Maxy will join the likes of Thalanga, Boree, Oombabia, Mumu and Nonda – whistlestops that have vanished with barely a trace.

In Hughenden, too, many homes are on their last stumps. Hughenden, like Richmond, has taken to marketing itself as a Dinosaur Town. A life-size, fibreglass Muttaburrasaurus prowls in front of the Grand Hotel. There's a dinosaur museum and the Outback Dinosaur Festival. Hughenden's green wheelie bins, like Richmond's, are encased in moulds shaped like dinosaur feet. Perhaps the professor paused to take a picture and admire the outback town's spirited display. Then again, he may have pitied it. Given Hughenden's sharply declining fortunes, the hard statistics of which he carried in his briefcase, the whole gimmicky shebang might have seemed wastefully hopeless. He wouldn't be the first to suspect that outback tourism, as an economical alternative for inland towns, amounts to little more than palliative care.

After Hughenden, the professor would have turned his attention to Richmond. Geometrically, it's a wonderful drive from Hughenden. For one hundred and ten kilometres the road aims at the same point on the hazy horizon. There's nothing to break the pattern: no hills, no creeks, not a single dwelling. Just a train line running parallel through an endless yellow prairie.

When Richmond shimmered into being, one of the first things to greet Stimson would have been a string of signs announcing a slew of Tidy Town Awards. With a flicker of trepidation, it might have struck him that civic pride in Richmond was a serious matter. And the town *is* tidy. Bougainvilleas blaze along the main street. Nature strips are green. Vacant blocks have been rid of debris. And, curiously, at least a dozen houses feature terracotta letterboxes in the shape of seahorses.

In the centre of town the Dinosaur Highway does a dogleg; the facing corner is graced by what looks like an enormous crocodile. At eleven metres long, with a three-metre jaw and fifteen-centimetre teeth, it's a life-size replica of *Kronosaurus Queenslandicus*, a dinosaur discovered on a nearby station. Behind it is a new museum about ancient marine life, which includes Richmond's only coffee shop, the Moon Rock Café. Richmond's main street peels off behind Kronosaurus Korner. The professor may have puzzled over the fact that, as in Hughenden, the main street is hidden from the highway. It's a legacy of rumbling road trains and the days before bitumen.

Even today, signs along incoming dirt roads request drivers to stop and 'dust your tyres'.

The shops look bright and colourful, as the Tidy Town judges must have noted. If the professor looked closely, however, he may have observed that the freshness is literally a facade. Though the fronts are newly painted, the shops' sides are slumped and peeling and several are empty. Elsewhere the town's a dustbowl of vacant lots and dilapidation. It wouldn't have been overly negative for the professor to surmise that Richmond was mutton tidied up as lamb. Good for a pit stop, perhaps, but you wouldn't want to spend the night. Let alone live there. But try telling *that* to those who do.

I ARRIVE IN RICHMOND late afternoon and check into the Federal Palace, a rickety old pub infused with the warm sulphurous smell of bore water. The railing along the verandah is loose and nails stick out of the floor, but there's a pleasant breeze. Downstairs, the pub menu stars Surf 'n' Turf and the barmaid sports a mullet. It's quiet, being the night before 'payday' for those on welfare.

I walk down the street to a showy brick motel, the Ammonite, diagonally across from Kronosaurus Korner. The man at reception looks familiar, but I can't place him. I ask him if Stimson's arrived. 'Yep. And we're not letting him go till we're done with him.' It's John Wharton, the mayor, and he's in a fine mood. Attracting Stimson proved a coup for his motel as well as his town. Journalists and municipal types have come from as far as Townsville and Mount Isa for the showdown. As well, a TV crew has checked in to film a segment on fossils for a holiday program. Wharton's impressed. 'It's Glenn Ridge, mate,' he intimates with a knowing wink. 'We got a professor *and* a celebrity in town.'

Wharton is a grazier who has invested in tourism as the future. As well as owning the motel, he's chairman of the council-operated Kronosaurus Korner. It's a rather cosy arrangement, as the owner of a rival business points out. Her struggling motel is located on a third corner, opposite both Kronosaurus Korner and the Ammonite. There are grumbles that the mayor has his finger in too many pies, and that Kronosaurus Korner has sent other businesses bust, like the bakery. But most Richmonders approve of Wharton: he's a charismatic leader and a sound salesman. For instance, Wharton likes to say Richmond's population is 1200. It's a very generous figure. Census figures show the entire shire just shades 1000. Richmond's population is actually about 650.

Wharton shows me into his motel dining room. 'Pick the academic,' he says, grinning. Stimson is sipping wine at the bar, surrounded by thick-necked station owners clutching beers. He's short, pallid and bearded. To my consternation, he also has a severe facial tic. Before I'd thought him brave. Now I'm concerned he's got a death wish. Surely Wharton, whose main affliction is a swagger, will wipe the floor with him at the next day's forum.

I approach Stimson and ask if he wishes to repair to the bar of the Federal Palace, which, presumably, is not owned by Wharton. But Stimson assures me he's all right. 'I'm not scared. I've done these kinds of things before,' he says. 'I'm here as a guest, not a captive. At least I think that's the case.'

At dinner it quickly becomes apparent that the professor is without a single ally among Wharton's dozen or so selected guests. Seated next to me is a moustached man from the Mount Isa Chamber of Commerce, who tells me he's 'wound up like a ball of twine' over Stimson's comments. The woman opposite mentions she expects no less than a public apology. Yet the initial mood is restrained. The mayor recommends the steak. The professor orders the chicken. Perhaps his twitch is keeping the critics at bay.

After dinner, however, tongues loosened by wine and beer, Stimson is asked to clarify his reported statements. In reply, he reaches for a copy of his presentation. It's a dry-as-dust dissertation on the statistics of rural decline. But Wharton waves it away. 'C'mon, Professor! You don't need statistics to see what's going on. You have a look around you. Is this town going backwards? Is it? I mean, come on! Queensland's tidiest town! In all of Queensland! What does that tell you? Going backwards? Going great guns, more like it. Tourists love these little towns. They get out here and they love it. You tell me we are dying. Go on, tell me!'

But Stimson is not given the chance to tell anything. Feebly he offers some salient points, but no one wants to know. 'Decline? What decline?' is the refrain. The discussion goes nowhere and certainly never reaches what I'd thought was Stimson's genuinely contentious point, that people living in dying towns be given incentives to move to more prosperous areas. Instead it's stuck on hubris. One station owner, the man who discovered the first dinosaur fossil, blithely asserts Richmond's population will one day stabilise at around 6000. As Stimson packs away his presentation, he says to me, 'All I can do tomorrow is give them the facts. If they don't want to listen, then that's that.'

THE NEXT MORNING ABOUT a hundred people show up at the Richmond shire hall. To pad out the show, and possibly to lend it a vestige of pomp and ceremony, John Wharton has put two politicians, including Bob Katter, and a pro-small-towns

academic on the bill as well. But the main stoush, the one everyone has come to see, or hear, is Wharton versus the professor.

Wharton's speech precedes Stimson's. It's a swashbuckling affair
delivered off the cuff with one thumb looped in his trademark
Wranglers. All Richmond needs, says Wharton, is water. And that
shouldn't be a problem; a couple of dams will do the trick, and the
plans are already in the pipeline. 'Because when it rains up here, it
really rains. Not like the drizzle down south.' After that, he
enthuses, the sky's the limit. Aside from a burgeoning tourism
industry, Wharton's vision for Richmond includes a vast expanse
of cotton fields and aquaculture ponds. At a stretch, Wharton sees
Richmond exporting red-claw yabbies, sleepy cod and barramundi to Asia. And goats. Hundreds and thousands of goats.
'Goats are the most eaten meat in the world, because all the
Muslims eat it. And there's a lot of Muslims,' he says.

Such is Wharton's bravado that the audience appears convinced. For a while I'm nodding along too. (Never mind that
Richmond's last mayor went broke trialling cotton. Or that even
if it does *really* rain in Richmond, when it evaporates, it *really*
evaporates. Indeed, the risk of salinity from wholesale irrigation
would be huge, especially over a former inland sea . . .)

But Wharton hasn't finished yet. He assures those gathered
that Richmond is not declining, that its young are not leaving
and that census figures are bogus. 'Don't trust data!' he urges the
paranoid, the gullible and the faithful. 'Being a cattleman, I
know cattlemen understate the amount of cattle for the taxman.
So if someone asks us how many people live here, you'll be told
two when there's another three hiding around the corner. We
don't deal with stats and data. We deal with reality. You try and
rent a house here: you can't. The place is full!'

Finally it's Stimson's turn. Data, the bare facts, are all he has.
'I'd like to talk about reality too,' he begins. His language is

emotionless but the figures are stark. He beavers through them, relentlessly and with barely a twitch. Laying out the effects of globalisation, he shows that nationwide, livestock farming is shrinking. The country no longer rides on the sheep's back. Nor on the cow's back, for that matter. And it's unlikely to be riding a goat in future. He shows how inland Australia's share of GDP has dropped and will continue to drop. He shows that the rural young will continue to be attracted to cities, where income growth is twice as high as in small towns. And he states bluntly that the bush needs to come to terms with the fact that it is nowhere near as important to the rest of the nation as it once was.

What he doesn't do is name the towns that have reached economic shutdown. But they're there, he says. Specifically, Richmond will continue to decline, but there are towns doing much worse, such as Hughenden. The latter's population has plummeted by twenty-five per cent in the last fifteen years, and by 2021 it is projected to become 'the oldest town in inland Queensland', with half its residents aged over fifty. 'We can't dispute these figures. We have to accept them,' the professor pleads. He goes on to say that while the towns may survive, their shires won't. Particularly in western Queensland, amalgamation is long overdue. It's a brave call, because Richmond, one of the smallest shires, would be one of the first to go, which means John Wharton would be out of a job. But no one reacts, because no one is listening.

Outside, on the steps of the hall, Wharton is met with a cordon of reporters and supporters. He's as triumphant as they are fawning. 'Well, we sure showed the professor what we're made of,' he says, nodding curtly to Stimson as he squeezes past.

Stimson gives a quick wave in return. He makes his way down the street alone but seems cheerful enough. 'Barramundi,' he chortles. 'I'd like to see that.' However, it turns out he's stuck for a ride back to Townsville, where he's due to catch a plane south. He approaches several of us for a lift. I tell him he's welcome to join me, but I'm heading west. 'No thanks,' he says quickly. 'This is far enough for me.' But his luck has run out, it seems. The only one heading directly east that night with room in his car is John Wharton. It's going to be a long, long drive.

CLONCURRY

In the Eye of Cyclone Bob

IF AUSTRALIA WERE TO accede to North Queensland's wishful thinking and anoint it a seventh state, Bob Katter would be premier. Katter, thumbs looped in his belt, is the North's man on the porch and his frequent tirades against 'all the over-educated pissant pygmies, parasites and petty obsequious nobodies running the joint' – by which he means Canberra politicians, Brisbane politicians, Sydney homosexuals, United Nations representatives, free trade apparatchiks, former colleagues, banana importers, anyone from Melbourne, the southern media, multinationals, supermarket chains, High Court judges, land rights activists, bureaucrats, economists, marine scientists – have won him many votes.

Bob Katter comfortably holds the federal seat of Kennedy, which covers the bulk of North Queensland. Stretching from the Northern Territory to enclose the Gulf, the Atherton Tablelands and most of the coast between Townsville and Cairns, Kennedy is Australia's fourth biggest electorate. Only seats based on deserts are bigger.

Katter has not one but two electoral offices, some 1150 kilo-metres apart, in Innisfail and Mount Isa. There are a further one hundred and forty towns in his electorate, each of which he likes to visit at least once a year. Like his father before him, he is, to all intents and purposes, wedded to his seat. He grew up in Cloncurry, lives in Charters Towers and works in Canberra under duress. He hates the nation's capital with a passion. This, if nothing else, makes him a man of the people.

His staff are fond of him: they refer to him as Cyclone Bob. There's a host of reasons, but fury is not one of them. Although he might come across as a shoot-from-the-hip maverick in the national media, his staff know it's an act. Within the mothering confines of his office his wrath is as sooky as that of a puppy scorned. Rather, his cyclonic tendencies include never being on time, a dizzying ability to seed confusion, and a front that's unrelentingly full-on. A colleague from Canberra once described joining Katter's campaign trail as follows: 'Imagine a date with Steve Irwin [the man behind TV's maniacal "Crocodile Hunter"]. Now treble the pain.'

Fortunately for his staff, Cyclone Bob cannot be in both electorate offices at once, even if this detail often seems to escape him. He has a habit of double-booking himself, and much of his staff's time is spent unravelling the resulting tangles. As one of them tells me, 'We try to leave a day or two open each week for Susie [his wife], but Bob never says no to anything. Besides, as soon as he's been home a few days, Susie will ring and tell us, "Please, you have him, I've had my turn."'

I'M ABOUT TO HAVE a turn, too, having rung Katter's office to request some time with him on the road. 'Hey, listen to this, we've got someone offering to look after Bob for three days!' a receptionist announces to fellow staff. A few days later his electoral secretary rings me with his itinerary and wishes me luck. 'Better you than me,' she says lightly. 'Ring us afterwards. You'll need debriefing.'

A week later, having left my car in Mount Isa, a Greyhound bus drops me off at 5.30 am in Cloncurry, the town that lays claim to being Australia's hottest for having once breached fifty-three degrees in the shade. The Post Office Hotel kindly lets me check in at six, and I spend the intervening time holed up at the only place that's open, a twenty-four-hour service station, captive to a manager spitting chips about local water restrictions. He's been fined three times in the past fortnight for sprinkling his garden, and it's only April. The rains aren't due for another eight months.

I've arranged to meet Katter at a meeting of the Country Women's Association, where he's due to give a speech. I walk across to the shire hall where a formidable, rigidly upright woman with tautly groomed hair, a pink silk scarf and red lipstick is supervising arrangements.

From the doorway, I watch her tick off a short, nuggety woman with a slight stoop. The latter, who turns out to be the Cloncurry CWA branch president, shuffles off muttering under her breath. Next the tall woman, who is the state president, rounds on me. 'And who are you?' she demands sharply. I bumble an explanation. 'You are here for Bob Katter? Are we not interesting enough for you?' Feebly I explain myself further. A hint of a smile plays on her lips. 'Three days with Bob? Are you not well, dear boy?'

I step back into the sun to ring Katter. It's a quarter to nine. He's parked on a lookout just out of town. 'I'm having a spiritual uplift on Black Mountain,' he says. 'A little nostalgia to start the day. I'll be there in five minutes.'

I tell him he's on at eleven.

'Oh? Am I? And it's at the RSL?'

'No, the shire hall.'

'Not the RSL hall?'

'No, you're thinking of the Anzac Day function. That's tomorrow.'

'So what's this today?'

'CWA.'

'Oh. And when am I on?'

'Eleven. After McGrady [the state member]. He's on at ten-fifteen.'

'Am I? I thought I was on at eleven.'

'You are.'

'Right. And where is it?'

I cross the blazing street to snatch breakfast at the bakery. After a few minutes a silver hire car pulls up in front of the council chambers opposite. Katter emerges with a phone clasped to his ear. He dons his white stockman's hat, tugs it down low over his forehead, runs a thumb inside the belt of his trousers and puffs his chest. A few elderly Aborigines are sitting on some steps nearby. Katter approaches them with arm outstretched. 'Bob Katter,' he announces. They laugh. 'Yeah orright, Bob. We know you. How you bin keeping?'

I head across to introduce myself, but Katter draws first. 'Bob Katter,' he says, hand out in a flash. 'Good to meet you. Wait here, while I go in and greet the ladies.'

He's back so fast he can only have run into one woman. 'Phew,' he says. 'It's heavy in there. Apparently I'm not on till eleven. Let's go for a drive.' He points his key tag at the car only to set off the car alarm with a shrill blast. 'Darn,' he says, pressing buttons in a feverish attempt to turn the thing off. I keep an eye out for the state president, but Katter eventually silences the car and we make a clean getaway.

In the car Katter immediately gets on the phone. With his free hand he steers slowly, absent-mindedly along the sun-bleached Cloncurry streets, up and down gravelly dead ends, to the aerodrome and back. I assume he's showing me the sights. We pass the stock saleyards, the cemetery, a donkey. All the while he rattles away into his phone. 'You know that man [a Queensland minister] is a contemptible bacterium. The blackfellas are ready to spear him. The bastard sold them out,' he tells one caller. And another: 'That woman [politician] has got a real chip on the shoulder. Mind you, if I was as ugly as her, I would too.' And to a banana farmer: 'That bloody [Minister of Agriculture]. If I get near him, I won't trust myself, I'll throttle him.'

I look at Katter behind the wheel. Side-on, he looks like a boxing albino. Beneath a thatch of snow-white hair his nose is hooked but flattened, such that its tip and his upper lip, which is drawn back in a semipermanent snarl, seem capable of grip. Every so often he interrupts himself to point to something: his family's old shops, the house he grew up in, the creek tangled with rubbervine where he was caught skinny-dipping and the grove of prickly acacias where he and his mates spied on young couples 'magnificently advancing the course of science'.

We pass the stockyards, the cemetery, a donkey. Again. The streets are wide and lashed with burn-out marks. I count three saddleries, four pubs and a gun-shop. The town subsists on cattle but booms and busts on minerals. Mostly it's copper but over time its craggy red hills have yielded lodes of gold, silver and uranium.

When we lap the donkey a third time, I let Katter know. We pull up overlooking the town dam, on Chinaman Creek. It's barely a puddle. 'I'll always love this town,' says Katter. 'I was born here, you know. Well, not technically. Technically I was born in Brisbane. But Cloncurry gave me the most exciting childhood anyone could have. Every day was a new adventure.'

KATTER IS NOT A complex man. As a kid, he longed to be one of the Curry boys. As a politician, that has not changed. Much of his political energy is spent playing up to the fears and prejudices within his electorate. For years he managed to do this from within the National Party, barking at shadows and snapping at the heels of its Coalition partner. But in the end it got a little embarrassing for the Nationals. Whenever the party wished to go forwards, Katter was peering backwards. An unreconstructed bush populist, he talks of globalisation, rationalisation and privatisation as diseases akin to foot-and-mouth. He wants a return to tariffs, subsidies and one-town shires.

'My motivation [for quitting the party] was a matter of tribal loyalty. I had to stick by my mates, the people of Kennedy. It comes well ahead of party loyalty,' he tells me. As an independent, Katter is all bark and no bite. It seems to be a role he relishes. He's been seen heckling former colleagues at public rallies and does a fine line in righteous indignation. Take an altercation on a Qantas flight not long after our meeting. While boarding a Townsville-bound flight in Cairns to attend a cane farmers' protest rally, Katter accosted a government mandarin by telling him he'd have blood on his hands 'when our poor farmers are killing themselves'. Katter was escorted off the plane but the resulting publicity only boosted his maverick status.

Katter's political nous resides in showing voters that whenever they hurt, he hurts. And whomever they hate, he'll bark at. (He's not really the hating type; he's a keen Christian. But he likes to impress his hardline mates.) In parliament he once voted against legislation overturning Tasmania's antiquated anti-gay laws, though those close to him claim he's no homophobe. Similarly, he attacked the Sydney Mardi Gras by declaring: 'If the poof population of NQ is any more than .001 per cent, then I'll walk to Bourke backwards. Mind you, if the percentage is what they say it is in the rest of Australia, I think I'll take to walking everywhere backwards.'

KATTER AND I RETURN from our three circumnavigations of the town for a bacon sandwich at his motel, adjacent to the bowls club. His phone lies on the table and every now and then he casts it a puzzled look because it's not ringing.

Back at the shire hall we pause at a Telstra stall laden with stationery and other giveaways. The CWA conference is being sponsored by the telecommunications giant as part of a push to win bush support for its planned privatisation, to which Katter is firmly opposed. I ask about the 'Dial Before You Dig' stickers on display. The representative explains that careless earthmoving activity by graziers and councils is behind a spate of recent communications blackouts in western Queensland. 'People think it's our fault, but it's not,' he says. Moments later Katter says to me, 'It is their fault, you know. Lying dogs.'

The conference delegates comprise about twenty-five women dressed in demure rural hues. Katter takes the lectern with a boyish swagger. His speech is off the cuff and folksy. It begins with a few hometown vignettes, switches to a meandering homily to his mother, and soon swings into a classic Katter rant against Canberra, awash with dubious data and punctuated by shrill screams of indignation.

Deregulation and competition policy are 'strangling our farmers', he says. Blaming free trade for rural population decline, he urges his audience to 'spit when they hear the term . . . If you don't fight, you will die,' he exhorts the women. 'Your towns will die and your country will die.'

The women remain unroused. Few wouldn't have seen Katter

perform before. But he's hardly in gear yet. He urges women to fight – by having babies. 'To the lady in the yellow shorts, how many people do you think we'll end up with if we maintain our current birthrate?' he asks the leggiest member of the audience. 'Well, I'll tell you. In 2101 we'll end up with just six million people.'

Several seniors nod. The CWA is traditionally safe ground for conservatives like Katter, a father of five himself. But when he takes a swipe at childless career women – 'of the ones I know, they've turned into bitter, twisted, lonely old people' – the state president, seated behind him on stage, rolls her eyes, and several of the younger members of the audience (who turn out to be nurses) exchange glances.

Katter barely pauses for breath. It's all one grand vision from here. He declares north-west Queensland can support a population of 80 million (about 2000 times its present level). 'Our black soil is the best in the world. It starts at the airport in Cloncurry and stretches all the way to Hughenden. All we need to do is water it and populate it.' Let's turn the rivers inland and dam them, he says. Let's farm the coast for prawns. Let's mine the beaches for silica. And let's take in 350,000 migrants a year.

It's unlikely the women are with him on this last point. And on the others, even a Greenie would be hard put to take him seriously. Katter winds up his performance with a Henry Lawson poem about the country being in possession of the banks, then takes his seat and switches his mobile back on.

At lunch I watch Katter insinuate himself into various huddles. When the women back away, he merely presses forwards, so that the huddle sidles across the floor, like a very slow waltz. His ploy is to relate local anecdotes which he regards as 'the stories of his tribe'. These he invariably finds uproarious. For instance, he relates the story of an unpopular local who 'walked into the

Kajabbi pub, laid his revolver on the bar and said, "I'm going to kill myself."' His voice ascends in pitch: 'Kill himself? Every second person . . . hee, hee, hee . . . in the place . . . hee, hee, hee . . . gave him their gun, including the barman.' At this, Katter's face screws up with convulsive laughter, yet no one else is smiling. (Interestingly, Katter always laughs with his eyes shut, which perhaps makes it easier to laugh alone.) Then, descending into seriousness just as suddenly, he adds, 'The unfunny ending, of course, is that he did end up shooting himself later. Poor bugger.'

After lunch a school principal rings to remind Katter he's running late for a flag presentation to some schoolchildren down the road. We hurry outside, where Katter gives chase to a woman striding to her ute. It's the young woman in the yellow shorts. By the time he reaches her she's belted up and about to start the car. 'Bob Katter,' he says, stabbing a hand through the window.

Katter finally makes it to his car, only to find he's lost the keys. After a fifteen-minute search, we eventually reach the school, where he poses for a photo, teaches the kids how to fold the flag and regales them with bush poetry. I excuse myself and leave them to their fate.

IF ONE MEASURE OF a good politician is not what he does, but what he's seen to be doing, then Katter is superb. Gradually I come to see there's method to his madness when, for instance, instead of holding phone conversations in private, he keeps his mobile glued to his ear while driving around or pacing along the street, popping in and out of doors, waving quick hellos. It maximises being seen.

Between leaving him at the school and meeting him for dinner, I learn he has popped into the shire offices for tea, as well as into the public bars of two hotels. And he's not even in campaign mode. The Country Women's Association dinner (a roast followed by pavlova) is at seven in the dining room of the Leichhardt Hotel. The red wine is poured from a chilled four-litre cask, but if it's good enough for the state president, it's good enough for me. She's turned into fine company: while sampling the mint-flavoured pavlova cream, she comments drily: 'Yum. Toothpaste.' The other women pretend not to hear.

After dinner, official courtesies are exchanged, song books are handed out and a guitar materialises. The women break into a Dolly Parton song but Katter doesn't join in. 'You're losing votes here, Bob,' the state president chides him. More songs are sung, mostly Girl Guide ditties and treacly patriotic tunes. Katter disappears. The state president requests a Bob Marley number, 'No Woman, No Cry', but alas, in vain. When the bush poetry starts, and Katter still doesn't return, I go looking for him.

I find him at the bar in animated discussion with three transport workers. The issue is Cloncurry's water supply. It's paltry and runs brown. One of the workers reckons the problem is 'too many over-educated deadshits. I could solve our water problems in a day'. He proposes to dig a trench to a river thirty-five kilometres away. 'Whoosh, arse over tit, down she comes.' Katter considers this and says, 'You're right, why the freak didn't I think of that?'

I bid them goodnight and return to my pub room. At 5.30 am, however, I wake to the sound of movement out on the verandah. Five quarry workers, having finished their night shift, are downing a few rums. Down below a huddle of people has gathered around the xenotaph in the middle of the intersection for Cloncurry's Anzac Day dawn service. Among them is Katter, his white noggin gleaming in the street light. 'Dunno about having it in the street,' says one of the workers. 'One road train and there won't be anyone to go marching.'

Two hours later I meet Bob at his motel. He's on the phone about the Curry's water problem. After snatching the comple- mentary biscuits and ordering a bacon sandwich to take away, he heads for Mount Isa, where he's due to lay a wreath at the city's Anzac Day service.

Once we're safely out of mobile phone range, I'm finally free to pick his brains. He tells me about his dream for North Queensland statehood. 'Australia is not the land of opportunity any more. North Queensland can be.' He proposes the coastal hamlet of Rollingstone to be the capital. 'Not Townsville. Everyone hates Townsville.' At fifty-seven, he hopes to see state- hood happen in his lifetime. 'What really hurt the new state movement was [former Queensland premier] Joh Bjelke-Petersen. Every time we in the North wanted something he bloody well gave it to us. It made it a bit hard to whip up enthusiasm.'

After trying his hand at copper mining, running cattle and selling insurance, Katter spent eighteen years in Bjelke-Petersen's arch-conservative government (while Katter senior held the fort federally). Though portrayed as a redneck down south, as a minister Katter junior was behind some much-needed reforms in Aboriginal politics, including the creation of community councils. He was also one of the few to emerge squeaky clean from the corruption scandals that ended Bjelke-Petersen's reign.

Katter still pines for those days. He tells me how he once accidentally tuned into Radio National, the channel favoured by left-leaning educated types. To his surprise he heard 'some sense for a change . . . This fellow I was hearing was saying terrific things. I thought he was a legend! And you know who it was? It was me! I didn't recognise myself because I'd done the interview so long ago.'

Apropos of nothing he breaks into a poem about angry cane cutters. We're driving at a hundred and thirty kilometres an hour, even though he's lost his licence for speeding on this high-way before. He slows down to take in the orange-red splendour of the hills. 'You know I've never been overseas?' he says. 'Not once out of Australia. People ask me why not, when as a federal parliamentarian I'm entitled to at least one first-class trip for two to anywhere in the world. But why would I want to when I haven't even walked the length of the Yamamilla Range?'

The which? 'These hills here,' he says with a wave of his hand at the parched domes around us. 'Mind you, declining these trips drives [my wife] Susie nuts. She loves to travel.'

Katter is not so much coy as deliberately circumspect about his racial heritage. I've read he's of Lebanese descent, and have been told one of his ancestors was an Afghani camel-driver, but he won't confirm or deny either. Instead, he hints that he may have some Aboriginal in him.

'I'm of dark complexion so I'm part of the Curry mob and that says a lot about me. I won't disown any of the racial back-grounds. So many people in the Gulf are of part Aboriginal descent, and I think that's a good thing.'

Katter tells me that like most kids in Cloncurry, he was raised on goat's milk. 'It was a goat-based society.' But his family were traders and relatively wealthy. They ran stores as well as the picture theatre, where Aborigines sat separate from whites until Katter senior lifted the colour bar.

In a town of miners' kids and ringers' sprog, little rich Katter felt a wimp. 'My mother sent me to school in socks and tie. I was the only kid with shoes.' He wanted to belong and got himself some mates who could fight. Sent to boarding school in Charters Towers, he suddenly found he was tougher than most. He also had the gift of the gab and he could run. He went on to study in Brisbane, where he met Susie.

When he returned to Cloncurry to run the picture theatre,

however, he found the social hierarchy unchanged. Stockmen's sons still spoiled to beat him up. 'I was a target, I'd been to uni,' he reflects. 'If you want to understand Australia, come to Cloncurry. We like wearing big buckles and shooting things and riding half-broken horses and wearing hats with holes. If you ride a broken-in horse or put in irrigation or go to uni, you're a sook. We've got to get past that.'

He got a similar homecoming when, years later, he stepped off the plane as a government minister. 'I was back to feeling like a little shit. You feel trapped in a small town. If you get bigger than your tribe, they cut you down. You better your peers at your own risk.'

Yet Katter also mythologises the Curry of his youth. He prides himself on coming from a town 'where there were blokes who could knock out a bullock with one punch'. He likes to mention his uncles Bert, a bookmaker, and Norman. 'My two uncles epitomised this country. They fought with their fists to become Australians and be accepted. And they succeeded.' And he tells me at least three times over three days that 'in Cloncurry, boys have their tear ducts removed at birth'.

We reach Mount Isa and Katter pulls into McDonald's for a cup of coffee. As we squeeze onto the tiny plastic stools attached to the low plastic table, I marvel again at his need to be seen. In an electorate as big as his you have to make the most of your opportunities, but Katter's public forays seem to go beyond strategy.

In the crowded restaurant Katter tells me about his father. Despite following in his footsteps, they drifted apart. His father was mayor of Cloncurry and Mount Isa before stepping into the federal arena, and the family saw less of him than Katter junior would have liked. Particularly when his father moved to Canberra.

'Dad was a distant man. He was always a bit conscious of not being a pure merino, if I can put it that way. Whereas me and my uncles revelled in it.' The eldest of three children, Katter junior grew very close to his mother, whom he remembers as 'a great beauty' and very strict. He didn't say the word 'bloody' until his army service, and he never learnt to use any stronger language until he went to federal parliament. Ma Katter, whom he refers to as 'Mummy' even now, would have washed his mouth out with soap.

Katter felt his father 'deserted' his mother. There were rumours of an affair, and in the years leading up to his mother's death, Katter and his young wife stayed with her in Cloncurry. Katter was twenty-eight when she died, and is said to have been furious when his father remarried relatively soon afterwards. Katter himself, however, will tell me only that his mother was left to live a lonely life in a lonely place. 'I still can't talk about it so don't ask any questions.' There are tears in his eyes, and people at other tables are noticing.

We're late for the march, but in time for Katter to lay a wreath, talk to maybe fifty people and help a disabled woman onto a bus. I can't keep up, and nap in the car. When he gets back he seems inordinately chirpy. He slaps the dash and says, 'The reason I'm such a bloody good politician is because I'm so good with people, if I do say so myself. I could have stayed there all day. I really, really enjoy it.'

We drop in at his office, which is closed for the day. At the coffee station there's a note for staff: 'Please restock with Malanda milk, Nerada tea, South Johnstone sugar and Mareeba coffee [all produced within the electorate of Kennedy]. Biscuits should be from an Australian-owned company and not under any circumstances from Woolworths or Coles. Signed: Cyclone Bob.'

He leaves me in his office to attend some meetings. I find a copy of his inaugural speech to federal parliament, delivered a decade earlier. It differs startlingly little from the speech he gave at the CWA meet, or the spiel I've been listening to in the car: the country needs more sawmills, more mines, more dams, more prawn farms and more people or it will continue to go to rack and ruin. It even finished with a patriotic bush poem, or it would have done had Katter not gone over time and had his speech cut short.

Over dinner that night at the biggest dining room in town, the Irish Club, Katter piles an ungodly amount of salt on his steak and chips. Some people up from Melbourne want his autograph. We also run into one of his campaign volunteers, who asks Katter whether he realises the September 11 planes were controlled from the ground by the CIA. I scan Katter for a response, but he lets it pass. 'She's one of my best workers,' he says with a shrug.

The next morning Katter picks me up from my lodgings, the Star Inn Single Men's Quarters, dressed in crisp new jeans, a bright red shirt and suede boots, as well as his trademark white hat. He looks like someone trying to look like a cowboy. In the main street, he double-parks in front of a diner called Burger Chief and dispatches me to fetch him breakfast: a bacon sandwich and a can of Coke. Unfortunately there's a line of red-eyed riverbed Aborigines stocking up on junk food in front of me. Katter honks for me to hurry up. It doesn't help.

Bound for Camooweal, we stop for fuel at a vast service station, frequented by road trains. As I fill the tank, Katter leans on the boot next to me and whips out his mobile phone. 'Christ, Bob, not here!' I yell in the nick of time. A station employee walking by laughs out loud. At the cash register, still shaking her head, she says to me, 'Bob'll blow us all up one day.'

An hour and a half later we're in Camooweal. It's no place to linger. Camooweal's a town of three-trailer road trains that spill hot cowshit, and old drovers who disgorge bush poetry. Katter reveals one of the latter has even written a poem in tribute to him, called 'The Reluctant Rebel'. To my relief, and surprise, Katter does not know it by heart.

Katter's in Camooweal to attend a lunchtime ringers' reunion and so – he's shocked to learn – is the CWA state president. She eyeballs him grimly for arriving late. After lunch we repair to the track for Camooweal's race day. I leave Katter to his glad-handing of locals. He neither gambles nor drinks, yet each time I spot him between races, he's got a can of VB in his hand. When it's time to leave, Katter recognises an Aboriginal man and offers him his beer. 'I don't drink,' says the Aboriginal man. 'Neither do I,' says Katter. 'I don't know why I bought it.' He hands it to me instead. It's warm and full to the brim.

URANDANGI

Town of Dreams

SOME YEARS BACK, IN his search for a sufficiently sun-dazed, saggy-arsed setting for his documentary of life in an outback town, film-maker Dennis O'Rourke checked out Urandangi. At least, he thinks he did. He can't actually remember *seeing* it. In any event, he settled for Cunnamulla, for he wanted a place 'at the end of the [railway] line', a town on the edge of mainstream Australia. Urandangi, by implication, has teetered off it. It lies two hundred kilometres south-west of Mount Isa, just inside Queensland along a rutted back road to Alice Springs. It has no mains power, and neither Telstra nor Australia Post acknowledges its existence in their compilations of Australian place names and postcodes. The landscape is flat and utterly fried. One British guidebook calls it 'GAFA country' – Great Amounts of Fuck All. And that includes Urandangi. The dot's one claim to fame is its knack for snaring the state's minimum and maximum temperatures on the same day.

Urandangi may not have a postcode, but it has a postcard. The snap, taken from the pub verandah in 1983, shows an enormous, rolling, billowing cloud, brown and thick as molasses, about to engulf the place. *Dust Storm – Urandangi* is a steady seller with tourists, meaning that the pub might sell one a week.

Several boxes of *Dust Storm* remain stacked in the pub store-room, ordered years ago in anticipation of the chimerical outback tourism boom. The postcards actually survived another apocalyptic event, the Great Flood of 1997. The entire town went under and flood pictures, taken ankle-deep from the same verandah, take pride of place on the pub wall. Indeed, *Flood – Urandangi* would no doubt rival *Dust Storm* for card sales, but there's no need to get carried away. The Dangi takes it one postcard at a time.

That the town exists at all amazes 4WD visitors. You hear them mutter about it in the pub. Why the hell would anyone live here? Meaning anyone white. They squint at the Aborigines drinking in the hellish glare outside, note the blare of generators and pick the scabs of congealed dust from their noses. They marvel that people actually live in the half-dozen peeling caravans plonked on bare-dirt blocks. They shake their heads at the ubiquitous clutter of disembowelled car bodies and other rusting debris. They laugh at the twin white horses that seem to have the run of the place. And they comment on the crows. 'I've never seen so many at once,' says one traveller. 'Except at the tip.'

Urandangi mattered once as an overnight stop along the Georgina stock route, when drovers brought cattle south from the Territory along the ephemeral Georgina River to the railhead at Dajarra, the nearest town 'at the end of the line'. But road trains and station mergers mean the cattle industry barely touches Urandangi these days. There's rarely a ringer in town. The Australian Agricultural Company, the country's third-biggest landholder, has swallowed most of the surrounding stations, and its base at nearby Headingly, a million-hectare spread straddling a hundred and fifty kilometres of the Georgina, has its own store and bar.

Yet Urandangi persists. Its eighteen permanent residents haven't lived here long, but long enough. Five, eight, fifteen years. Too long to leave, too short to share a past. Everyone's a local in Urandangi. What's more, they'll tell you they were *attracted* to the place. They came for jobs, affordable dwellings, the lifestyle, even love, or at least lust. It's like anywhere else, really, yet it can still come as a shock: Urandangi's a town of dreams.

RAY'S PLACE, FRIDAY NOON: 'I'll crank up the generator and make us a cup of coffee.' Ray Cantrill, fifty-nine, lives in a tin carport on a concrete slab and hasn't left town for years. Inside it looks like the Unabomber's den. There are rows of salvaged car batteries, piles of mechanical innards, hollowed appliances and an immense spaghetti of electrical wiring. Every surface is covered in a cruddy film of brown dust, rendered browner by the dim light, for the windows are boarded up with beer hoarding. Amid the clutter is a foam mattress and a makeshift desk with a home-wired computer and ashtrays three-deep in butts. Behind a tin partition is the rudimentary kitchen and the toilet – a bucket. A black dog called Pig is tied to a short leash at the back door.

'Bit of a step up from the old bus ay?' he says. And it is, it is. When I last saw him, four years ago, Cantrill's home was a rusting bus chassis on the other side of town. It was just months after the Great Flood, and everything was still damp or crusted with red-baked mud. Cantrill had lost his guitar, his stereo, the TV, the lot. Drowned, too, were his budgies, his poetry, his books and an album of his prized Urandangi sunset photos.

Cantrill still longs to have the bus-shell towed to his new block, if only for the memories. Fifteen years ago, Cantrill, then forty-three, and his newlywed twenty-four-year-old wife crammed what they had into the bus and quit Queensland's central coast for a new life. Towing a Holden HQ panel van, they made it as far as Winton when the bus motor blew up. They tried towing the bus with the HQ. It blew up too. The pair hooked their bus to a road train and scored work on a nearby station, but two years later Cantrill's wife fell ill and was rushed to the coast for tests. She never made it back, succumbing to leukemia within weeks. Left alone with an infant son, Cantrill had his bus towed to a vacant lot in nearby Urandangi, between the pub and the overgrown cemetery. 'I was as pleased as I was going to be at that stage of my life.'

There he squatted for a decade, accumulating debris, acquiring a palsy (and a nickname: Shaky) and befriending feral cats. His son ran wild and was taken away by the Department of Family Services, known to Cantrill – and only to Cantrill – as the Corned Beef Society. Then came the Great Flood. It was a turning point, he reflects now. With his compensation money he bought a quarter-acre block ($200), a carport ($5000), and, over a period of months, he shifted his possessions, wheelbarrow by wheelbarrow, up the street.

Since then he's got himself a cheap digital camera and is again taking pictures of sunsets, which he photoshops and tinkers with on his computer. Slumped shirtless behind the terminal in his splattered shorts and battered hat, chain-smoking and typing with one trembling finger, he transmits the pictures around the world, and people email back saying Urandangi must be very beautiful. Cantrill chats to them about the outback. His generator often rumbles well into the night and a recent month's Internet bill came to over $1000. Lying face-up next to his computer is a small framed photograph of a stylish middle-aged woman. 'That's Linda,' says Cantrill. 'My lady friend from Toronto. We've been chatting online for two years. She's coming to visit me next month.'

THE DANGI HOTEL, FRIDAY evening: At the dog-legged bar of the Dangi Pub, Cantrill's cyber relationships are a running joke. At least they were. Too many women have actually made the romantic pilgrimage to Urandangi. There was one from Victoria, another from New South Wales, and a third from Queensland. The last stayed for months. Janne Anderson, the brassy Danish-born publican, recalls one heavily made-up woman inquiring after Cantrill's 'house'. 'She put on all these airs and graces. I just stared at her and pointed down the street at his bus. Then I said to Tony [Anderson's husband], "She'll be back in five minutes." But she didn't come out of that bus for a week.'

'She probably fucking fainted,' interjects Dennis Burrell, a crusty bar regular. But no, says Anderson, the dame emerged chirpy. So chirpy, in fact, that when a rumour went around that a wealthy Honolulu woman was coming to see Cantrill in a private plane complete with spa and queen-sized waterbed, some in town believed it.

Burrell suddenly calls out from the verandah. 'Journo! Carn have a look at this cunt!' I rush outside to find him admiring the sunset. 'Best in the world,' he drawls, a roll-your-own bobbing on his lip. 'You'll wanna photograph that.'

We watch Cantrill's silver carport, two blocks away, turn steadily orange. Cantrill's red station wagon is in front, on blocks, its bonnet up. 'Last time Shaky got that thing going was two years ago, when the gearbox packed it in. For months he was driving it around town in reverse,' says Burrell. 'Now he reckons he'll drive to Mount Isa backwards if he has to, in order to pick up that Canadian sheila. He may as well. The country looks just the fucking same arse about.'

An elderly black man with a crooked jaw, a useless arm and a walking stick joins us on the verandah. 'Johnny's this area's traditional owner,' says Burrell. 'He once tried to put a land claim on the pub, didn't ya, Johnny?'

Johnny Age nods and limply offers me his good hand. 'G'day, I'm an alcoholic,' he says. Age's leg injury came in a horse fall when he was a ringer, but his wonky jaw was dealt him by his wife, Jessie, who sports a scar or two herself. The couple live under a yellow tarpaulin across the street, on a block Jessie bought. She no longer drinks, or fights, and is saving up for a caravan, if only her family would stop 'borrowing' her savings. The extended Age clan make up most of the Marmanya mob, a community of six neglected houses on flood-safe land three kilometres out of town. Each pension day, the families migrate to their camp in town, known as the Village, which includes Jessie's block, to drink themselves numb under a desert oak. Come Sunday, broke once more, they drift back to Marmanya.

Sally Tweedie, on the other hand, drinks in the pub. She's married to a white man, John 'Cookie' Tweedie, a camp cook at Headingly. The Tweedies have two children and live in a caravan next door to Sally's mother, Jundu Kamara. Jundu is an Arrernte woman, from Tobermorey, across the border. Relatives often visit around pension day. Her block is well away from the Village, on the other side of the pub, for the Marmanya and Tobermorey mobs don't always get on.

Anderson jokes she'd go broke without the Tweedies. They are so devoted to the pub that they are its de facto security team. Their sprees, however, can get hairy. A few years ago, in a fit of rum-fuelled madness, Cookie Tweedie pulled a gun on his wife and mother-in-law and burnt down their caravan. He stays off the rum now, mostly.

This Friday night a silver-haired couple from a station down the road, known to all as Kenny and Dolly, have dropped in. The night gradually gains in warmth and vigour, mostly thanks to Sally, who likes to hog the jukebox and hug the nearest male while singing 'True Blue' in his ear at full blast. By the time the pub shuts, Bryan Ferry's 'Let's Stick Together' is being played for the fifth time and everyone joins in for the midsong howls. Burrell, who is flush with cash after having a $5000 bank loan approved for a $2500 generator, invites everyone back to his place. Meanwhile Cantrill's generator hums until 2 am. After all, it's only noon in Canada.

DENNIS'S PLACE, SATURDAY MORNING: I'm up early after being woken by one of the two white horses farting right outside my tent. Walking by Burrell's block, I stop to say hello to the stooped figure of Karen Jorgensen, Janne Anderson's grand-mother. She lives with Nils and Lis Knudsen, Anderson's parents, in the restored former post office, diagonally opposite the pub. Every morning she pushes a wheelbarrow around Urandangi to scoop up the previous day's dung. I've been told her tomato plants are three metres tall.

She doesn't return my greeting, however. Instead there's a shout from Burrell, who is warming his hands with Cantrill over a fire outside his van. 'Oi! Journo! She can't speak a fucking word of English! All she knows is horseshit!' Jorgensen, who left the Danish coast eight years ago, gives me a startled look. Her eyes are the palest blue, and it strikes me that in Urandangi a language barrier might be a safety net. Things are rough enough already.

Burrell is a short, wiry sixty-year-old with an unshaven face that readily creases into a toothless leer. He's a grader driver for Headingly Station and has a room there, but he moved to town 'because I can't stand fucking jackaroos. The cunts are forever hammering away at their fucking leatherwork or banging the fucking screen doors while I'm trying to watch the fucking TV. And that music they play – Jesus Christ all fucking mighty. What the fuck's wrong with Slim Dusty?'

Burrell lives in a caravan next door to Cantrill, who regularly pops over to sift through Burrell's junk and drink his beer, when invited. This morning they are discussing renovations to the van. It turns out Burrell's fold-out dining arrangement is no more, because Sally Tweedie sat on it at last night's postpub party. 'She went straight through it,' says Burrell. 'She's got an arse two and a half axe handles wide. I had plans to replace it anyway, but not this fucking early.'

Burrell's proud of his van. It's the biggest and best appointed in town, he tells me. 'You know what's got me where I am today? Working like a fucking cunt, that's what.' He throws an empty plastic coke bottle into a bin, thinks again and retrieves it. 'Want it?' he asks Cantrill. 'Yep,' says Cantrill, and wedges it into his jacket pocket. He glances at me and explains himself: 'Cut it in half and you've got a funnel *and* a screw container.'

Talk turns to how Cantrill is going to pick up Linda. The publicans are driving to Mount Isa for supplies on the same day, but have refused him a lift. Janne Anderson claims Cantrill only comes into the pub if the beer is on someone else. Neither does he buy food from her, which has her baffled. 'Shaky never leaves town, so somebody must be smuggling it in for him,' she says, casting me a suspicious look. 'It's not you, is it?' Anderson also claims Cantrill doesn't wash because he doesn't buy soap – 'I can show you the books' – but, in truth, Ray doesn't smell too bad. He just looks like he might.

No sooner has Ray wandered home, toting a can of beer as well as the salvaged chipboard from Burrell's dining ensemble, than Burrell shakes his head. 'Fuck he's a tight-arsed cunt. Wouldn't shout if a shark bit him on the balls. You know me and him used to share his generator? I was pissing diesel just so he could sit there jackhammering his dick all night in front of his computer. Then the cunt reckons my freezer uses too much power, so he unplugs me, just like that. By the time I found out, I'd lost half a bullock. I was so fucking mad, I was going to put a stick of gelly under his shitcan and blow the cunt up.'

FRANK'S PLACE, SUNDAY BREAKFAST: It's been a bitterly cold night and Frank Juhasz is rugged up in two jumpers, waiting for the sun to kick in. He's reading a hardback edition of *Robinson Crusoe* and his mug of coffee contains a generous shot of mango whisky, a vile-tasting eighty-proof substance that he distils himself. Juhasz has two vans, a study van and a bed van, as well as a solar shower, outside his-and-her bathtubs, a paved courtyard, a wood stove and a concrete table featuring an inlaid goanna pattern, made by Sally Tweedie. A sprinkler system keeps the desert at bay. There's a passionfruit draped over the outside toilet, laden with fruit; as well as wild plums, coolibahs and even a young rain tree.

Yet the set-up is only a weekender. During the week Juhasz resides in Mount Isa, where he also lives in a van, under a mango tree in the backyard of his rented-out home. Juhasz is a well-preserved sixty-five. Clean-shaven, well read and politely spoken, he seems quite debonair for Urandangi. 'This town is not full of intellectuals, but you don't come here for that,' says Juhasz who, alone among the non-Aboriginal locals, doesn't run a generator. 'You come here for the peace and quiet.'

Things have got louder across the road, however. For ten years there was nothing between Juhasz and the rising sun. Now there's Cantrill and Burrell. 'I am deaf in one ear,' he says. 'It's not deaf enough.' Juhasz recently bought the block behind his.

It's flood-prone, but quieter. He plans to put a third caravan there.

Juhasz, from Hungary, met Nils Knudsen, a Danish cod fisherman, in Sydney in the late sixties. The pair went to Mount Isa to work in the mines, but Juhasz was drawn to the outback. He became a grader driver, sleeping in a swag by the side of the road for months at a time. Meanwhile Knudsen stuck it out in the mine. 'I was working at Headingly and Nils came to visit. We went to the Dangi pub, and Nils could see the place was a gold mine,' says Juhasz. 'Most of the [Aboriginal] communities across the border are dry, and the pub is the only place around where the blacks can cash their cheques. But it's only a gold mine if you work sixteen hours a day, seven days a week, for ten years, as Nils did. He bought most of the town for $40 a block and gave half away to family and friends as Christmas presents. That's how I got mine.'

Having been married four times (to a Hungarian, two Fijians and a Filipina), Juhasz has resigned himself to the fact that his twin longings for isolation and female company are incompatible. Shortly after his last marriage ended, however, an old school friend from Hungary contacted Juhasz and he invited her to Urandangi. She came once, twice, and is coming again to drink red wine with him at sunrise. 'She was the perfect wife forty-five years ago, and I didn't see it,' Juhasz says wistfully. Without envy, he points up the road at his friend's house. 'Nils is the lucky one. He married Lis at twenty and has been happy as Larry ever since.'

NILS'S PLACE, SUNDAY AFTERNOON: Urandangi's town plan is a crossroads. The tracks leading north and west peter out at the cemetery and the pig-churned banks of the Georgina respectively, while those pointing east and south connect Mount Isa to Alice Springs. Nils and Lis Knudsen own each of the well-watered corner blocks, which are home to four generations of women. There's Janne Anderson in the pub, her mother and grandmother in the restored post office and, in a high-set miners' donga, Anderson's eighteen-year-old goth daughter. She works as a teacher's aide at the Marmanya school and lives with her boyfriend, a thirty-three-year-old unemployed ringer. The fourth corner is a private park, dotted with young trees. It's fenced to keep the Village out.

Locals call Knudsen the Old Man, though, at sixty, it's not that he's old, more the Town Father. Each month he makes the 600-kilometre round trip to sit on the Boulia Shire Council. Knudsen is a strong-armed, barrel-chested man but he's less gruff than he lets on. Both Jessie Age and Jundu Kamara speak highly of him.

Knudsen rules the town with a barman's touch. He wheels and deals in blocks and caravans, and Tweedie, Burrell and even Cantrill will do most things for a few cans of beer, be it burning rubbish, collecting firewood or hard labour (Tweedie only). And pub prices aren't cheap. A slab of beer costs $44, a loaf of bread $4 and diesel $1.30 a litre. Then there's the Dangi Pub line in T-shirts, windcheaters and caps – everyone in town wears them, black and white, young and old. The pub gets a further $20,000 a year from the Bureau of Meteorology for doubling as a weather station. And to cap it all, Knudsen's mother-in-law collects his manure. Really, the Old Man has it made.

To call the Knudsens' home a palace, as Burrell does, might seem a bit far-fetched. But pile carpet and airconditioning are luxuries here. Not to mention the ornate patio, the Japanese garden, the porcelain garden gnomes, the gleaming workshop, the enormous vegetable garden, three fat pet kangaroos, a pen of even fatter pigs and – in the desert! – an orchid house. At night the place is lit up with fairy lights. To a humpy-dweller, it's a Ferrari showroom.

The Knudsens emigrated with their three daughters in 1970, spending their first eighteen months in Mount Isa in a caravan. Twenty years later they took over Urandangi. 'It was a dump back then,' says Lis Knudsen. Of course, the tourists still say that, but the changes are subtle. The roadsides are slashed. The pub has banned cask, flagon and glass bottle sales. Aborigines own land and pay rates. There are no roaming, mangy dogs. The Tweedies have planted street trees and make a point of picking up litter en route to the pub. 'People have got a bit of pride in the place,' says Knudsen. Even Burrell seems to have caught the bug. He's talking of putting up a white picket fence around his van.

The recalcitrant one, in Knudsen's eyes, is Cantrill. The Knudsens' sunroom, where we're sitting, faces the park. Next to it is a vacant block, and next to that is Cantrill's chaotic pile. Cantrill originally tried to buy the block next to the park at auction, but he was told he was outbid by a 'mystery buyer'. It was Knudsen. 'I didn't want Shaky or Dennis there,' he admits. 'I could sell it tomorrow, but only to the right people. I was behind the bar in that pub for eleven years. When you have to look into those faces every day, hour after hour, it can get really get to you.' His ice-blue-eyed wife looks at him with feeling and says, 'One day we'll put a six-foot fence around Ray, won't we?' Other than that, though, the Knudsens seem content to have ceased building. Their little empire is complete. Asked if he'd like to see Urandangi grow in future, Knudsen says no. 'Just the trees, that's all.'

JUNDU'S PLACE, MONDAY MORNING: Jundu Kamara is cooking yellow-bellied perch, caught in a Georgina waterhole yesterday afternoon. She's being watched at a respectful distance by her seedy-looking daughter Sally Tweedie and a red heeler tied to a stake in the sun. 'She's mad because I've been drinking all weekend,' says Tweedie. 'I don't think she'll take us goanna hunting today.'

An enormous blaze somewhere to the south has left a hot, heavy haze over the land. It's as if the whole town is hungover. Frank Juhasz has left for the week, as has Cookie Tweedie, out with a stock team at Headingly. Johnny and Jessie Age have gone fishing. A Headingly bore-runner passing through town tells me the station manager's wife has lost her collie off the back of a ute, and the station has the chopper out looking for it.

I wander over to Cantrill's place. His head is sore, and all the sorer for being rung out of bed at 5 am by a mad-as-hell Janne Anderson after her shower ran out of water. The Boulia Council pays Cantrill $240 a month to clean the public toilets and keep an eye on the town's water tank. The pump is solar powered and Cantrill is meant to start the back-up generator if the level's low. But last night Cantrell fell in bed drunk before the sun went down. Says Burrell: 'When Shaky gets pissed, the whole town dries up.' Cantrill, however, blames the Knudsens for running their sprinklers at night.

I wander back to Jundu Kamara's. Her mood has improved. She grabs her handbag, her grandkids and a crowbar and we drive into the Territory's scrubby red-dirt plains. Jundu explains that the reptiles are holed up underground, waiting for the first thunderstorms. Prodding with the crowbar, she finds them soon enough. One carney (bearded dragon) and one goanna. She kills them with whiplash and a little later we sling the reptiles into the back of the ute. The carney rights itself and opens an eye. 'That bugger,' she says. She grabs it by the tail and cracks its head a second time on the dirt. The commotion seems to have roused the goanna. 'Here, gimme that.' Whack. Back at her place she guts the lizards and cooks them over coals for lunch. The carney's a tad lean, but the goanna's not bad. 'Cookie reckons bush tucker tastes like boot,' says his wife, Sally. 'But that's because he's only got one tooth.'

Meanwhile Burrell has packed his swag. He'll be gone for a week, grading the Headingly airstrip. That evening there's no one in the bar. Not a soul. From the pub verandah, I watch the smoky sky turn scarlet, and wish I had my camera. Across the intersection, the fairy lights blink on at the Knudsens', while over at the Village I can make out Johnny and Jessie Age, huddled around a campfire. At Cantrill's carport, for once, all is dark and quiet.

RAY'S PLACE, TUESDAY MORNING: The postie has arrived with a package. It's a DIY kit for the car's gearbox. Cantrill opens it and examines the O rings. 'Hmmm, I dunno,' he says. He invites me in to check my email, and afterwards checks his – four messages. Nothing too personal: an American woman would like to see more pictures of 'The Outbacks', his son says he might visit next weekend and a Victorian penpal is off to the hairdresser's to have her roots done. Finally, Linda from Toronto wants to know if she should bring her fleece.

I ask him if he's sent Linda pictures of Urandangi in daylight. Sure, he says. He opens a file of pictures that he has mailed her. There are plenty of sunsets, but there are also shots of his junkyard, his stricken car, his tin home, a crow, Dennis Burrell, Pig the dog, his kitchen, a new fluorescent tube he's just installed in the ceiling, his face, him shirtless – he really hasn't left much out at all. Did she say anything about the mess? I ask him. 'She did. She told me not to worry. She said she's coming for me, not the place.'

AROUND THE GULF

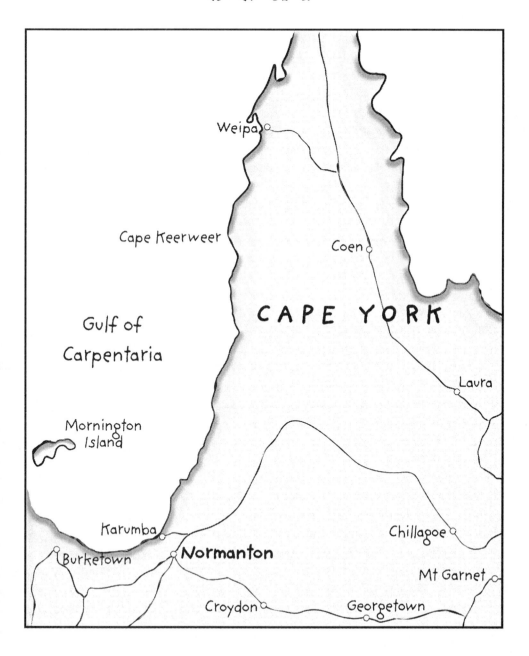

Weipa

Cape Keerweer

Coen

CAPE YORK

Gulf of
Carpentaria

Laura

Mornington
Island

Karumba

Chillagoe

Burketown

Normanton

Mt Garnet

Croydon

Georgetown

Travelling North III

In mid '93 I was offered a job editing the *Northern Beachcomber,* a tiny subsidiary of the *Cairns Post.* The position came with an office in Trinity Beach, north of Cairns, and an editorial team of one – myself. My beat would extend from Palm Cove to Yorkeys Knob. The job sounded as ideal as it did idyllic. Sure I preferred to write fat, long, topical features rather than reports on lawn bowls and real estate, but I'd at least be a journalist rather than a tour guide who dabbled on the side. Especially one whose fat, long features routinely earnt rejections.

Before I started, there was time for one more freelance trip. A photographer I'd met in Melbourne, Emmanuel Santos, was keen to document an Aboriginal cultural festival. We'd been told of one in Normanton, on the Gulf of Carpentaria. All the Gulf communities would be coming – Doomadgee, Mornington Island, Kowanyama, Burketown. Would there be traditional dancing, Emmanuel wished to know? I checked it out. Yes there would, I advised him.

I didn't know Emmanuel well, but I knew he was good. He was the friend – and mentor, inspiration and role model – of a friend. He worked for arty magazines, specialised in cultural documentary photo essays and was being courted by the world's top photo agencies. Emmanuel talked of publishing the trip's gleanings in European magazines such as *Stern* and *Paris Match.* Professionally, I was way out of my league, but I was cocky enough to think that a shared passion for Aboriginal culture meant we were ideological brothers, as if this might suffice.

I picked him up in the Kombi from Mount Isa airport. With him was Dominic, a studio photographer specialising in fashion and top-end advertising – one of Melbourne's best, and with the lifestyle to match. Dominic knew he was in for a shock, but that was why he'd come. Emmanuel was his mentor too.

We drove north into the Gulf savanna, a bleak landscape of introduced tree trash, road kill and anthills like tombstones. In Normanton, we checked into the top floor of the Purple Pub and went in search of the cultural festival. What we found instead was a football carnival, as well as legions of drunks.

'You call this cultural?' Emmanuel asked me.

Oops. I might have argued that football had come to play a central role in Aboriginal life. As had drinking. But I should have done my homework. The traditional dancing that I'd promised Emmanuel was restricted to a semiprofessional dance troupe performing on Friday and Saturday nights. As it was, the Friday night show was called off – the dancers were too drunk. Instead a troupe of South Sea Islanders took their place. We watched as an intoxicated Aboriginal man staggered out of the crowd to shake a leg with one of the prettier dancers. Suddenly an Aboriginal woman, presumably his wife and no less drunk, walked up and belted him across the face. Dominic, who was taking photos, lowered his lens. What an introduction to Aboriginal Australia he was having.

The publican of the Purple Pub expected riots between rival groups over the weekend, as did the police. But we stayed. We'd come so far and I'd got a sniff of a story. Normanton was gleaming with new indigenous infrastructure and its work for the dole scheme was said to be the best in the country, yet all was not what it seemed. Against a backdrop of impending festival riots and simmering racial tension, I pursued all that was rotten with the eagerness of a novice. I found out that the festival organiser was a sly grog runner, that the publican sold alcohol out of licensing hours and that up to eighty per cent of the social welfare money propping up the town was spent on alcohol. Emmanuel, however, seemed strangely disinterested and only reluctantly took the pictures to go with my story. I got the sense that he'd come to photograph only the dignity of Aboriginal people, not their reality. Whereas I went looking for grit, Emmanuel wanted the romantic, censored version. The politically correct image. Or so it seemed to me.

What I couldn't see then was that Emmanuel did not wish to engage his subjects on the political level at which journalists operated. For him, ideology came second to something deeper. Born in turbulent times in his native Philippines, he was renowned as a humanist photographer (although at the time I hardly knew what the term meant), who knew how to photograph joy, sorrow and suffering. The Jewish diaspora was a favourite subject, for instance. His work was gentle, celebratory, reflective – never cynical. Nothing like a newsman's, in other words.

In any case, the three of us were glad to leave Normanton, perhaps each thinking he'd been taken for a ride. But we were in luck. The following weekend was the Cape York Cultural Dance Festival, a dry (alcohol-free) event held every two years at Laura, inland from Cooktown. About twenty Cape and Gulf communities would be performing traditional dances in the *bora* (corroboree ring) over the three days, and we elected to extend our trip.

We spent much of that weekend with the Wik people from the Gulf community of Aurukun. Although as ravaged by alcohol and violence as any other community, the Wik had held on to their traditions better than most. Their dances were intricate, their dreamtime stories complex and their preparations extensive, even if they did wear board shorts underneath their grass skirts.

The most powerful men of the Wik were two brothers, Clive and Francis Yunkaporta. Between them they were custodians of their clan's cache of Dreamtime stories and oral history, including the account of their ancestors' skirmish with the Dutch in 1606, Australia's first encounter between black and white. Though courted by numerous media types at the festival, Emmanuel alone appeared to win their respect. His communication seemed innate, almost tribal. And perhaps it was. He later explained, for example, that he made sure that Clive faced the morning sun, because that was how village chiefs in the Philippine highlands liked to be addressed.

Still, I envied Emmanuel his grace and effortless charisma. Elders, both men and women, took him deep into Wik culture, far deeper than the rest of us were able to go. I recall emerging from my tent one morning to see him doing his Tai Chi exercises. Around him were a dozen Aboriginal kids, copying his every stretch.

Meanwhile Dominic and I floundered. At one stage Dominic took a photo of Francis Yunkaporta without asking for permission. An hour later, he suddenly lost his voice. Emmanuel wasn't surprised. He took Dominic to see Francis, who affirmed that Dominic had offended the spirits. At a ceremony arranged for the following morning, Francis called out to the spirits in his native Wikmungkan language and wiped his hands repeatedly under his arms to pat Dominic on his hair and body. This conferring of smell was a blessing of sorts, so that the Wik spirits would leave Dominic be. Remarkably, he regained his voice within a few hours.

The night before, I'd stumbled across the youngest of the Aurukun elders, Stanley Kalkeeyorta, on a walk back to camp. Looking like a man possessed, he grabbed my arm and ordered me to sit down. I sat. His head was lolling from side to side and his arms were swaying mystically. He proceeded to spit in each palm and rub his hands on my legs and arms, all the while moving with a kelp-like rhythm. Then he rubbed his armpits and patted me all over. Flummoxed by his intensity, I let out a nervous laugh. 'Don't laugh!' he snapped, and carried on rubbing and patting. When he stopped, he held my arm for what seemed like an inordinately long time and said, 'Now you not get sick.' Then he let go of my arm and keeled over. He was drunk as a parrot.

We left Laura a little wiser in some respects but not in others. I did not yet know that my fat, long pieces on the Wik (too earnest) and on Normanton (too bleak) would be comprehensively rejected by editors. In the Kombi on the way back, Emmanuel's pitch for international magazines still seemed feasible. And his enthusiasm for freelancing was infectious. You can do what you want to do, he urged. Write to your passions. Follow your dreams. I stopped at a phone booth to advise the *Cairns Post* editor that I wouldn't be joining the *Northern Beachcomber*.

Consequently I didn't sell another piece for six months.

Nonetheless, Emmanuel was right. Freelancing might well be a professional wilderness, or even a desert at times, but I could go where I wanted, stay weeks at a time. As for following dreams, what dreams? I just liked driving.

BURKETOWN

Killing Time with Murrandoo

WHITEFELLAS OF THE GULF country don't like Murrandoo Yanner, the activist. They say he's not even black. Chinese, they reckon. But they liked his late father, Phillip Yanner. A fine blackfella, they say. A credit to his race. Like his son a leader of the Waanyi community, granted, and a champion of his traditional heritage, but he played by the rules. Whitefella rules. The ex-stockman was a shire councillor, respected his mayor and kept his eight kids in line.

They were good kids when the old man was alive. Tough, but on the rails by and large – a sound parental achievement in the Gulf, where the black communities of Doomadgee and Mornington Island rate among the country's most dysfunctional. Phillip Yanner's second-eldest son was a police liaison officer in Mount Isa. The younger ones showed promise, too, at school as well as in the ring. But Jason, a middleweight who'd knocked out a teacher at fifteen, was widely regarded as the clever one. He went to uni and was in the second year of a journalism cadetship with the Australian Broadcasting Commission when a heart attack felled his father in 1991.

Streetwise and media savvy, Jason Yanner was asked to return and lead his people. As well, he 'felt a personal call to come back and pick up the spear'. He was nineteen. To win the respect of the elders, he endured a bush initiation with an old *kadache* (traditional law) man called Blue Bob. He emerged from 'the business' minus a foreskin but with a new name, Murrandoo, meaning whirlwind, or, in his words, 'an unpredictable and uncontrollable force of nature'.

For the backers of a billion-dollar zinc mine planned for Waanyi land, and their biggest supporter, the Queensland Government, he certainly lived up to his name. As the head of the Carpentaria Land Council, Yanner blocked, obstructed, cajoled and generally frustrated negotiations at every turn. He mobilised his people for mass sit-ins, hid traditional owners from government spruikers and at one stage bluffed he'd trained a hundred men to form a Bougainville-style resistance army.

When a former governor-general was called in to negotiate, Yanner laughed in his face. Editorials accused him of holding the country to ransom. If so, it worked. The mining company eventually agreed to pay the Waanyi, most of whom live in depraved conditions, an unprecedented $60 million worth of education, health, infrastructure and employment measures. (Once the deal was sealed, Yanner brazenly applied for a position as trainee powder monkey [in charge of explosives] at the zinc mine. The application now hangs framed in the mine manager's office.)

While the fight for Waanyi land rights made good ground in the courts, Yanner, drawing inspiration from the likes of Malcolm X and Xanana Gusmao, also fought by his rules. Holed up in Burketown, he drew his brothers, cousins and friends around him to form a posse of local toughs. He avenged insults, defended relatives and beat up local publicans. He stole stock from graziers, hunted protected wildlife and shared the meat among his supporters. He staged further sit-ins, occupied national parks, held fiery lectures, charmed journalists, roughed up local businesses and channelled Waanyi funds to buy them.

To boot, his slipperiness was the stuff of legend. Despite appearing in court some fifty times (mostly for assaults), he was never jailed. Once, famously, he was let off when a witness to a bashing in Mount Isa failed to identify Murrandoo in a line-up with his brothers. Australia hadn't seen street-fighting politics like it since the days of Koori hard man Gary Foley, as Foley was to acknowledge himself. 'I love you, brother,' the angry old man of black politics gushed after bussing from Melbourne to hear Yanner speak in Townsville five years ago. 'I wanted to see if you were as good as they said you were. And I reckon you're better.'

WHEN I RING YANNER at his home in Burketown to arrange a visit, he sounds suddenly on guard. 'How d'you find out about this business? I haven't told anyone yet,' he says.

'What business?' I say.

'The fucking raid last night.'

It's news to me. It turns out that armed police burst into his house as well as the homes of six associates overnight. The troupe, said to be twenty-strong, included members of Townsville's drug squad, Mount Isa's dog squad and the stock squad from Cloncurry. The stock officers seized some suspect beef from his fridge. The drug squad seized a bong. And the dog squad seized a pistol from under his bed, as well as a sawn-off shotgun and three firecrackers, later referred to in the media as 'explosives'.

'They want to put me away,' says Yanner, who only a week earlier had been committed to stand trial over knocking out a Townsville publican. 'I'm on an eighteen-month suspended sentence at the moment, so any conviction on any charge will land me in jail. Thing is, I can handle being a target. But what I can't tolerate is goons barging in with guns and scaring the shit out of my wife and kids.'

He tells me he'll be appearing in Burketown court in three weeks time. 'That will be the best way to catch me, because I'll be in town. I never miss the circus. Anyway, it'll just be a mention, shouldn't take more than five minutes. Or maybe ten, because the cops reckon they got me on seven or eight charges out of last night. Petty bullshit, all of it – I need the pistol for self-defence – but they're not mucking around. They're really gunning to put me behind bars.'

BURKETOWN MAKES FOR A sound strategic base. The corrugated access roads run through some of the most clapped-out country imaginable, keeping out – and in – all but the most determined. And Burketown itself is no oasis, but for a gushing hot water bore which sustains a small, sulphurous wetland. Most of the town's trees have been shredded by the thousands of corellas which rise and fall as one all day. The only intact gums are those in the van park, a near-empty haven of green in the middle of town, where the caretaker cracks a stockwhip as soon as the shrieking white cloud descends.

I circle the town twice and drop in at the office of the Carpentaria Land Council. Yanner's not in, but I'm sounded out by two of his brothers, Bull and TJ. (Pa Yanner's first two sons, Shane [Bull] and Jason [Murrandoo] loathed their 'sissy' Christian names so much that they were allowed to name their younger brothers – Bruce Lee and Trinity James – after their favourite action stars.)

TJ explains Murrandoo's asleep, having arrived home that morning after a twenty-hour drive around the Gulf from a men's meeting and buffalo hunt in Arnhem Land. TJ points up the street to a modest house behind a high fence. 'That's Murrandoo's place, but you can't call in. His pitbulls would go you. We'll let him know you're here. If Murrandoo wants to see you, he'll let you know.'

I check in at the Burketown pub and bide my time. Every second year or so, the pub famously claims to run out of beer when the Wet sets in. It's nothing but a publicity stunt, but the media falls for it every time. The previous year a Victorian brewery chartered a flight to drop off a hundred and twenty cartons plus a TV crew. The publican, not expecting cameras, had to scramble to clear the far from barren coolroom in order to keep up appearances.

I find the surly bar clientele are happy to run their town down. Within minutes I learn Burketown has lost its rodeo, its annual show and its race meeting over the past year. 'The town has lost its soul,' laments a ruddy-faced occasional tradesman. 'The good people are leaving.' Not surprisingly, he blames the blacks. 'They run the town; we just do as we're told. If you volunteer to do something, people think you're up to something. So nothing happens. The only event that's survived is the Abo [football] festival. That and the barra fishing comp. I tell ya, if it wasn't for that Chinaman dickhead Yanner, Burketown would be boomin'.'

At this the barmaid perks up. She's a braless girl from London here on a three-month stint, dropped off by mail plane. Evidently the publican subscribes to a backpacker employment agency, a sound business practice in a town of forty women and a hundred and forty men.

'Boom town? This place?' she scoffs. 'You're having a laugh, aren't ya?'

The tradesman turns to address her nipples. 'It was thanks to Yanner's mob that the [zinc slurry] pipeline from the mine went to Karumba [three hundred kilometres away]. It would have been better for the mine to ship out of Burketown and we'd have been boomin', bloody boomin'.'

At the bar and elsewhere, locals will speak to me about Yanner only on the basis of confidentiality. They may sneer and call him Jason behind his back, but they'll never do it to his face. For underneath its blokey crust, Burketown is soft with fear. The whites are scared – you can see it in their faces, you can hear it in their voices, and eventually some will even admit it. Stories abound of bashings and burnings. When the vacant old hospital building blew up and burnt to the ground a few years back, it was seen as a warning to the rest of the town. The female mayor has been verbally abused. Senior shire council staff have been beaten. So has the publican, numerous times. When the council's building inspector decided to press charges after an assault with a beer bottle, his 4WD was torched and 'YOU'RE NEXT' daubed on his wall. He dropped the charges. And the fear extends to Normanton, where a shop owner told me it was well known that anyone offending a friend of the Yanners could expect a visit from a few of his heavies. It's said even the local cops are scared.

But the Burketown Pub remains the prime vent for violence. Its windows are barred, there are security cameras inside and out, guard dogs are trained to attack anyone running, and the publican, Tim Trad, is not averse to using pepper spray to clear the bar. More than once the Flying Doctor Service has been called out to attend to the victims of bar-room bashings, including Trad himself. A few years back the hotel was broken into under cover of a thunderstorm. Thirty thousand dollars worth of grog and cigarettes were trucked to Doomadgee, where most of the Waanyi live, a hundred and twenty kilometres south of Burketown. No one was charged and nothing was recovered.

The publican is stubborn, however. He won't leave, though his family has. The bullying at school was bad enough, but when Trad's wife was chased out of a parent–teacher meeting by a Waanyi woman swinging a chair, she took the kids and bolted. Meanwhile the Yanners continue to chat up travellers at Trad's bar (he wouldn't dare ban them) and his barmaid's sleeping with the land council lawyer. But if Trad feels under siege, he won't talk about it. All he'll say publicly is: 'You can let people know the pub's for sale. Maybe there's someone else out there silly enough to buy it.'

Down the street I meet Tom (not his real name), who spends his winters in Burketown to fish for barramundi. Like everyone else, he's got a boat to take him into the Gulf, forty-five kilometres downstream, where the famous Morning Glory clouds roll in come October and the fish are there for the taking. He won't drink at the pub – 'At those prices you've either got to be a tourist or black.' But he feels for Tim Trad. 'It's as if the cops can't touch Murrandoo. I've heard blokes here say that if they were dying, they'd take him with them. One bloke was going down [to Mount Isa] for cancer tests and reckoned he was coming back with two bullets. One for himself, and one for Murrandoo. Something will happen one day, a fight, a piece of four-by-two, and it will all be over, no questions asked. Maybe not here, but in the Isa. I know they look out for him there.'

That evening, Bull Yanner and friends are in the bar for a session. Murrandoo doesn't show up, however, and I retire early to my room above the bar. Shortly after midnight I wake to loud shouts and bangs from down below. It's Bull Yanner, the former police liaison officer, abusing the publican.

'I'm going to fucking kill you, you cunt! You think you are a big man, but you're no big man. Murrandoo is the big man in this town. And when he ain't here, I'm the big man! You fucking cunt! You'll be dancing to my fucking tune, you'll see!' There is a loud smash and the tinkle of breaking glass. Then a door slams and the shouts and threats fade down the street.

Next morning, at a leisurely hour, I drop in at the land council office. No one's there, but Bull Yanner is tucking into some bacon and eggs next door, on the steps of the land council lawyer's pad. The barmaid's there, too, and Bull motions me over for a coffee. 'Murrandoo won't get up before eleven, he's a bit of a nocturnal fella, a cockroach. But he'll be here.' He points at the shire council offices across the street. 'We've got some business over there later. They keep getting new people and we keep having to break them in.' He laughs. The most powerfully built of the Yanner brothers, he shares Murrandoo's looks, if not quite his charm. He tells me he has a house and family in Townsville, but he much prefers Burketown. 'In Townsville no one knows you, people look right through you. Here, I get respect. People watch us all the time. Like down at the pub, the publican has got eight security cameras. Eight of the fuckers! Just to spy on us, to catch us.' Then he chuckles. 'Well, seven, actually. We smashed one of them last night.'

THAT AFTERNOON I GO fishing. There's nothing else to do, but at least the evening's covered. Earlier, when I finally got hold of Yanner over the phone at midday – he'd just woken up – he'd suggested a crocodile hunt ahead of his court case in the morning. Though he'd have to okay it with Bull first: 'He's the man with the boat. I'm just the guy with the ideas and the spears.'

Meanwhile my fishing guide is Pete, who runs the van park. En route to the Gulf we spot four large crocodiles and when I mention the night's entertainment, he quickly says, 'Don't tell Murrandoo about my crocs. I need them for the tourists.' But he's on good terms with him. He's taken the Yanners fishing and they've taken him out hunting. He tells me how a fortnight earlier, after a successful hunt, Yanner parked his car bang in front of the pub with a large crocodile draped over the roof. 'He'll make sure he gets you a croc. He loves to show off.'

Crocodiles have been protected since 1972. When Yanner was charged with killing a crocodile in the mid nineties, however, he argued that as a native title holder he had the right to hunt for meat on his land. He took his case all the way to the High Court, and won. The ruling set a precedent for Aborigines everywhere.

That said, traditional hunting, Yanner-style, has made some concessions to the times. As well as bringing along a spear and a wop (traditional harpoon) for the night's hunt, he's taking a rifle, a shotgun, an esky of beer, a homemade bong and an anonymous red-eyed mate with a bagful of ganja.

His brother Bull, however, is staying home. Murrandoo, his mate and I drive the short distance to the river and back the boat down a muddy trail through the mangroves. The moon is full, the river inky black. Flying foxes flap overhead. His brother's boat has seen better days. 'It used to have a canopy but we streamlined it,' explains Murrandoo. 'Now it's a lean mean killing machine.' We cast off into the ink and motor downstream for a while, slowly, drinking beer. 'People say drinking and croc-hunting don't mix, but you find the crocs are a lot bigger,' Yanner offers. It's my job to hold the torch and pick up the red eye-shine. The further apart the red reflectors, the bigger the croc. We pick up several sets, lurking at the waterline along the bank, but each time we approach, the beasts duck under before Yanner can get a shot in.

When we get to Pete's wharf, we turn and head back upstream. 'We leave his crocs alone,' says Yanner, who estimates that he and his brothers have shot some thirty to forty crocodiles in the river over the last ten years. No wonder the beasts are wary. His father used to work in the crocodile industry in the late sixties. 'The whites shot them, the blacks skinned them and lugged them. That's how it was back then.'

Yanner's father's father was of Spanish descent. In line with government policy, Phillip Yanner, being a mixed-race child, was destined for the Mornington Island mission, but his Aboriginal mother hid him from authorities until he was old enough to work on a cattle station. Murrandoo's mother, however, was not so lucky. Also of mixed descent, she was taken from her family and institutionalised on Croker Island, in the Gulf.

'You know, when I was a kid I used to hate being called a blackfella. They'd shame me at school. They'd call me "boong", and I'd lash back. Now that I'm over that and proud of my heritage, the same lot who used to called me a boong say I'm a yellafella!'

The torchlight picks up two livid red retinas set well apart, high up on the bank. Yanner grabs the gun and fumbles for a cartridge. It's a good-sized croc, over three metres in length. BLAM! The croc launches itself forwards and glides into safety. Murrandoo picks up the cartridge and curses. 'Red! Fuck! It should have been a black one. The red shot is all right for ducks and corellas, but you need those black ones for cattle and horses. That croc would hardly have felt that.'

The water becomes gradually less brackish. In 1841 Captain John Lord Stokes anchored his ship HMS *Beagle* (the same ship that was to ferry Charles Darwin around the world) off the river mouth and paddled eighty kilometres up the Albert in a longboat. Impressed by the river's width and fresh water, he initially believed he'd discovered the chimerical waterway to the country's centre. Perhaps he was sunstruck. Stepping ashore at one point, he called the surrounding drylands the 'Plains of Promise' (a phrase repeated without evident irony on the front of Burketown's tourist brochure) and further gushed that he 'breathed a prayer that 'ere long the now level horizon would be broken by a succession of tapering spires rising from the Christian hamlets that must ultimately stud this country'.

Real estate promoters in southern cities pounced on his flowery journal, land unseen. And in England, aristocrats dreamed of a colony to be called Province of Albert with Sweers Island, off the river mouth, as a new Singapore. But subsequent visitors were less enthusiastic, particularly after two famously perished on their way back: Robert O'Hara Burke and William Wills in 1861. In addition, once a town was finally established in 1865, an Asian fever almost immediately wiped out half the population.

'They should have left the place to us blackfellas from the beginning,' says Yanner. 'It would have saved us the hassle of trying to win it back.' His vision is for the Waanyi to run the town, including the pub. But he denies his mob is using fear tactics to achieve its ends. 'We're just looking after ourselves better, that's all.'

The thirty-year-old father of five is fiercely protective of his wife, the daughter of Papuan missionaries, their children and his mother. He points out that his own home was burnt down four years ago and he and his family continue to receive death threats. He also maintains the publican is no victim – after all, until the practice was banned a few years back, Trad was one of the last publicans to sell 'Monkey Blood', a lethal alcoholic concoction mixed in forty-four-gallon drums and sold to Aborigines in flagons. Says Yanner, 'For a hundred and fifty years rednecks have run the show up here. Now we're running it, and if the rednecks won't change, we'll get rid of them. They reckon we held a gun to Australia's head over the [zinc] mine. Yeah, so what? What about our mob? What about the gun held to the Waanyi nation? Blackfellas have been held to ransom for two hundred years. Whole communities are fucked. People's lives are fucked. We've been locked up, stitched up, grogged up, paid with our lives, but it was always our land. Even the courts acknowledge that now. If some mine wants to dig it up, they can fucking well pay for it.

'Basically, we got bugger all to bargain with, but what we've got, we'll use. Look at them mobs in the Torres Strait. The Islanders are in control of quarantine up there. If one mango full of bad-arse bugs gets through from New Guinea, bang, there goes the neighbourhood. There's huge power in that. If I were them, I'd use it. If it gets a better deal for your people, why not?'

If Yanner's stoned, it doesn't show. He's smoked as much as his mate, who can no longer string a sentence together. But then Yanner thrives on provocation. He talks like he fights: dancing, taunting, one punch. (A month earlier, a Townsville publican had testified in court: 'Mr Yanner said to me, "You won't see the next one coming." Next thing I knew, I landed in the pot plant.') And he plays politics the same way: sparring with the like-minded, softening up journalists, moving all the time, keeping opponents guessing. Alone among black activists, he claims to like cowboy MP Bob Katter, for instance. Neither does he mind King Billy Cokebottle, the comedian who tells Aboriginal jokes. Hell, he tells them himself: 'I've got an uncle who married a Thai woman. You know what we call the kids? Tycoons.'

By now we're getting cold, and hungry. We pull up at a bald spot on the bank, in among the she-oaks, and prepare a fire. Yanner tosses on two live mudcrabs that we got from somebody's crab pot – possibly his own, though I doubt it. Meanwhile Yanner and his mate pack bong after bong, while I keep a nervous eye on the river.

'We'll get a croc yet,' says Yanner, sniffing the aroma of roasting crab. 'The tail is best but the belly meat is good too. And croc spare ribs are quite a delicacy.' Yanner's taste for wildlife has not endeared him to Greens. Park rangers in particular remain livid over an infamous month-long squat at Lawn Hill National Park, when the Waanyi asserted their land claim by openly fishing and turtling in the gorge. Yanner remembers it fondly. 'At one stage we were having a cook-up, all the boys sitting round the fire, when down comes the main ranger's wife. She looks at our group and suddenly starts screaming, "Max, oh no! Max! Max!" We're all looking round. "Max? Who's Max? There's no Max here." Then we look at the giant catfish on the fire and think, "Oh, right, Max."'

After finishing the crabs and the beer, we get back on the water. Croc after croc submerges before Yanner can take aim. We still spot the occasional saltie, but more and more crocs are of the smaller freshwater species. The river has narrowed and the trees almost touch overhead. Every few hundred metres the stench of a nearby fruit bat colony wafts across us. Captain Stokes would have turned back by this stage, all those years ago, his hopes of an inland waterway well and truly dashed.

The August night air is freezing. Yanner's in front, a cigarette in one hand, the spotlight in the other, rugged up in a beanie and gloves but still barefoot. Yanner's mate cuts the engine and we drift up to a freshwater crocodile semisubmersed in weeds. Murrandoo grabs the wop instead of the gun but at the last moment the beast gives a mighty swish and the harpoon misses. Foiled again.

It's well after midnight – we've been out five hours already – but Yanner's ego hungers for a croc. To rouse us he pulls out a can of bully beef from underneath his seat, along with an onion, a tomato and some bread, and we each make ourselves a splendid sandwich.

Finally, just on 3 am, in the remote upstream shallows of the Albert, Yanner thrusts his three-pronged cray spear and nails a croc. It's a baby freshie, barely eighty centimetres long, mottled black. Yanner ties up its slender snout – he hasn't killed it yet – and gives it to me to hold, one hand around its snout, its body between my legs. Its belly is white and soft and its back, too, is surprisingly supple, not horny. Its claws are harmless as a duck's, its eye feline. Every now and then it emits a soft, plaintive mew sound, like a kitten.

Ominously, the spot Yanner chooses to cook my new pet is marked by a telltale curved depression. 'Big fella, that one,' says Yanner, but we stay put. We stoke a blazing fire and warm ourselves over the flames while the baby croc is strung upside down from a nearby tree. When there's enough coals, Yanner clubs the croc, cuts its spine and severs the tail, which he heaps on the coals. Twenty minutes later it's done, the skin peeling off like aluminium foil. The white meat is coursed with strips of yellow fat, and doesn't taste like chicken at all. More like eel. Yanner grins at me. 'By the way, I don't mind if, for the sake of the story, that little fella turns into a three-metre whopper. Gotta look after my reputation.'

Cold, greasy and dog-tired, I'm desperate to head back, but Yanner's mate has fallen asleep in the mud and is snoring loudly. Yanner walks to the boat, rummages around and tosses me a gun bag and a safety vest, for bedding. 'We'll sleep here the night, by the fire. It's too cold to get back on the water.' Within minutes he's snoring too. I'm left staring at the inky river, no more than two body lengths away. Someone has to keep watch. The last man taken by a crocodile in the Gulf was seized from a riverbank just like this one.

I wake up to the sound of the bong bubbling. It's Yanner's mate. The sun's up, too – it's 7.20 am. I wake up Yanner. He's due in court at nine, and we're at least an hour upriver. On top of that, the engine won't start. It takes fifteen minutes of Yanner's bush mechanics for it to splutter into life. Motoring back, the river steams in the morning sun. Yanner's in no rush. Halfway down, we come upon a croc washed up on the bank, belly up. It's been dead for some days. Its belly is purplish and the stench is terrible. 'Maybe Bull shot and wounded it last time,' says Yanner. 'He's been ripping into them lately.' He moors the dinghy upwind and searches for his knife. 'Can't let a good skull go to waste,' he says, leaping ashore. He returns with his nose pinched and the rotting head poking out of a bucket, bristling with maggots.

We make it back to Burketown just on nine, in time to see the judge's plane land. Yanner wanders up to the courthouse bare-foot and shares a joke with two reporters from Mount Isa. They know each other well. Semidetached from the police station, the courthouse is tiny, no bigger than a lounge room inside. The police prosecutor reads out the charges:

Unauthorised possession of a pistol
Unauthorised possession of a bong
Possession of a dangerous drug
Possession of an unlicensed weapon
Failure to legally secure weapon
Possession of an illegally shortened shotgun
Possession of pyrotechnics

No plea is required, and the matter is adjourned for four months. Yanner looks like he's smirking, but more likely he's just wasted. Outside he poses for a photo by leaning against the POLICE sign and giving the V signal.

I ask him if he really thinks he can beat the charges this time.

Probably not, he says with a shrug. 'But you never know. I've faced hairier things than this and come through all right. What the powers that be need to understand is I'm not the leader here. If they send me to jail there are other boys around, just as capable. I just happen to be the bloke on TV because of my journalism background.'

He shrugs again. 'Anyway, half the people in Stuart Prison [in Townsville] are from the Gulf. My mob includes some of the most violent men around, so I'll probably do all right in there. Who knows, I might end up running the joint. And in that case, they'll want to let me out early.'

CHILLAGOE

The Shirts Off their Backs

DONNA BURTON, THE PUBLICAN of Chillagoe's Post Office Hotel, is delighted that someone was able to replace the town's regular portraitist at the eleventh hour. 'We're so pleased. Have you photographed many nudes before?' she asks as Dot, the bald barmaid, pours me a second welcome. 'Not a lot, no,' I confess. (None, actually. I'm not really a photographer at all – just a writer with a camera – but then they're not really models.) 'Oh well, doesn't matter,' says Burton, a slim, silver-haired woman of not quite fifty with a taste for sparkling strawberry wine. 'It will be easy. We're used to getting our gear off in this town.'

For the third year running, Burton has convinced Chillagoe, or at least its drinkers, to strip for a charity calendar. They didn't need much convincing. Such are the bonding benefits of disrobing, and such is the money raised for the local hospital in the process, that Burton admits it has almost become a compulsion. But she vows *Chillagoe Couples* will be the last instalment. Too many other towns have been getting in on the act lately and she's worried the novelty value is wearing off. She points to a string of copies of *Chillagoe Chicks*, 2002's effort, hanging behind the bar, on sale for $15 each. Of a thousand printed, there are almost two hundred left, and it's already mid September.

Miss September, Burton herself, smiles back at us in triplicate. Her figure is wedged in the fork of a paperbark above the caption: 'I'd rather be in a tree-some than in a ménage-à-trois!' Burton grabs a copy for us to leaf through. The black and white portraits are a little tame, she concedes. Chillagoe's finest are draped decorously and without parody on rocks, among trees and in water. Several have had their hair done like debutantes, heaped high with horse-mane fringes. Any burlesque touch is restricted to the captions – 'Slippery when wet', for instance, and 'Plenty of milk around here' (beneath a woman handfeeding a calf).

The town's first calendar, on the other hand, was overtly silly enough to be an instant sell-out. *Chillagoe Charmers* featured men brandishing the tools of their trade – a drill, a pick, a gun, a detonator – to barely cover the tools of their sex.

Burton tells me calendar participants must again come up with their own poses and captions. Most have already submitted their ideas. One couple wants to straddle a ride-on mower. Another's on the golf course: he's teeing off, she's lying on her belly with a ball between her buttocks (caption: 'Bummer of a shot, ay'). A few may need some guidance, says Burton, but basically the job's half done. However, as far as the women are concerned, she'd like me to extract 'a bit more, ah, a bit more, umm . . . '. 'Tit,' interjects her husband, John Burton, who is wiping beer glasses in the corner. 'We need more tit.'

A young woman dressed in no-nonsense clothes strides in off the main street. For a moment she pauses a few steps short of the bar, as if assessing the tableau: the nude calendars, Dot the bald barmaid, Dot's husband the drinker, Donna Burton and myself. (John Burton's ducked behind the beer fridge.) Then she introduces herself. 'Hello, I'm the relieving police officer.' She announces she'll be in town for a fortnight while the resident constable, a popular figure who knows not to lean on locals, is on leave. Burton offers her a welcome drink. She declines.

She's heard about Chillagoe's calendars, she says, staring at the row of naked Donna Burtons behind the bar. But she doesn't appear amused. Instead she has some questions. Where will the new calendar be shot? How long will it take? What is it for? Will participants be partying? Burton patiently explains. Around town. Over the weekend. For the local hospital. Hope so. The policewoman nods earnestly. Following a further briefing on the town from Burton – 'everyone here's pretty good really; we rarely have any trouble' – she takes her leave to call in at the 'bottom pub', a somewhat rougher affair where ringers spree and locals rumble, and where public nudity – in the words of one regular – is for poofters.

No sooner has she walked out the door than John Burton, who looks like a cop himself, pops back to say, 'She'll book ya.' His wife ticks him off gaily. 'Oh, John, how can you say that? She seems okay.' But her husband shakes his head and goes back to wiping beer glasses. 'You can tell. She'll book ya in a flash.' He taps his ring finger. 'That's why she's not married, see.'

ONLY A TRIO OF crumbling smokestacks remains to hint at Chillagoe's starry past. In the early decades of last century, the smelters processed copper, lead, zinc, silver and gold. Spearheading northern development, the town sustained the country's worst mining disaster, produced two premiers and spawned corruption scandals big enough to bring them both down. Now, viewed from a central limestone ridge, Chillagoe lies strewn about the surrounding savannah as if its owner left in a desperate hurry. The railway and hospital lie on one side, the two pubs on the other. Scattered among them are dwellings cobbled from tin, vans, buses and besser block, the typical window a shutter of corrugated iron propped open with a stick. Beyond the town limits is a rim of limestone pinnacles famous for its caves. Dormant marble pits – ringed with twenty-tonne cubes of marble to prevent horses and cattle tumbling in – further pockmark the landscape.

Located three hours west of Cairns, Chillagoe, population one hundred and fifty, is on a dirt road to nowhere. In the main street there's a fading map of the region: its 'You Are Here' tag points to a spot a hundred kilometres to the east. Yet the town is not dying. Not any more. It's just sleepy. Black and white live side by side without the tension found in other communities. Locals leave their cars and homes unlocked. Like the museum, the souvenir shop ('Arts, Craft and Laundromat') is left unattended. Should some tourists trickle through, a beeper sounds and a woman moseys across from next door. I end up buying a marble knick-knack out of a niggling guilt that I've woken her up.

I wander by the local hospital, where the beds are old and clunky and the Director of Nursing is still called Matron, and dawdle in the shade of mango and frangipani trees. Matron Teri Lambert spots me from the verandah. I learn that she's ordered a portable vital signs monitor with the $7000 raised so far from the women's calendar, and that she hopes the couples' edition will fund a new ECG machine. When I say I'm the photographer, she laughs. 'Your subjects will say they're doing it for charity, and of course they are, but some of them are old enough for it to be a personal investment.' She walks me around the back to show me a steel structure protecting her ambulance from the sun. 'I'm very proud of that shed,' she says. 'That's what the blokes [calendar] built.'

IF CHILLAGOE'S HEALTH GETS a lift from charity, its social life positively spins around it. That Friday evening at the Post Office Hotel, as well as meeting many of the calendar couples, I'm struck by the number of bald people. It transpires that twenty-odd people had their heads shaved a week ago to raise money for the Leukemia Foundation. Others arrived on foot from Dimbulah, a hundred kilometres away, in aid of the same cause. 'It was a great night,' says Donna Burton, one of the walkers. 'And we raised a heap. Dot's head alone went for $700.'

As arranged by Burton, a three-man Channel Nine crew from *A Current Affair* shows up midevening. The reporter is banking on a 'TOWN'S GONE STARKERS' story and wants to schedule as many couples as possible the next day. This proves tricky, however, as most of the women will be attending a bridal shower for one of the participants. Given that it is also variously referred to as a ladies' morning tea, a prewedding brunch and an afternoon sausage sizzle, how long it will take is anyone's guess. 'You're on Chillagoe time now,' Burton says.

The calendar's most senior couple are Bill, fifty-eight, and Margaret Korsch, sixty, though Bill, an asthmatic marble miner, is not exactly comfortable with the idea. He takes me aside to propose a pose. It's cute and I tell him so, but he remains on edge. 'Margaret and I are not going to be in any funny business,' he tells me sternly. The penny drops. I explain I'm as new to the caper as he is, and relief washes over him. 'I was a bit worried about where these kind of pictures might end up,' he says. His wife takes his hand. 'We're doing this to help out the town, like everybody else,' she says. 'Also, when Bill and I are in a nursing home in twenty or thirty years time, we can hang the picture on the end of the bed and say, "This is what we did when we were young."'

The next morning begins apace. In a cave outside town a local ranger strips and wriggles into what looks like a particularly nasty piece of bondage apparel. It's a caving harness. 'I really should have practised this, shouldn't I?' she says, squirming beneath the straps. 'Youch!' Meanwhile her husband reclines naked on the cave floor with his legs stretched either side of a two-metre stalagmite, which she'll pretend to scale. Fortunately, no unsuspecting tourists clatter down the steel stairs while we're thus engaged.

Back in town, John and Donna Burton disrobe on the marble bar of their hotel with practised ease. (Since his appearance in *Chillagoe Charmers*, locals have taken to calling their publican 'Mr Bush'.) They've barely covered up when a folk-singing duo turns up with two guitars. I take them out to a nearby field of anthills, where the hardest thing – as with all folk singers – is to get them to stop. 'But we've got twenty-seven verses to go,' one of them protests.

Next are station hand Ashley Pashen and his one-armed girlfriend, 'Indiana' Pippa McLean. The arm was lost in a sawmill accident four years ago. Her upper thigh bears a large tattoo of an Indian chief, a twenty-first birthday present from her father. We head out to the paddock where Pashen's horse, Flagon, is tethered, along with two nags called Plonk and Bundy. Pashen's plan is to ride Flagon and lasso McLean. 'It's a cowboy and Indian theme,' explains Pashen. The man-ropes-armless-girl image doesn't quite grab me, however, and even the TV reporter appears to have some qualms about it. In the end Pashen is persuaded to sling his partner across Flagon's rump instead.

Four months down and it's only 10.30 am. We repair to the pub, where the word is out: the new constable means business. She's been up and about all morning, pulling people up for failing to indicate, wear seatbelts and abide by other regulations that are considered pointless at best in Chillagoe. 'It's a scandal,' jokes one part-time miner. 'Next a man won't even be able to drink and drive in his home town.'

Two quick beers later we're bound for Koolatah Station in John Burton's six-seater Piper Cherokee, the only plane on the Chillagoe airstrip. He bought it a year ago for $1900. 'Cheap? Sure, but I've done a fair bit of work on it,' he says as he bends a recalcitrant flap of nose fuselage back into place. Inside, he pulls out the operator's manual. I assume he's kidding, though maybe the camera crew knew something I didn't when they opted out of this trip. As we taxi downwind, Burton checks the controls out loud, like I'm his instructor. A couple of wallabies bound across the runway ahead of us. I ask if he's ever hit one. 'Christ no,' he says. 'We'd be shrapnel.'

Flying across the base of Cape York, the country quickly flattens out into a vast, scorched plain, scratched by myriad bush tracks. All are impassable in the Wet, when Burton does grog runs on request until the airstrips go under as well. At Koolatah, Helen Zutt is nervously waiting in a sarong and battered 4WD. Her husband, 'Big Dick' Zutt (Dick's a very big man) is bringing his grader along for the photo. Zutt is the station's 'yardie' (general handyman). Helen's the cook. They live in a donga away from the homestead, which stands empty during the Wet. The station manager, his wife and kids, their governess and the stockmen don't return until March. 'Not a whole lot happens out here,' says Helen. 'That's why we reckoned this calendar could be a bit of fun. But then, we'd had a few at the time.'

On the return trip clouds are massing. We fly between them, under them, over them and around them, but never through them. 'I like to see where I'm going,' explains Burton. 'I don't like to rely on my instruments.' Closer to Chillagoe it's raining and the limestone pinnacles glow purple beneath a leaden sky. Burton swoops low over the pub to let his wife know he's home and lands his craft with a bump. Says Burton: 'A good landing is one you can walk away from. An excellent landing is when you can use the plane again.'

Back at the pub, we hear there's bad news and good news. The bad news is that a 4WD car has rolled near Wrotham Park, a station which Burton had earlier pointed out to me from the air. The good news is that the constable has left town to attend the scene. Later in the afternoon couples pose in the local bogey (swimming) hole and in a cattle trough. The last light is reserved for Bill and Margaret Korsch. En route to the old smelter yards in their rattling ute, we pass a couple trudging along the road, carrying saddles. I'd seen them the evening before, too, walking with their saddles. 'That's the nearly-weds, Greg and Nita,' says Margaret. 'You're photographing them tomorrow. She's the girl that had the bridal shower this morning. They are probably looking for their horses. They're always looking for their horses.'

We drive on to an expanse of black copper slag and unload the dinghy. 'For our caption we thought of "Waiting for the tide" because this all used to be sea once,' says Bill. All the same, it's been a 450-million-year wait. Their set-up is an elaborate one. They've brought pillows, hand lines, a fishing rod and a home-sewn lace brassiere to tie to a makeshift minimast. Bill has even made Margaret a spectacular if perilous-looking necklace of barramundi lures to drape over her breasts.

'We had a rehearsal at home,' Margaret explains. 'The neighbour couldn't figure out what we were doing, sitting in the boat in the backyard, trying different positions. At least we still had our clothes on.' Just as they're ready to face the camera, a second ute turns into the smelter yards. 'Oh no,' says Bill, recognising the vehicle, 'it's . . .' when suddenly there's a yelp from his wife. Margaret, having turned to look, had forgotten about the barra lures.

Fortunately it's just a few scratches, revealed to much laughter later that evening at the 'top pub'. But it's another set of scratches that brings the house down. It transpires that 'Xena', as the overly zealous policewoman has been dubbed, rolled her car on her way to the roll-over accident. She's spending the night in Mareeba hospital, nursing a broken wrist and bruised pride.

The night flares in her absence. As well as the stars of *Chillagoe Couples*, revellers include stockmen, mustering pilots, the TV crew, a contingent of Dutch, Swiss and German endurance cyclists, their entourage (including a brace of leggy masseuses), and two off-duty policemen from nearby Dimbulah who pretend to be scorpion hunters engaged in the live pet trade. Even one of the nearly-weds' horses gets a look-in halfway through the night. The folk singers sing, the bald barmaid yodels and the Germans are taught a Slim Dusty song. By midnight one of the off-duty police is having his backside signed by the masseuses, while Pippa McLean, the one-armed calendar girl, is goading the TV cameraman to bare his in return for having filmed hers. He obliges by challenging a diesel mechanic to a naked race down the main street. It's an unusual run – with their underpants around their ankles and a lit length of toilet paper dangling from between their buttocks, the men don't get very far. But the so-called Dance of the Flaming Arseholes does raise another $34.50 for the hospital.

THE ENGAGED PAIR, GREG Todd and Nita Burdell, live at her mother's place on the outskirts of town by the old limeworks. Crows caw overhead as I ease past a donkey at the front gate. 'Watch her, she'll kick ya!' It's Todd, the groom-to-be. He's slouched in a chair on the patio, wearing a week's growth and a battered hat. As I approach I pass a couple of dogs. 'Don't go near that black bitch cos she'll bite ya!' I stay standing. 'You've found your horses, I see,' I say. 'Yea-ep,' he says. 'We always find 'em.' His fiancée emerges wearing a veil. Though well into her twenties, her shyness is disconcertingly childlike and I'm grateful for her mother's presence.

On the way back I stop by Tommy Prior's 'truck farm', an assembly of lovingly restored World War II trucks and burly Fords. Prior, jockey-sized and sixty-four, creeps out from behind one of them to pop the bonnet of a deep blue 1946 V8 ute. His harelip initially makes him difficult to understand, though when I ask, 'Does it still go?' there's no mistaking the phrase: 'Like a shower of shit!' (Prior is famously sensitive about his speech impediment. He once knocked out a station hand for daring to answer him with the same slur. 'That'll teach ya for having a go at me, ya bastard,' he'd reputedly growled. It turned out the poor fellow had a harelip as well.)

He kicks the engine over and we listen. Next he pats a Ford Blitz, a hulking war truck with tyres that come up to his chest. 'This is my four-wheel drive. Wouldn't bother with that shit they're making now. Done over a million miles and not a rattle in him.'

Prior was born in Chillagoe, 'unlike all them Johnny-come-latelies you've been talking to'. He reassembled his first Ford engine at the age of nine, started a local carrier service in 1958 and holds countless regional speed records. 'Did Mareeba to Cairns in twenty-four minutes [fifty is fast] in this one, and Cairns to Townsville in two and a half hours,' he says, fondling a hefty '45 Ford. 'And that was on the old road. Can't do it no more because of the cops, but I reckon it's disrespectful to go any slower.' Disrespectful? 'To the Ford. It's all about respect. I used to go from here to Cairns to Townsville to Charters Towers and back in a day [about 1200 kilometres], put her back in the shed, and she'd hardly be warm.'

I return later in the day with Margaret Korsch's son, Danny Lee, and his ex-girlfriend, Liz Bishop, who's a good friend of Prior's. Lee and Bishop have been ice cool for a month but on impulse they've agreed to pose in the back of Prior's antique V8 ute. 'Are you staying to watch, Tommy?' asks Bishop as she rolls out a swag on the tray. He laughs. 'Nah, I think I'll go inside and watch *Oprah*.' But he doesn't. After all, it's been a long time since his ute got this level of respect.

JUST ONE COUPLE TO go. They're an hour's drive away and there's not much left of the day, so John Burton offers to fly and half the merry bar elects to come along for the ride. We grab a slab of beer for the station, pack a small esky for the flight (all ten minutes of it) and arrive above Crystalbrook Station to find its airstrip dotted with cattle. Burton buzzes them once to clear the strip. Station owner Adam Hill seems unfazed by the number of spectators, who happily declare they've come see his beautiful wife naked. If Chillagoe has an 'it' couple, it's the Hills, whose ringer-meets-nurse romance forms part of a long and sustaining outback tradition.

We quickly arrange the shoot in the cattle yards and corral the visiting drinkers in a distant pen. After finishing the calendar, and a good part of the slab, the dying sun provides just enough light for us to make it back to Chillagoe without Burton having to resort to his instruments. In the half-light I spot two horses ambling down the main street, from the direction of the old limeworks. A 4WD police car is cruising towards them, from the direction of Mareeba. 'Looks like she's back,' I shout at John Burton over the noise of the Piper. 'She might not be quite so gung-ho now.' But Burton shakes his head and shouts back: 'Either that, or she's going to be very, very cranky.'

CAPE KEERWEER

Everything but the Scurvy

THERE WAS MUCH LAND, for the most part waste, and inhabited by wild, cruel, dark, barbarous men who killed some of our sailors, so that the true nature of the land and what might be produced or desired could not be understood and the farthest point in the discovered land was given the name of Cape Keerweer [Cape Turn Around].

From a report given to Abel Tasman by Dutch authorities in Java, ahead of his 1644 voyage to Cape York.

'IT STARTED WITH A girl,' says Silas Wolmby, sitting cross-legged on the poop deck of the regally reconstructed *Duyfken*, surrounded by a handful of crew. 'Oh, she was a fine-looking woman. She must have been, ay. The more beautiful the woman, the bigger the fight. And this was a big, big fight, so . . . ' The Wik elder and one-time tent boxer makes an appreciative sound with his tongue. The ship's artist, sensitive soul that he is, blushes.

Wolmby's story of Australia's first encounter between black and white fills the balmy afternoon. The Gulf of Carpentaria is as placid as a pond and Cape York's western coastline is a distant, dun-coloured crust. The skipper, Peter Manthorpe, is waiting for a light northerly to puff us through the night to Cape Keerweer, where Wolmby's ancestors fought the original *Duyfken*'s crew in a wild free-for-all in 1606.

Manthorpe did well to invite Silas Wolmby, along with his brother Ray, to come sailing after the morning's welcome ceremony in Aurukun. Particularly after having Wolmby, spotted white at the time and wearing a diadem of ibis feathers and a grass skirt over his pants, brandish two quivering spears under his nose.

'My people, the Cape Keerweer people, saw them come, the Dutch mob,' Wolmby continues. 'It was black under the trees; there were two, maybe three hundred blackfellas. They watched the Dutchmen row ashore in a boat with nine, maybe twelve empty barrels. The Dutchmen dug a deep well. Every night the Dutch rowed back to their ship.

'One day, the Dutch turned up with tobacco, flour and soap. They didn't know my grandfather [ancestor]. He was a very big man with a terrible temper. My grandfather, that silly old man, he threw away the flour. He spat out the soap. "I own this land," he said. "Who are these people? What is this rubbish?"

'This beautiful girl was standing near one of the Dutchmen. Her hair came all the way down her back. That Dutchman grabbed that girl. Right there, with the white hand on the black arm, there was trouble. My grandfather hit the Dutchman in the back of the neck. Knocked him out stone-dead. The Dutchmen began firing their guns, but my grandfather shouted to kill the others. He speared one man, then another. They killed all of the Dutchmen there, in the well. Then they burnt the [row]boat.'

'Sounds a bit like payday,' someone comments, nodding in the direction of Wolmby's Aurukun community, infamous for the social mayhem of its weekly hit of welfare money.

Wolmby, a teetotaller, smiles grimly, 'Payday's worse, brother.'

'How many Aborigines were killed?' another asks him.

'Oh, eighty, maybe ninety. But you know, what I wonder is why that old man had to kill that Dutchman. Maybe my grandfather wanted the girl for his wife, I don't know. Who was to blame? The Dutchman? Or my grandfather?'

'The Dutchman,' Robbie Jefferson, the ship's artist, says quickly. 'He should have been more polite.'

Wolmby grins. 'True, brother, true. But I wonder, ay. Think, think of the beauty of that girl. Her eyes, her breasts, the way she stood. Long hair down to her waist. Maybe she smiled at the Dutchman. Maybe their eyes met. What would you do, brother? That fella had been lonely for a long, long time.'

Wolmby leans back to let the crew ponder that one. They have been lonely for a long while too. Manthorpe asked his girlfriend to marry him just days before sailing out and hasn't seen her since. The *Duyfken* left Fremantle four months ago, bound for the nutmeg island of Banda, Indonesia, where the original voyage of discovery began. Now the novelty of sailing this stunning replica, built from European oak and authentic down to its steering wheel (it's a stick), crew living quarters (there are none) and bilge pumps (the ship leaks), is wearing thin. 'A pitching, lurching barrel of bruises,' is how Manthorpe describes his vessel, albeit affectionately.

Conditions on board are not all that different from four hundred years ago – no showers, no meat, minimal lighting, too much rice and someone always snoring somewhere. As for pay – don't tell the Maritime Union. The leading hands get just $8000 a year with twenty days leave – no weekends – and pay their own medical expenses. Their skin is permanently cruddy with tallow, tar and salt, and many sport weeping tropical ulcers the size of dollar coins, with three crew requiring hospital attention in Weipa. 'At least no one has scurvy; that's a bonus,' says Nicole Gardner, one of three leading hands.

But people cope. None better than Gardner, nineteen, who spends her leave working on the boat as a volunteer. She rang her mother from Weipa to say she wouldn't be going back to university. She says her family had hoped an all-girls' school might mend her tomboy ways, 'but they realised all was lost when they caught me mending my school skirt with a sailing needle and wax twine'. Her main gripe is that the ship has often had to resort to the noisy engines to stick to its schedule, which includes a string of fundraising appearances.

Just twenty-two metres long – half the length of James Cook's *Endeavour* – the ship looks remarkably undersized to have been given the task of discovering new lands. Captain Willem Jansz left Banda in the *Duyfken* (Dutch for 'little dove') in February 1606, at a time when the Dutch East India Company, known as the VOC, was ruthlessly expanding its influence. Armed with ten cannons and up to twenty crew, Jansz was seeking to discover gold and spices in the fabled land of New Guinea. Instead, he found Australia, the first European to do so, at the Pennefather River, just north of Weipa, a hundred and sixty-four years before Cook struck a reef and stopped for repairs on the other side of the Cape. Jansz was not impressed: 'River with the Bush' is how he marked the occasion on his chart, which is all that remains of his journey.

By the time Jansz got as far south as Cape Keerweer, he'd encountered nothing but barren lowlands, treacherous shoals and crocodile-infested estuaries. Presumably the loss of a rowboat and several men was the last straw. He cut his voyage short (keerweer means 'turn around' in Dutch) and turned for home. Heading north, Jansz lost another man to Aborigines at present-day Mapoon, and still more at Irian Jaya.

The only written account of Jansz's tribulations was by an English trader, Captain John Saris, who saw the *Duyfken* limp back into Banda. After inquiring what had passed, Saris noted that 'in sending their men on shore to entreat of trade, there were nine of them killed by the Heathens, which are man-eaters. So they were constrained to return, finding no good to be done there.'

If, as some evidence suggests, Jansz lost up to five men in Irian Jaya, at least three were killed at Cape Keerweer. Silas Wolmby, however, is adamant that his ancestors killed nine of Jansz's men. Although no words exist in his Wik-Gnathan language for numbers beyond three, he distinctly remembers his father, and his grandfather before him, knocking down a stick nine times to signify the number killed. 'Nine Dutchies for sure,' says Wolmby. 'Must have been young fellas. I'm thinking of that girl . . .'

A shout from Gary Wilson, the workaholic first mate, signals that the lazy afternoon has come to a close. A light evening breeze has arrived on cue and it's all hands on the anchor cable. 'Two, six, heave! Two, six, heave!' goes the cry.

It's the hardest job on the ship, hauling in this monstrous weight from the deep. Hard enough for Jefferson to wonder if this degree of authenticity is absolutely necessary. 'Even eighteenth-century technology would have been nice,' he mutters.

'Carn, you wimps! Pull it like you're pulling a sailor off your sister!' urges Wilson from the beakhead. Once the anchor is roped into place, the sails are raised, yanked and tweaked into position in accordance with Wilson's square-rigging gibberish. 'Tail on the burden,' he yells. 'Halyard up fo'd!' Something like that.

There's hardly enough breeze to billow the sails, but the Aboriginal flag is flying aloft for the first time, a present from the Aurukun community. Night falls as a large ship passes to the west, laden with zinc ore bound for a smelter in Rotterdam. It seems the Dutch have finally found some riches. To the east there is a smudge of fire, possibly a burn-off, but otherwise no sign of life. The coast looks the same as it would have done in 1606. If anything, it is more thinly populated today.

Dinner is eaten by the light of the moon. Afterwards, Wolmby, a former chairman of the Cape York Land Council, returns to the poop deck with his 'little' brother Ray (who is fifty-nine) to kick back and enjoy the ride. The pace is a knot or two at best. As the ship ghosts along in the dark, the brothers begin softly singing and clapping traditional songs.

'We feel happy about this ship,' Wolmby says later. 'Oh, some people might say, "Don't let them in, old man. You should be angry, old man." But when I saw that fella Peter jump out of that dinghy, when he asked me for permission to step on our land, I only felt, "Oh, welcome, brother, welcome."'

At first glance, Peter Manthorpe, thirty-nine, looks too mellow to be the skipper. He'd make a likelier ship's artist. He sleeps in a hammock, wears a straw hat and plays guitar on deck on moonlit nights. Back home in Adelaide he drives a Kombi, keeps chickens and plans to build a boat with his father, Pep, a former harbourmaster, to whom he remains very close. As well as his master's ticket, Manthorpe has a degree in English literature and anthropology. He likes to read Conrad to the crew in the evenings, and posts an entertaining log on the Web. Mindful of the Invasion Day protests that greeted the First Fleet re-enactment, he admits to having had some early doubts about the voyage. The Indonesians could hardly be expected to remember the VOC fondly. And would the *Duyfken* really be welcome back in Cape York? But the crew received a royal welcome wherever they went. 'The ship is such a beautiful thing, it has become the focus of any number of people's imaginations,' says Manthorpe. 'Particularly in Cape York, the people seem to understand what we're doing better than we do. Suddenly we find we have sailed right into their oral-history tradition. It's what they do, keeping history alive with ceremony, with song and dance.'

Informing the rest of Australia about its discovery, however, has not been easy. The crew, several of whom have sailed on the *Endeavour* and the *Bounty* replicas, suspect that the Australian public is 'tall-shipped out' after several re-enactment voyages over recent years. And they wouldn't put it past the eastern seaboard to think Australian history began with the discovery of Sydney. Says Wilson, the second-in-command, 'It's kind of understandable, I guess, this bias we have towards Cook. The *Duyfken*'s voyage might have been first, but it didn't lead to anything, whereas Cook's voyage did. It's the winners who write the history books, after all.'

It wasn't until the 1970s that anthropologist Peter Sutton learnt several Cape York languages in order to record more oral history, including about the Cape Keerweer incident. The story presented to Sutton differs slightly from Wolmby's, in that the Cape Keerweer 'grandfather' apparently 'lent' the Europeans his two wives. (Sutton notes this practice was not rare, which is hardly surprising when you consider that the Wik-Gnathan word for wife, *pu'eth*, literally means 'has vulva'.) Only when the Dutchmen held on to the women for too long did all hell break loose.

In the oral history of the Wik, the Dutch appear as 'the first mob' and 'the second mob'. The second mob arrived seventeen years after Jansz, in the Arnhem and the Pera, led by Jan Carstensz. Carstensz was under instructions to shanghai Aborigines in order to extract information about spices and minerals. Not surprisingly, his attempts met with considerable hostility, and his men were beaten off by large tribes at several points along the coast. Carstensz, too, made it no further than Cape Keerweer.

Twenty-one years later, in 1644, the Dutch sent Abel Tasman to see what he could find. Although no log remains (and although Tasman made it well beyond Cape Keerweer – all the way to Western Australia, in fact), his Cape York experience cannot have been encouraging, either. The Dutch did not visit the place again for another one hundred and twelve years. Nor did anyone else, for that matter.

FIRST LIGHT HAS THE *Duyfken* at anchor off Cape Keerweer. The Wolmby brothers are awake, conversing animatedly in Wik-Gnathan. They are pointing at an unbroken stretch of flat-lands in the dim distance. Cape Keerweer is actually the mouth of the Kirke River, which runs north behind a narrow tongue of low dunes for five kilometres, parallel to the beach, before finally elbowing its way inland.

According to Silas Wolmby, Jansz's men dug their well about halfway along the narrow spit. Following the slaying of the boat-load of crew, Wolmby's ancestors fled by swimming across the Kirke. Meanwhile, the remaining sailors regrouped to go on a punitive rampage on the south side of the river, killing scores of unwitting people from a different clan. 'They never got that crazy old grandfather,' he says.

After breakfast Wolmby summons a bucket of seawater and lines the crew up on deck for a protective dose of *awel*, or 'underarm smell'. 'There are too many spirits here to mess around,' he says, removing his shirt. 'I don't want anybody to get sick.' Wolmby runs his hands under his armpits and rubs the sweat over each crew member's hair, shoulders and belly. Calling out to sea, he implores the spirits of his dead ancestors to recognise this stranger as a friend. He completes the ritual by rinsing the hair with a palmful of seawater and blowing through it. Only the ship's artist baulks. 'You want to swell up like a pelican, with a big neck and small eyes?' Wolmby asks him.

Jefferson quickly steps forward, eyes shut tight. 'Just the back and sides, thanks. And no wash.'

A leading hand ferries us ashore in the rubber dinghy in groups of four. Carstensz called this 'the most arid and barren region that could be found anywhere on Earth'. But Wolmby will have none of that. 'There are lots of wild fruits here. Also crabs, fish, birds, dugong, goannas, sea turtle. I was born here, and I will die here. My nephew is always saying to me, "Uncle, whenever you want, we will take you home." There is lots of trouble at Aurukun, lots of violence and rape. I want to be well away from that. I'm tired of young drunks saying, "Hey, old man, give me tinned meat." "Old man, give me cigarette." "Give me fifty, old fella."'

Wolmby is keen to show Manthorpe an old well. The pair meander barefoot across the dunes, between the river and the sea. He points out dune berries that taste like snowpeas. 'Very good for VD [venereal disease],' he tells Manthorpe, who nods politely. Suddenly a dog barks from a fisherman's camp by the river. A wild-looking character appears shortly with his young family, offering to drop off a bag of barramundi in return for a tour of the *Duyfken*. He tells us he has been coming here for twenty years, and in that time the river mouth has shifted at least a kilometre.

But Wolmby is unfazed. He eventually stops at a large sandy depression near a couple of tall casuarina trees. Bleached bailer shells as big as bread loaves lie abandoned around it, and it is partly overgrown with beach hibiscus. 'This belongs to the second mob,' he says. Could this really be where Carstensz and his men dug for water in 1623? It seems incredible, and yet . . .

'The first mob dug over that way,' he says. 'That's where the bodies are buried, under those trees.'

'We don't need to go there,' says Manthorpe.

'No,' says Wolmby.

They sit down and gaze at the *Duyfken*, a burr on the horizon. Wolmby lays a hand on Manthorpe's shoulder. 'Peter, my son, we have been telling the *Duyfken* story for a long time. Now you've made the old story new again. I will never forget you, Peter.'

Manthorpe remains quiet. Later he writes in his log that the old man reminds him of his dad – 'the eyes that see detail in the distance, the low but arresting voice, and those endless stories . . .'

The skipper and the elder stay put for most of the morning. Finally Wolmby says, 'You know, I can't stop thinking of that girl. When my father told me how that Dutchman grabbed her, I ask him right away: "That girl, was she very good-looking? Or so-so good-looking?" "Very, very good-looking," he told me. Now I'm thinking, why did she stand so close to that Dutchman? He must have been good-looking too. Maybe – I don't know – but maybe she liked that fella?'

AT THE TIP

PAPUA NEW GUINEA

Boigu Island

Saibai Island

Stephens Island

Buru Island

Erub
(Darnley Island)

Masig Island
(Yorke Island)

Yam
Island

Mabuiag
Island

Poruma
(Coconut Island)

Badu Island

Moa Island

Naghir
(Mt Ernest Island)

Warraber
(Sue Island)

Hammond
Island

Thursday Island

Muralug

Horn Island

(Prince of
Wales Island)

Somerset

Bamaga

AUSTRALIA

Travelling North IV

TUCKED BEHIND A MANGO tree in Thursday Island's main street, Stan Pedler's shop doesn't look like a travel agency. More like a video library. The sign above the door reads 'Sower Christian Bookstore, Agent for All Pest and Weed Control'. But then, on TI, it obviously pays to diversify. The newsagency sells kitchen utensils. The supermarket sells fridges. See Hop Investments is a bakery that sells hard-boiled eggs. And Stan's an insecticidal Bible-thumper who sells plane tickets.

'If you get to the outer islands and you want God on your side, then I'm your man,' Stan tells me with a kindly smile. 'Otherwise you can hop in a dinghy like the rest of these jokers and run on a prayer.'

Stan's a modern-day missionary. A large, effusive fellow with a colossal colonial-style moustache, he has two life stories to tell: his own and Jesus's. Fortunately, his own gets main billing. He keeps a copy of it behind his desk – the unpublished auto-biography, *Kid from Bongeen*.

A failed cotton farmer and unlucky in love – 'God shut all doors: I couldn't get the lowest-ranking cotton-picking job' – Stan flew north in his little Cessna as far as he could, to Mer, in the eastern Torres Strait. There, at last, he again felt the warmth of God's pres-ence. There was no fishing on Sundays and the Islanders' biggest party of the year was the Coming of the Light, in commemoration of the arrival of the first missionaries in 1871. But Stan sensed another presence too. He shows me a diary entry: 'God in the morning, the devil in the afternoon. Everyone's in the canteen.'

A year later he returned to Mer in a yacht laden with picture Bibles and Jesus videos. Calling himself New Light Ministries, he moved on to nearby Stephens Island, a tiny place of a dozen households where every television ran off the chairman's. 'What he watches, everyone watches, so I'd get him to screen my videos at prime time.' Meanwhile he narrowly survived a mango tree falling on him at an island building site. 'Everything just went green real quick. This great big massive branch just missed me. It was God's way of saying thanks for the good work, keep it up.'

My travel agent pauses to twirl his moustache. 'So I did. I went all around the Strait before setting up shop here on TI. Now, where do you want to go?'

'North. As far north as I can. To Saibai.'

'Saibai? There's nothing there. I left some videos there once. You know where I found them again? At the rubbish dump. Why do you want to go there?'

'I want to look at Papua New Guinea.'

'Why don't you just go to Papua New Guinea?'

'I'd like to see Saibai, too.'

'Can't say I didn't warn you. What else do you want to see?'

'Badu. I read a book about it as a kid.'

'*The Wild White Man of Badu.* By Ion 'Jack' Idriess. I got it right here. You know, that's what first drew me up here, one of his books. *The Drums of Mer.*'

'And Hammond Island. I'd like to see the church.'

'Ah, Hammond's lovely. Owned by the Catholics – trust them to end up with the best real estate. But you can catch the school ferry across to Hammond. So you want to fly to Badu, Saibai . . . What about Yorke [Masig] on the way back? Friendliest people in the Strait.'

Why not, I said.

'So what's your purpose? You can't lob at these communities without a reason.'

'I'm writing a book.'

'What kind of book?'

'Kind of a travel book.'

'You don't look like you're travelling. You just look lost.'

I look at him blankly.

'Do you know what you're doing here? Look, son, I see people come up here all the time. They say they're here for this or that, but nine times out of ten they are running from something. They hang around the island until they realise they can't afford the rent, then they drift back down to Cairns or Cooktown. Where are you staying?'

'Upstairs at the Federal.'

'Ah. That's too close to the devil for my liking.'

'It's where Jack Idriess stayed.'

'Jack knew the devil. Listen, son. Take my advice. Go to church.'

As it happens, I do want to go to church. As a fan of the Mills Sisters, TI's septuagenarian musical exports, I'm keen to take in a TI gospel session. Attending church is also the best way to meet the locals. But which church? There are fifteen on the island, and even the Mills Sisters are divided among them. TI congregations have been fragmenting for decades, apace with the push for autonomy. Within the Pentecostal sects, Islanders, particularly women, found much more freedom to express themselves. These sects split and split again to become more like clubs than churches. But the biggest schism came in 1996, when the Anglican Church, by far the dominant Church in the Strait, all but ended up a splinter group. Fed up with being run by mainland Anglican bishops, indigenous clergy broke away to form the Church of the Torres Strait, taking with them not only

157

entire congregations on most of the islands, but also annexing the church buildings themselves.

The following day, a Sunday, ambling from church to church in search of song, I walk past 'Rumah Ross', a small, aluminium-clad house adorned with fishing buoys and bailer shells. A handwritten note rather bravely proclaims it to be the home of the Society of Islam. Intrigued, I knock, and meet Balfour and June Ross, a sweet, wry-humoured, sixty-something couple of Malay and Ambonese origin. In its pearling heyday, TI boasted a Japtown, a Malaytown and a Chinatown, and Islanders were banished to muddy reserves. But now, jokes Balfour, 'We are just a few Muslims in a sea of Christianity and it is all we can do to keep our head up. But not too far up, or someone will kick it.'

June, who wears the hijab outside the house, says a prominent pastor warns his flock not to mix with her. But she can handle herself: 'People say, "Why do you Muslims kill everyone?" And I say, "Well, I never killed anyone, but I'll start with you, shall I?"'

The day after September 11, Balfour received a visit from a detective. 'He told me President Clinton was staying in Port Douglas and he wanted to know if there were any dangerous Muslims on the island. I said to him, "How do I get to Port Douglas?"'

I'm still laughing when the phone rings. It's a crew of Muslim missionaries from Lakemba, in Sydney, who are driving up the Cape to TI and visiting various Aboriginal communities en route. Balfour eventually puts down the phone, chuckling to himself. 'Those poor fellows. They told me they were arriving tomorrow. I told them I know. I've had reports of their progress all the way, from the federal police. They're in a big hire car. Everyone thinks they are either a travelling al Qa'ida cell, or refugees fleeing a detention camp.

'This is the first lot of missionaries we've had since September 11. Everyone here is very jumpy. But they're just coming to keep me in check. It's good for June and me. It keeps us devout. They'll be staying here, sleeping on the floor, for about a week. And they want to go to Badu, to check out some Muslim surnames.'

I mention that they'll have to buy their tickets from a man who yesterday had been enthusing about the benefits of 'nuking Mecca'. 'Oh,' says Balfour happily. 'You've met Stan Pedler? He's a good friend. We argue all the time. He gives me his videos, I give him mine. Stan has a bee in his bonnet about Muslims taking over the world. I point out that June and I are childless, which is a poor premise for world domination.' In fact, says Balfour, his eyes brimming with mischief, Stan once asked him to run the shop while he was away. 'Can you imagine? A Muslim in a Christian store. On TI! Of course I said yes.' (Unfortunately, the pastor who subsidises Stan's rent later vetoed the plan.)

On my way out Balfour gives me a booklet on Islam. He does it almost apologetically: 'The missionaries will bring a new stack of propaganda, so I better get rid of the old lot.'

My next stop is the Assemblies of God, whose church is a portable classroom up the hill. Taxis drop off the old, the infirm and the obese. The congregation consists of mostly women, all dressed in colourful dresses with puffy sleeves and lace necklines. They wear their hair in buns adorned with hibiscus, and have brought pillows and blankets for their kids. Several women have tambourines, one is on guitar and another on base. The singing is as joyous as I'd hoped, but after three rousing numbers I've had enough rapture for one night. As the hallelujahs and mercies and praise-be's build to another crescendo, and everyone is sway-ing trance-like on their feet with their eyes shut, I seize my chance to slip out unnoticed.

A few days later I return to Stan's shop to return some books

I'd borrowed. The four Muslim missionaries, two of whom are in robes, are just leaving. Apparently they've decided against going to Badu. 'Too much controversy,' explains their turbaned leader. 'It would freak everyone out too much.'

I'm left with Stan, who is still shaking his head behind his desk.

'Did you see that, son? The two blokes in sheets? They were dinki-di Aussies. Now tell me they're not lost. What did I tell you? Everyone that comes up here is running away from something. Even from God.

'The problem here is that the Torres Strait has two mango seasons. They fruit in August and again in December, so we get twice the usual madness. Those blokes wanted to buy tickets to Badu. I told them they were silly as a cut lunch to go in clothes like that. The Badu mob would have them for breakfast. They used to eat people, you know.'

I tell him that I had dinner with the missionaries last night and they seemed nice enough.

'Yes, that's what's so tragic,' he says, twirling his moustache. 'Lovely people. But God has decreed there is only one way to salvation, and it isn't theirs. Now, are you still going to Saibai?'

I nod.

'And have you figured out why you want to go there yet?'

I shrug. Perhaps Stan should call himself an anti-travel agent.

SOMERSET

The Great Jardine

WAYNE BUTCHER, THE YOUNG Aboriginal leader from the Cape York community of Lockhart River, once told me that whenever he and his mates ended up further north at Somerset, it did them good to piss on the grave of Frank Jardine, John Jardine's son and the so-called Father of Cape York.

'Nothing more than that?' I asked him.

'It's been done,' he replied grinning. 'But it wasn't us. You know, if that bastard copped a crap for every blackfella he killed, the pile would cover him standing.'

THE DRY'S DAILY LEGIONS of 4WD tourists dusting up the peninsula's spine are sure to do two things. First, they will all stand on the Cape's rocky tip – mainland Australia's northernmost point – and think they have achieved something special. It's a great tradition, this. A mini carnival. Those from overseas are often accompanied by a guide. If so, he will supply the props for the photo: champagne, usually, and something 'Aussie': a flag perhaps, or zinc cream. I've watched six Germans don blue singlets, and two Danes pose next to a giant stuffed kangaroo. Australian men, however, prefer to hold something. They may pose with a stubby or with a fishing rod. But what's remarkable is how many come up with the idea to stand on the continent's very last rock and piss off the edge.

The second certainty for the Cape Crusaders is that each and every carload will spend more time whingeing about the cost of the Aboriginal-owned ferry across the Jardine River than they will waxing lyrical about any other part of the trip. The five-minute crossing is just a few bone-rattling hours from the tip of the Cape. For this, the Aboriginal custodians charge $80 one way, per vehicle. It's exorbitant, without a doubt. Daylight robbery, really, for there is no other route. But no one turns back.

To get their money's worth, many tourists like to linger north of the river. They'll probably explore Jardine National Park. They may spend a night at the Jardine Hotel, recommended in most guides as the safest place to stay on Thursday Island. And they may deviate to beautiful Somerset Bay, just south of the tip, where Frank Jardine lies buried next to his Samoan 'princess'. Still, by the time they get home, the name Jardine likely won't mean a thing other than the name of that river where they got ripped off by the blacks.

DURING THE EARLY TO mid nineties, great strides were made in recognising – even righting – past wrongs against Aborigines. Massacres were mapped, regrets offered and land rights conceded. Since then, however, there has been a backlash. Those on the conservative side of politics have been enraged not so much by Aborigines themselves, but by the whites agitating on their behalf. In a previous time these would have been called 'nigger lovers'. Nowadays right-wing columnists and think tanks prefer terms like 'do-gooders', the 'politically correct', the 'Aboriginal industry' and the 'black armband brigades'.

The backlash flared during the late 1990s as part of the hick patriotism of Pauline Hanson's One Nation Party. Before and since, however, it has been fanned by the Prime Minister, John Howard. Like the One Nation stalwarts, he feels that to dwell on the wrongs of the past is overly negative and 'un-Australian'.

More recently, the Right has turned up the heat. One of its trusted lieutenants, Keith Windschuttle, has been set the task of proving in three vast volumes that past wrongs against Aborigines have been greatly exaggerated. In his sights are the 'black armband' historians whose sleuth work has proved seminal in various landmark land rights cases. These historians stand accused of relying on suspect oral history, of selectively quoting from the documentary evidence, of operating solely in hindsight, of letting ideology cloud their judgment and even of passing social work for scholarship. The latent, deeper charge, however, is one of treachery. By rewriting history, so the patriots claim, the black armbanders have obfuscated the efforts of the heroic pioneers who have made this country great.

On Cape York and in the Torres Strait, Frank Jardine is that heroic pioneer. His story is known well enough there. As reviled by Aborigines as he is revered by graziers, the middle voice – that of tour guides, say, or travel journalists, or teachers – likes to uphold him as a tough man for tough times. Having overlanded cattle on an epic journey fraught with marauding blacks, Frank Jardine and his brother Alex joined their intrepid father at lovely, lonely Somerset, where they battled the elements and yet more savages. Frank Jardine went on to pioneer the pearl-shell trade and in total spent over half a century at the tip. As one guide-book to the Cape concludes: 'It is indeed sad that we seem to have forgotten that it took people like the Jardine family to make this country what it is today.'

Naturally, the indigenous version of Jardine's contribution is somewhat different. From Kowanyama to Mapoon, Jardine is remembered as a despot who shot terrified Aborigines out of trees, cracked the skulls of babes on tree trunks and wiped out entire tribes.

But even if this oral history is dismissed out of hand, as the likes of Keith Windschuttle insist it must be – his contention being that black oral history is no more reliable than white oral history – enough written documentation remains to arrive at a darker judgment than currently prevails. Although his journals of his Somerset years are lost, Frank Jardine wasn't the only literate chap around.

THERE'S A LITTLE-KNOWN footnote in the history of North Queensland that I like very much. It concerns the day that the 'Father of North Queensland' beat up the father of the 'Father of Cape York'. The former was George Elphinstone Dalrymple, by then the founder of Bowen. The latter was John Jardine.

In 1863 Rockhampton society was abuzz with the rumour that Dalrymple, a young aristocrat with a taste for adventure, was dallying with a married lady. Dalrymple demanded that Jardine, the police magistrate, investigate the slander. When Jardine refused, Dalrymple rode up to him outside the police station and said: 'You've prejudged my case and, I have the satisfaction of telling you, you are one of the most damnable scoundrels in Queensland!'

Jardine, who was also on horseback, countered it was the wrong time and place to raise the matter, whereupon Dalrymple said, 'By God, I've made it a proper time and place!' With that he stood up in his stirrups, raised his hunting whip high and cracked it on Jardine's head, again and again.

That same year, Governor Bowen was sailing by Somerset Bay, a secluded cove opposite Albany Island, off the tip of Cape York. Observing the rainforest spilling down to a small, palm-lined beach hemmed in by rocky headlands, Bowen was so taken with the spot that he declared it would become 'a new outpost of Christianity and civilisation'. Less than two years later he sent John Jardine, by now mired in financial scandal, to Somerset by boat to found a government settlement.

At the time the nearest mainland settlement was Rockingham Bay, now Cardwell. Seventeen years earlier the ill-fated explorer Edmund Kennedy had set out for Albany Passage from Rocking-ham Bay with thirteen men, several wagons, twenty-eight horses and a flock of sheep. Only Kennedy's loyal Aboriginal guide, Jacky Jacky, made it to the rendezvous point in Albany Passage, his boss having died in his arms just days earlier after being speared by Yardiagan warriors.

Jacky Jacky's rescuers, the crew of the *Rattlesnake*, recovered what bodies they could and buried them on Albany Island, opposite Somerset. The graves would have been a stark reminder to John Jardine of the dangers of trespassing on Aboriginal land. (Not that he needed it. As Rockhampton police magistrate, he oversaw the reprisals for the massacre of nineteen whites at Cullinlaringo Station in 1861, after which scores, possibly hundreds of Aborigines were killed in revenge.) However, Jardine would also have been aware that the *Rattlesnake* crew had remained in the area for a total of three months and established friendly relations with the resident tribes, including the Gudang.

IN 1864 TWO OF Jardine's sons, twenty-three-year-old Frank and twenty-one-year-old Alex, set out for Somerset with two hundred and fifty cattle and forty-two horses from a Gulf Savanna station. It was an ambitious journey up the length of Cape York, and one they did not take lightly. There were ten in the party, including four black troopers. All were heavily armed. The native police bore carbines and the six whites carried breech-loader rifles as well as revolvers. From the outset, as the expedition journal makes clear, the Jardines, unlike explorers such as Leichhardt or Burke and Wills, set off with the mindset that the best form of defence, in the event of an encounter with Aborigines, was attack – or a 'shindy', as they called it.

The Narrative of the Overland Expedition of the Messrs Jardine from Rockhampton to Cape York was published two years afterwards. A journalist called Fred Byerley, who convinced the Jardines that their achievement was sufficiently heroic to warrant celebrating in print, attributed the delay in publication to Frank Jardine's 'modesty'. More likely, however, it was due to Jardine's fear of self-incrimination. Shooting blacks for sport was hardly legal, after all.

Significantly, what was published was not Jardine's journal, but his edited account as told to Byerley. In most instances the number of Aborigines killed was unspecified, doubtless to protect the Jardines. It's also worth pointing out that the killing spree would have been worse had the party not lost half its ammunition in an accidental fire at the start of their trip. Even so, the Jardines owned up to killing between fifty-five and eighty Aborigines. Most of these were shot in the back, as the following digest of their own account shows:

Nov 14, 1864: The party shot a number of Aborigines to instil fear in those following them.
Nov 20: Frank Jardine uttered the words 'exeunt [leave the stage] warriors' as he shot several more.

Nov 22: Frank Jardine shot an Aborigine who loitered too close. The rest ran off, 'but before they could cross the bed of the river, which was dry, clear and about 300 yards wide, he was able to get two good shots at close range'.

Nov 23: The 'scarcity of [bullets] and of horseflesh alone prevented the [Jardine] brothers from giving their enemies a good drilling, which, indeed, they richly deserved' for 'treacherously waiting'.

Nov 27: Frank Jardine shot an Aborigine while looking for lost cattle. Meanwhile the rest of his party also had a shindy. After some spears were thrown, they killed several Aborigines and shot those dragging away the wounded.

Dec 16: The Jardine brothers, riding ahead, shot eight or nine blacks 'only regretting that some of the party were not with them so as to make the lesson a more severe one'.

Dec 18: The party came upon a tribe of blacks fishing on the Mitchell River. As the Aborigines reached for their spears, the cattlemen were 'determined this time to give their assailants a severe lesson' and opened fire.

Either by accident or through fear, despair or stupidity, they got huddled in a heap, in, and at the margin of the water, when ten carbines poured volley after volley into them from all directions, killing and wounding with every shot with very little return, nearly all of their spears having been expended in the pursuit of the horsemen. About thirty being killed, the Leader [Frank Jardine] thought it prudent to hold his hand, and let the rest escape. Many more must have been wounded and probably drowned, for 59 rounds were counted as discharged.

Riding back to camp Jardine encountered one last 'savage' and shot him dead too.

Dec 21: The Jardine brothers chased Aborigines on horseback and returned to camp 'laughing heartily'.

Dec 28: 'Some' more were shot.

Jan 14: Two Aborigines were shot and Frank Jardine 'owns to a feeling of savage delight at the prospect of having a shine with these wretched savages who, without provocation, hung on their footsteps dogging them like hawks'.

MEANWHILE, BACK AT SOMERSET, their father and resident police magistrate, John Jardine, was similarly 'dispersing' blacks. Indeed, when the Jardines finally made it to Somerset, they had to take care that John Jardine's marines didn't shoot on sight their four native troopers.

Governor Bowen's high hopes of friendly coexistence with local tribes soon lay in tatters. When a Gudang boy was flogged for stealing an axe that hadn't been stolen after all, Somerset ended up under siege, and two marines were speared, one fatally. In retaliation at least eight Gudang men were killed, including four in a turtling canoe and one hiding up a tree. The Gudang took to stealing horses, spearing stock and removing survey markers. Even Frank Jardine's native troopers ran amok and became mutinous, raiding the station and killing Jardine's favourite 'boy'. In reply Jardine executed two of them in cold blood.

By the time two missionaries arrived at Somerset in 1868, they found Aborigines were being shot on sight. Reverend Jagg, who befriended the Gudang while his colleague visited tribes in the Torres Strait, reported that the Jardines justified their actions with false claims of Aboriginal violence and infanticide. He wrote, 'At Somerset . . . the Aborigines have been described as the most degraded, treacherous and bloodthirsty beings in existence by . . . those whose only idea is to shoot them down whenever they were seen.'

It was a similar story in the Torres Strait. Attacks on whites were met with violent reprisals from Frank Jardine and his contingent of native police and marines. He particularly targeted the Kaurareg, who lived on Murulag, or Prince of Wales Island, where in 1872 a visiting missionary noted 'the scene of more than ample revenge exacted by the whites'.

The discovery of pearl-shell beds in 1869 brought a new level of lawlessness to the Strait. Lugger skippers kidnapped Islanders for work and sex, and their indentured South Sea Islander crews behaved little better. On some islands they outnumbered the local tribesmen by four to one. Rape and murder were commonplace, including the massacre of at least nine Murray Islanders by rampaging Samoans.

As the resident police magistrate, Frank Jardine chose to join the pillage. He used the government cutter for pearl-shelling and put his divers on the government payroll as marines. Mixing pearling and policing proved very lucrative. As shipping inspector and in charge of all government business, he harassed competitors and quickly amassed a fleet of six boats and some forty divers.

Jardine's main concern became not the divers' crimes but their wages, as he lamented in 1872:

The great grievance and thorn [for the pearling masters] is the South Sea Islander who will not remain the heathen Polynesian that he was, but keeps pace with the times, and is already becoming too civilised and knowing to give 12 months service for a butcher's knife, a nine-penny tomahawk, and a dab of red ochre quarterly on each cheek, as was the case in the Old Times, but has already learnt the love of money, is a good judge of Queensland rum and uses a toothbrush.

The following year Jardine pursued and married a sixteen-year-old Samoan girl, Sana Solia. She was the niece of a village chief, destined for missionary work.

Word eventually filtered south of Jardine's corruption. An official inquiry ensued, but Jardine had little to fear. The then Premier of Queensland was a mate of his father's as well as his brother Alex's brother-in-law. As a rival pearling master put it in 1872: 'I question if any Government would tolerate, but Queensland, what is done in Cape York.'

Jardine resigned as police magistrate and switched his pearling base to Mount Ernest, or Naghir, where his men had executed the leaders of the resident tribe just four years earlier. A familiar pattern of tribal decimation followed, aided by a measles outbreak.

In 1877, when the government decided to move its business to Thursday Island, Frank and Sana Jardine returned to Somerset. They lived there for another forty-two years, in relative quiet, on the headland overlooking the beach where they now lie buried.

Today, visitors to their graves see only romance. They don't know that he died a leper. Nor that she was no princess. They can't see the remains of the coconut tree where Jardine tied up scores of Gudang and flogged them. They don't know that a third grave is that of Jardine's grandson, who blew his brains out in a TI outhouse in 1963, exactly one hundred years after Somerset Bay was declared a future Singapore. And they don't see the ghosts of the Gudang.

'WOULD YOU GO TO Uganda and stay in the Idi Amin Motor Inn?' the Aboriginal activist Murrandoo Yanner once asked me. The hotel named in Jardine's honour is the 'resort' of choice for politicians, bureaucrats and journalists visiting Thursday Island.

Its pale blue, bunker-like design makes no concessions to aesthetics and appears to have been built with Port Moresby's troubles in mind. Inside its high cement perimeter there's a small pool, flanked by an odd-looking, glass-enclosed cage. This is the bar. It has all the charm of a smoker's room at an Asian airport.

Lest Islanders be under any illusion that they are welcome, the legend of the Jardines is celebrated in the form of framed newspaper articles. One of the pieces describes Frank Jardine as a fair and just man, who 'by all accounts' shot only in self-defence. There's even a novel twist on the Mitchell River massacre, with Frank Jardine presented as a man of mercy when he pleads with a raised hand: 'Let the poor devils go.'

In 1968 the anthropologist Bill Stanner called the nation's wilful ignorance about the fate of its Aboriginal people the 'Great Australian Silence'. Until then, the victors – white Australia – had been allowed to get away with a version of history that was insensitive at best. Yet it is this version of history that today's so-called patriots, the Prime Minister included, cling to and wish to resuscitate. If only someone could convince them that listening to the losers needn't lessen the standing of the nation. God knows, it might even boost it.

BADU ISLAND

The Wild White Stories of Badu

'STAYING AT THE BADU Hilton?' the pilot asks me. 'Better you than me. Been there before? You haven't heard this one then: How many Badu Islanders does it take to change a light bulb? Thirty-three. One to change it, two to yarn with him, and at least thirty rellies to attend the light-bulb-opening party.'

I smile politely. I'm the only passenger on his Badu run. Taking off from Horn Island, we skim by Thursday Island to fly over a succession of reefs – large, cigar-shaped shoals of sparkling pool-blue separated by furrows of deep azure. I peer in vain for dugongs. Within twenty minutes the plane is swooping over the biggest settlement in the Strait outside TI. The Badu community, 1100 strong, lives in a string of glinting homes along a beach facing neighbouring Moa Island, four shallow kilometres away to the east. Stretching west, the hinterland is a lightly forested slab of low ridges and dimpling gullies. It's big and wild enough to get lost in. Its caves are said to house skulls from the headhunting days. Death adders are found in higher densities than anywhere else in Australia, and resident crocodiles measure up to six metres in length. Little wonder that pets die young on Badu.

The early morning walk from the airport is pleasant if already hot. A distant stereo booms gospel music. Unlike in Aboriginal communities, the streets are neat and the houses have gardens. The dogs look well fed and less cowed. So, too, do the people.

Badulag men are widely regarded as the biggest and strongest in the Strait, a reputation forged both by their ferocious warrior past and their present-day football-playing prowess. They play hard and party harder. A recent audit of indigenous councils criticised Badu's for spending over $20,000 on 'office' Christmas drinks. Though widely reported elsewhere, it wasn't news in Badu, where people considered it money well spent. It was quite a night, apparently.

My first stop is the council building to let the chairman know I'm here. Officially visitors need council permission, a regulation which helps keep Badu that rare gem — a speck of paradise uncharted by Lonely Planet. But obtaining a permit can be a long, fraught process and, if caught at short notice, generally an excuse other than sight-seeing will do.

Mine is idle curiosity. While on Thursday Island I re-read Idriess's *The Wild White Man of Badu*, which paints a fearsome picture of a European castaway who became chief of the Badu headhunters. I'm keen to find out if any oral history persists to back up Ion Idriess's story. While academics tend to dismiss the documentary value of Idriess's work, many on the Cape and in the Strait, both black and white, continue to regard his books as gospel.

After dropping a note in at the council offices, I check in at the Tamana Mudh Motel, set on a sandy back street. Two girls are doing the cleaning, while a boy tends a square-metre of garden. They move at a Polynesian pace but the motel is spotless.

I walk down the street and a bus pulls up. The driver seems as surprised to see a passenger as I am to see a community bus. There's no one else on it.

'That will be two dollars,' he says.

'Where to?' I ask him.

'Anywhere you like. You can go round and round all day, for two dollars.'

The driver's name is Haley Nona. He's also a pastor. 'I used to be with the Assemblies of God, but then I formed my own Church, the United Torres Pentecostal Outreach.' I'm not surprised. If my time on TI taught me anything, it's that Islanders form Churches like mainlanders upgrade their cars. For now, however, Nona's happy to be my tour guide. We pass the football oval, the island's true spiritual centre. Enclosed by a two-metre fence, it boasts a decent grandstand, comes equipped with spotlights and lies smack in the middle of the community, next to the pub.

Nona points out his relatives' homes. The houses are painted in different colours and the roofs feature solar hot water systems. Curiously, like the football oval and pub, every house has a new timber fence. Nona explains it's a recent initiative to keep out the wild pigs and horses. Elsewhere tens of new homes are being built on a low dune. 'We need more houses. People that left years ago to work on the mainland are coming back to their island home,' says Nona. 'They hear how beautiful our village has become.'

It's almost a shock to see an indigenous community look this good. White North Queenslanders often rationalise the differences between Islander and Aboriginal communities by asserting Islanders are a prouder race. Unsurprisingly, Islanders are partial to this explanation as well. But this is unfair. Unlike Aborigines, Islanders traditionally lived in villages and have not been dispossessed to anywhere near the same extent. Although Islanders also lived under the dreaded Aboriginal Protection Act, and have likewise been pillaged, converted and ripped off, they were mainly invaded by other Islanders – missionaries, pearl divers and bêche-de-mer fishermen from the South Seas. Many of these invaders married in, learnt the language and went fishing. Their children, though technically half-caste, were neither seized by authorities nor ostracised by their communities. Consequently there's no Stolen Generation as such, and traditional adoption codes – *kupai omasker* – persist.

Take my preacher guide. Nona's grandfathers were God-fearing pearl divers from Samoa. His mother adopted him out to extended family. He speaks Creole and Kala Lagaw Ya, the Western Island language. And he has native title.

HALEY NONA DROPS ME off at the island shop, where I meet Helen Bowie, the larger-than-life shop manager. She arrived on Badu as a nurse twenty years ago, married an Islander and raised six children on the foreshore 'without losing a single one to a crocodile – yet'. (Her labrador was not so lucky.) Loud and rambunctious, and dressed in pink and purple, Bowie doesn't mind one bit my telling her she looks like the Wild White Woman of Badu. 'I'm a bitch,' she says happily, 'but no one seems to care up here.'

We jump in her truck for a tour of her life, starting with the crayfish factory owned by her husband, Badu's deputy chairman. 'His great-great uncle was a member of Badu's last great cannibal raid in the 1860s,' she tells me. Their home is next door, over-looking Moa Island. It looks idyllic, yet it's not a patch on the family's holiday 'shack' on the 'back beach' (the island's west coast).

The shack is a house and the back beach consists of a succession of beautiful coves, each tufted with coconut palms and fringed with reefs where children pluck crays at low tide.

Bowie and I sit down under the palms. In front of us are the remains of several *kup mari* cook-ups, shallow pits ringed with baking stones and turtle bones. Bowie, as it happens, is a little turtled out. Turtle was the main fare during three days of funeral feasting earlier in the week, and again the next day, when her husband caught a 'fruit platter' (a medium-sized turtle) with which he taught his eight- and ten-year-olds the finer points of turtling. Bowie describes how her husband tied one end of a rope to a fore flipper and the other end to a fishing buoy. The boys then practised diving after it in turn, clasping it from behind, hooking their arms under the front flippers and steering it to the surface. 'They are naturals,' she says proudly. 'They'll be bringing the big ones home in no time.'

Personally, though, she prefers dugong meat. It's tastier, she says. 'Nothing like chicken.' But she concedes dugong are getting scarce. The use of motorised dinghies has upset the balance of the traditional hunt. Surveys in the mid nineties, for instance, showed Badu Islanders *wopped* (harpooned) a dugong every three days. Islanders from Mabuiag, to the north, took even more, and researchers estimated the overall catch in the Torres Strait at a thousand a year. Such a catch was unsustainable, and the dugong population has declined sharply since then. 'I think we are starting to realise we'll have to go easy on them,' says Bowie. 'Or there will be none left to eat.'

Badu's death rate – the average lifespan is fifty-five – hasn't helped the dugong. Nor the turtles, for that matter. Each death is honoured with not one but two traditional feasts – one for the funeral and one for the tombstone opening a year or so later – and each feast lasts up to four days. Earlier, at the main Anglican church, I noticed a flyer for a 'hoopla' fundraiser: 'HOOP THROWING AND SALE OF TURTLE MEAT TO RAISE MONEY FOR TOMBSTONES.'

Death is a constant theme on Badu. Rock crevices are avoided for fear of finding skulls in them, and a patch of tea trees with blood-red leaves marks the site of a massacre by headhunters from another island. Although the island is overwhelmingly Christianised, many Islanders rumour there are still practitioners of *pouri-pouri*, or black magic, among them. Strange coincidences have added to the rumours. Within twelve months, sixteen members of one family died of separate causes. Then there were the mysterious coma deaths of a man and a boy in 1996. They were later determined to be victims of Australia's first outbreak of Japanese encephalitis, a mosquito-borne virus, but for a while everyone feared being next.

Black magic was also implicated in events a week before my visit. A utility had overturned heading back from a party at the back beach. The dual-cab was carrying thirteen passengers, twelve of them children. Seven were riding on the tray. One sixteen-year-old girl was crushed, and a three-year-old boy suffered brain injuries. But the trauma didn't end there. When the pregnant sister of the dead girl was told of the accident, she miscarried and lost her seven-month-old foetus. The family is burying the baby tomorrow. There will be a feast, albeit a modest one. Turtle only, no dugong.

ON A STROLL THAT evening I meet two teachers who inform me I'm headed for the 'piggery'. As feral pigs are the main carrier of Japanese encephalitis, quarantine authorities keep sentinel pigs to test for the virus's presence. (Apparently one goes missing every now and then, though it usually turns up the same night on a spit at some feast.) The teachers, Greg and Di, ask if I'm immunised. When I say no, Greg says, 'Well, everyone else is. But that's all right because death is quick. And you have a one in four chance of recovering completely.'

I decide to forgo the piggery in favour of a beer at their place. 'At last,' says Di, rapt at the break in routine, 'someone to talk to about something other than homebrew and football.' We drive to the back beach for sunset and emerge at a different cove to the one Helen Bowie showed me. If anything, it's even prettier. We walk along the beach and cross a tidal stream to access a semi-detached headland. The sand is very fine, the water glassy, and delicate whelks are there for the taking. Lean-tos and beach huts are spaced every fifty metres or so and shallow sand ovens ringed with turtle bones dot the high-tide line.

At the base of the headland, in the midst of a small clearing, is a one-metre pillar cupping a large spherical rock of pink granite. It looks like a giant golf tee. 'This is the warrior stone,' Greg says. 'Would-be warriors used to gather here to prove they were men. The idea is to lift it above your head with your arms held straight. Try it.' But I can't budge it. Greg manages it with his arms bent, but then he teaches physical education. He confesses to having once taken a set of scales here: it weighed precisely 40 kilograms. On the other side of the headland he found a tiny cove filled with similar boulders, tumbled by the tide. He even lugged home a 39.5 kilogram warrior stone of his own. 'You have to do something to pass the time,' he says with a shrug.

The sunset is lovely, but then, as Di points out, they always are. I ask them if they're bored. 'God yes,' says Di. 'How can you not be? This is paradise, after all.'

THE TEACHERS ARE UNABLE to enlighten me about the Wild White Man of Badu but like Helen Bowie they recommend I talk to Ate (Uncle) Walter Nona, the grand elder of the vast Nona family. I run into him the next morning on Nona Street, sitting underneath a map of the community in front of the council offices. The map shows the location of every single back-yard mango tree, for Badu is a hotspot for Asian mango pests that like to island-hop to the mainland, and the trees, like the pigs, are regularly monitored.

A lean and kind-looking man of eighty-eight, Ate Nona's already dressed for the afternoon's baby funeral in a cotton shirt and black lava-lava skirt. When I ask him about Badu's Wild White Man, he nods patiently. As grandpa to all on the island, he has told the story many times. Ate Nona tells me he has never read the book, but he was told the story by 'the old blokes'. (Ion Idriess also claims to have gleaned his story from the 'grey-beards', though most of these were drinkers at Thursday Island's rough-house Federal Hotel.)

Ate Nona proceeds to recount how a murderous white convict castaway called Wini became the bloodthirsty Chief Wongai of the Badulag people. He tells the story precisely as it is in the book, without missing a single plot twist. Several other Islanders sitting near us listen and nod. Ate Nona's story ends as abruptly as the book ends, at the point where Chief Wongai failed in his bid to capture a white girl castaway living with another tribe. 'That's the story of Wini,' he says.

But is it? It's certainly Idriess's story of Wini, chapter for chapter. Yet Wini is known to have lived for at least another twelve years. Tellingly, Ate Nona can't say how many children he had, what happened to them, how Wini died or where he's buried.

Haley Nona, the bus-driving preacher, helps me meet the man most likely to know more. His name is Peter Getawan. He's sixty-four, very big and very, very black. Silver fuzz spills from his blue worker's singlet across his back and shoulders. Unlike Haley and Ate Nona, Getawan won't wear a South Sea-style lava-lava.

'There's not much Samoan in me, not like these other fellas,' he says. We're sitting on a porch overlooking the foreshore.

Several dinghies can be seen heading out to hunt turtle for the funeral. Across the passage lies Moa Island, where the Wild White Man supposedly did most of his killing and conquering.

Getawan has lived a typical Islander man's life. He dived for pearls and trochus shell. When the advent of plastic sunk the market for trochus buttons, he left to work on the railways. Later he skippered boats and drove taxis in Brisbane. But now he's come home. His new house is almost finished and he's planning a big house-opening party. 'After that I'm just fishing, fishing, fishing.'

On the table is a big bag of native *wongai* plums, which Getawan eats like grapes. Spitting out the pips, he tells me the Idriess story is rubbish. 'They should have made it a comic book,' he says. 'It may as well have been about Borneo. My grandfather was a Badu man, from out the back here. He told me there was a white man here, Wini, but he wasn't wild. He was a tame one, some sort of teacher. Taught us how to grow things. I can show you the cave where they put his skull. Tomorrow, or maybe the next day. When I'm feeling fitter.'

Unfortunately I don't have the time, as I'm due at the airport. But I suspect Getawan's take on the Wild White Man of Badu is probably all that's left of the island's corroded oral history. The Samoan influence seems to have been all-pervasive. When Idriess's story was published, the author himself noted that the oral 'threads' had probably vanished. And that was over half a century ago.

But there is some relevant written history too. The castaway white girl whom Wini pursued did exist. Her name was Barbara Thompson and she spent five years with the Kaurareg people from Muralug, or Prince of Wales Island, between Badu and Cape York. In 1849 she was rescued by the crew of the government survey ship, the *Rattlesnake*. On board she was quizzed about her exile by the ship's zoologist, John MacGillivray, and by the ship's artist, Oswald Brierly. Both men recorded her account in their journals, though only MacGillivray's – by far the briefer and less reliable of the two – was available to Idriess. Thompson herself was illiterate.

Her rescuers seemed rather taken with her. MacGillivray described her as 'though not very pretty, she has a soft, feminine and very pleasing expression', and Brierley wrote that when 'appropriately dressed and restored to health she would be not bad looking'.

From Brierley's meticulous recordings of his conversations with Thompson, who met Wini once, it's clear Wini was no chief. Rather, he 'belonged' to two brothers – like Thompson, he'd been recognised and accepted as a *lamar*, a ghostly reincarnation of a lost relative. His real name was Gino and he did not speak English. He'd alighted on Badu in a lifeboat in about 1840 after killing a fellow castaway, whereupon he made himself useful by mending canoes and establishing gardens. Though he accompanied headhunting raids to Moa, and was present at the murders of at least one shipwrecked European crew, he was no warrior. When it came to turtling, for instance, he paddled while another dived. And he remained unmarried, whereas his warrior 'brothers' claimed three or more wives. Although he had three sons to two unmarried women, he told Thompson he dared not speak to the wives of warriors for fear of being speared. He asked Thompson to live with him on Badu, but she refused.

So how did tame Wini become Chief Wongai? In all likelihood Ion 'Jack' Idriess, having read MacGillivray's wildly misleading passage on Wini, put two and two together and came up with a ripping yarn. After all, as Idriess wrote in his foreword, it was in the pub 'that it dawned upon me that Wongai, chief of chiefs, beloved of Sida, God of the Crops, beloved of Kwoiam, God of War, had really been a white man'.

In any event, the truth is wild enough. What happened to Wini's sons? They seem to have vanished without a trace. And what happened to Wini? Was he one of the many killed by the men of Frank Jardine?

Idriess, who saw Jardine's journals before they were lost, claimed Jardine wrote 'of this great news [Wini's slaying] with the liveliest expressions of satisfaction'. Yet Idriess was of the opinion that Jardine's men got the wrong man, a mourning Badu Islander whitened with pipeclay. He might well be right about that (or perhaps they shot one of Wini's sons who would have been in their twenties by then), because a visiting missionary noted that Wini had died 'six turtle seasons' before Jardine arrived on the scene.

But Idriess never saw that missionary's account either. Instead, he asserted that Wini/Wongai 'cunningly' disappeared and 'lived to be an old, old man' who witnessed the pearling boom. But then Idriess would write that. In the epilogue to *The Wild White Man of Badu*, he was already advertising a sequel.

MASIG ISLAND

Coconut Tourism

IN THE HIGHSET GUESTHOUSE of tiny Masig, a stone's throw from the council fish freezer, I find a folded copy of the *Cairns Post* newspaper on the table. It's a month old, quite possibly left by the previous tourist.

I glance at the front-page headline: PORT GOES NUTS: LEAVE OUR COCONUT PALMS ALONE. I read on to find that the residents of showy Port Douglas, north of Cairns, are in a flap over council moves to chop down coconut palms to reduce the public liability of falling nuts. They've formed an action group, Preserve Our Palms (POP), to lobby the council to 'de-nut' the palms instead. POP feels the culling of palms will ruin the town's 'general tropical ambience' and possibly bring its tourist industry to its knees.

Sometimes the mainland must seem like a weird world to the people of Masig, formerly known as Yorke Island, deep in the Torres Strait. Coconut palms cover the cay like fur, as they do the surrounding islets. Indeed, Masig's tiny grid of sandy streets is draped with coconuts, and dozens upon dozens thud down each day. Before the day is out I watch a man on a bicycle swerve to avoid a falling nut and careen into the shrubbery. After he has dusted himself off, he introduces himself as Uncle Willy.

'Have you ever been hit by a falling coconut?' I ask Uncle Willy.

'Oh yes, *bala* [brother],' he said. 'Coupla times. Bang on the head. But I just keep going. I seen people get hit time to time, people just standing around and yarning. But I never seen anyone knocked out. One bloke, he got hit by a young one, a green one. I saw it. All of a sudden, bang! Split right open.'

'His head split open?'

'The nut, *bala*. He a little bit dizzy, but he all right. No worries, *bala*.'

I'VE COME TO MASIG partly as a tourist and partly – because Masig doesn't officially accept tourists – to look at its preparedness for tourism. Of the Strait's so-called Outer Islands only one, Coconut Island, welcomes tourists – but its resort is exclusive and very expensive. Yet there are many prettier islands, including Masig, and the potential for tourism is vast. By definition, an outer island is more than one tinnie (dinghy) fuel tank away from Thursday Island. There are over a hundred of these, of which thirteen are inhabited. Most have airstrips and no less than five different airlines patronise the region. You can even fly from Cairns to Masig direct.

Tourism is a vexed issue for Torres Strait Islanders. Their islands are beautiful, and they are all the more beautiful for being unspoilt by tourism. But the people's idyllic lifestyle is almost wholly government sponsored. A few jobs exist aboard prawn trawlers and as crayfish divers, but there is little else in the way of enterprise. The use of marijuana, much of it powerful PNG Gold, the fabled cannabis grown in the New Guinean highlands and regarded as the world's purest, is rife among the young and the bored, many of whom eventually move to Thursday Island, Cairns and Townsville.

Newly arrived, with my Kombi on the banks of the Daintree, 1993.

Cane farmer Laurie Fabrellas flies one of the three flags of North Queensland.

Bowen mayor Mike Brunker officially opens the Big Mango.

Russell Doig and his thong museum, Alva Beach.

The rodeo crowd at Mt Isa.

Cricketers' fashions at the Goldfield Ashes, Charters Towers.

Dinosaur town: Hughenden's Muttaburrasaurus.

Flinders Highway, near Hughenden.

Bob Katter on the Flinders Highway near Camooweal.

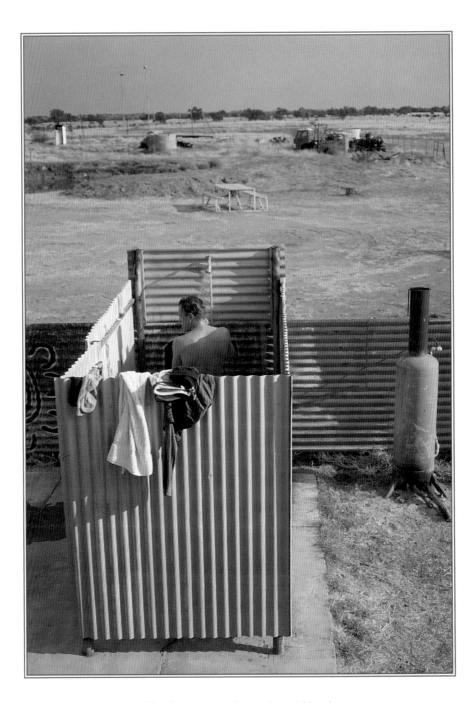

The bathroom, Urandangi Hotel.

Jundu Kamara, ready for a goanna hunt, Urandangi.

Traditional dancing at the Laura Festival.

Murrandoo Yanner, Burketown.

'Duyfken', from the crow's nest.

Silas Wolmby, Aurukun.

Chillagoe Couples calendar shots, Mr and Ms May and
Mr and Ms September.

Mango tree, Thursday Island.

Sunday at the Anglican church, Thursday Island.

Uncle Willy and the thong pole, Masig (Yorke Island).

Oma and George snorkelling (almost).

Silkwood's Three Saints Festival.

The view from Queensland's second highest mountain, Bellenden Ker,
to Queensland's highest mountain, Bartle Frere.

Main street, Tully.

Albert Pennisi on his Euramo property, a favourite landing spot for flying saucers.

Kids chasing a piglet, Reedy Brook Station, Upper Burdekin.

Guano Lager poster, Willis Island.

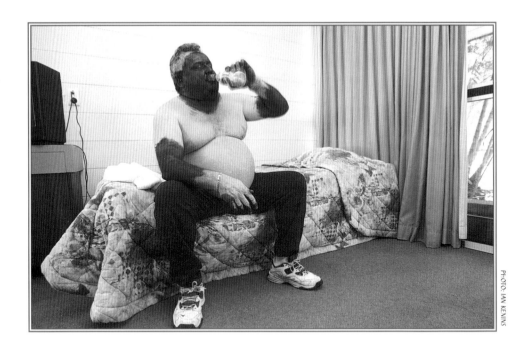

PHOTO: IAN KENINS

PHOTO: IAN KENINS

King Billy Cokebottle, Townsville.

With my dog, Guinness, Headingly Station, near Urandangi.

Yet it would seem Islanders much prefer welfare to tourism. Perhaps it's a case of better the devil you know. Church leaders, always prominent in the Strait, are loath to welcome the free-wheeling spirit of backpackers into their culture. Others fret that tourist ventures will either undermine or entrench traditional island hierarchies, particularly at a time when things are already tense between some families following recent disputes over native title. The government, too, seems reluctant to push tourism, especially budget tourism. It has enough problems policing the Strait for drugs, illegal immigration and exotic fruit pests, without the emergence of an island-hopping hippie trail. And there are other, more immediate obstacles. Take Badu, a large island with more to offer the intrepid traveller than most, and which is toying with the idea of commencing sailfish fishing charters. A community leader pointed out to me that tourists would be shocked to see dugongs and turtles being carved up on the front beach. 'We need a slaughterhouse,' he explained. 'Turtle is all right, but dugong is messy.'

MASIG'S AIRPORT TERMINAL IS a grove of casuarinas, from where a pleasant paved street leads to the hub of the cay – the community council offices, the police station and the shop, but, happily, no beer canteen. Big women in colourful dresses greet me kindly as I traipse by. Enticing side lanes bear names like Barney's Road, William's Road and Dan's Road. Kids on their way to school cycle round and round a central roundabout while two men noisily sweep the paved street with leaf blowers, pausing and stooping every now and then to remove the night's yield of fallen fronds and coconuts.

At the council offices, the receptionist tells me the chairman, Don Mosby, is in Cairns. So is Dan Mosby, another elder I'd hoped to meet. Ditto for Ned Mosby, the senior policeman and Anglican deacon. But I can see the deputy chairman, John Mosby. (Almost everyone on Masig is a descendant of 'Yankee Ned' Mosby, a Boston whaler with several wives who ran Masig as a base for his bêche-de-mer operations.)

John Mosby, a big man of about thirty with bloodshot eyes, unlocks his door to usher me into his airconditioned office. He looks a little under the weather. Perhaps he was asleep. 'Tourism ay?' he says, fingering the receptionist's scribbled message. 'That's not something I can talk about just like that. That's something to think about.'

He picks up a pen, twirls it and glances around his office – at the walls, the ceiling – with what almost seems like a 'where am I?' look.

'Anyway, welcome. Do you like the island?'

How could I not, I reassure him, and steer him back to the topic at hand.

'What sort of tourism you mean?' he asks.

An expanded guesthouse, perhaps. Or a modest swimming lagoon open to locals as well as visitors. Maybe kayaking tours. Fishing tours. Or a museum recreating Masig's wild past, which is spoilt for gripping tales. (For example, in 1836 rescuers looking for survivors of a nearby shipwreck found the skulls of seventeen sailors arranged around a ceremonial turtle shell.) There's even the potential for renting out entire desert islands, for Masig is surrounded by tens of uninhabited cays just like it.

Mosby taps his pen and looks puzzled. 'I'm not sure that is the tourism we want,' he says. 'We're thinking of putting Americans in luxury huts, like Coconut [Island] is doing. Big dollars in that.' He adds that he'd like me to talk to some 'old fellas'. However, he first has to ask the old fellas if they'd be happy to talk. And that could take time. 'How many days you got?'

Two, I say.

There's a slow expulsion of air through pursed lips. 'That's not long,' says Mosby. 'If you come back later, tomorrow maybe, maybe I have something for you. Maybe I can talk to you about tourism. When I've had a think.'

TEN MINUTES AFTER LEAVING John Mosby to think his thoughts, I run into one of his 'old fellas', Father Napoleon Woria (pronounced 'warrior'), who is collecting coconuts in a wheelbarrow. 'Going to make coconut oil,' he explains. 'For moisturiser. It's hard work but it's something to do.' I accompany him to an open-sided tin humpy with a sand floor, where he parks his barrow. The shack is his church. There are mats, plastic chairs, a guitar and a portable fan. Bunting of the kind you find in used-car yards flutters around the awning.

We sit down at a table looking out to the seafront and his old church, a pretty, whitewashed building containing three guitars and eight portable fans. Father Woria broke away from it in 1989 over the Anglicans' support of ordination for women, and took his family with him. No Mosbys joined him, however, which hasn't left him with much of a congregation.

'I think tourism is a good thing,' Father Woria tells me. 'I think it's happening already. I see people come for a day and go again. They must be a tourist, I suppose. We need them, to bring income into this community. Fish tours would do well, you know? I took the bishop fishing once. He went back with an esky full of coral trout, big ones. He was very happy.'

As we chat, a gleaming 4WD pulls up with little international flags flapping from the bullbar. It's Joseph Mosby, the island's chairman for thirty-five years until he lost the last election to his nephew. He, too, wants tourism but his notion of tourism seems to date from the days of passing cruise liners. He tells me, 'You tourist, you come here and you want to see us do traditional dance at night and making baskets, mats and maybe *lagetoi* [a traditional vessel]. You look and then you buy for big money. But we are not ready. First we have to learn to go back to the old way.'

Not necessarily, I say.

'No, you listen,' says Joseph Mosby. 'White man want old culture. My plan is to put tourists out the back, behind the airstrip, so they mind their own business. Start small, ten huts or so. The council will run it until it can give the business to a family to run. But we must start with white manager first, because we have never done it before.'

But I'm not convinced. As it is, Masig is my kind of retreat. It's a fine place to string a hammock, play soccer with the kids, meet the locals after church and feast on barbecued seafood. The community fish freezer is stocked with cheap prawns, Spanish mackerel, coral trout and crayfish, and there's always someone to take you out reef fishing if you shout the fuel.

The catch 22, of course, is that much of Masig's appeal is its innocence. If the Islanders' innocence must be broken (and surely it must – at the end of the day, welfare is no less corrupting than tourism), it best be done at a time of their choosing and with their informed consent. After all, it's inevitable that a Lonely Planet writer will reach Masig eventually. And one day, though I hope it never comes, someone will campaign to have Masig's palms de-nutted.

SAIBAI ISLAND

Lucky Island

FROM THE AIR SAIBAI Island looks every bit as unappealing as I've been warned. It's one vast swamp in a bog-coloured sea. King tides inundate the entire island, which measures twenty-four kilometres long by eight wide. A village encrusts its north-western edge, just five turbid kilometres from the mangrove jungles of New Guinea which expand north as far as the eye can see. To the rough-necked contractors maintaining the Torres Strait's infrastructure – builders, plumbers, sewage treatment plant operators – a stint on Saibai is the raw deal. They know it as Club Mud.

As on other northern islands of the Strait, everyone on Saibai, even visiting tradesmen, has been immunised for Japanese encephalitis. Unlike those islands, however, no sentinel pigs are kept to warn of the virus's breaches of quarantine. It's simply assumed Saibai gets whatever New Guinea's having.

Locals say that come the monsoon, which may last from December to March, forty-knot winds bear Papuan mosquitoes in clouds so thick that they hit the windows with a thud. But the storms also harbour other undesirables, such as the banana skipper butterfly, the melon fly, the Asian honey bee (its passenger mites are the problem), the papaya fruit fly, the mango pulp weevil, the red-banded mango caterpillar and the flesh-eating screw-worm fly. Not to mention a fungus called sugarcane smut. The names may be as colourful as a fruit platter, but each has the potential to devastate tropical crops and livestock.

Saibai forms part of the vast Fly River delta. Islanders are closely related to neighbouring Papuan tribes, sharing a similar language, dance, headdress, taro diet and totems. Early missionaries were forced to flee for their lives on four occasions. Far from the pearl-shelling beds, Saibai was largely spared the South Sea Islander invasion of other islands, but a measles epidemic in the mid-1870s cut the population in half, to three hundred. As recently as eighty years ago Saibai Islanders were still being subjected to canoe raids from West Papua's Tugari warriors, who lopped off their heads, smoked them, ate the cheek meat and hung the skulls on ceremonial trees.

That Saibai is Australian at all is an historical artefact. As recently as the mid-1970s there were moves to place it under Papuan administration, but these were vigorously opposed by the Islanders. After World War II, repeated flooding, overcrowding and disease led the Australian government to establish a new town for the people of Saibai, on the tip of Cape York. They called it Bamaga, after the chief who led his people there. Many followed, but not all. Some returned. Now some four hundred and fifty people again reside here, though village facilities lag behind those of other, less populous islands in the Strait.

I turn up on a steamy Friday afternoon. The village, surprisingly, is a hive of activity. Friday is both payday and market day, and there's a special meeting organised by Customs at the open-sided town hall, which I long to attend once I hear I'm not permitted to. It has been called in response to intelligence reports that people smugglers will soon be targeting the Strait following the Australian government's clampdown on boatloads

of illegal immigrants elsewhere. Papuan chiefs from impover-
ished villages across the way have been ferried across to listen to
the case for border protection. The Australian navy, too, is in
attendance. A patrol boat lies anchored offshore.

I learn that about a dozen foreigners have made it to Saibai in
the past twelve months, including a dinghy-load of four
Pakistanis in suits. The mind boggles at the image of them
trudging ashore at steamy, stinking, staring Saibai. What were
they expecting? Sydney?

Saibai's town plan essentially consists of two streets. A cement
esplanade runs along a two-kilometre lip of land raised enough
to bear homes, albeit on poles. The dyke is mostly just a single
house wide, cupped by lagoonal marshland on one side and
mudflats on the other. A second street meets the esplanade
perpendicularly. It runs inland to the shop, the clinic and the
school. Cars are few, the main transport being bicycles and four-
wheel motorbikes sometimes dubbed 'Saibai tuk-tuks'.

The village centre is the T-intersection where these streets
meet. The surrounding buildings, including the council office,
Customs office, grog canteen and takeaway satay stall, are ugly,
makeshift structures constructed from corrugated iron and old
shipping containers. Beneath a fig tree on the mud-front,
Papuan traders have spread out their wares. They come each
Friday when the tide is up, in up to fifteen long tin boats.

The Papuans are lean and muscular. Wading through the
mud, they bear the tucker that the Saibai Islanders, now fattened
on welfare, used to hunt and gather for themselves. There are
trussed-up mudcrabs, bags of fist-sized mangrove mussels and a
range of fish. Often as not, the catch of the day includes fresh
turtle and/or dugong. Sometimes the meat is sold dried, as jerky.

By midday, all that's left are the household things that tourists
(should Islanders ever want tourists) would prize as souvenirs, at

prices they would leap at. There are snake-skin *kundu* drums, for example. Pandan mats, palm baskets and straw brooms. And *wongai* spears, four-metre *wops* (harpoons), shell necklaces, goa nut (matchbox bean) castanets, carved face-masks, machetes and bows and arrows.

I head west along the esplanade. The smells are strong and damp, of mould, rubbish, sewage and mangrove rot. Saibai doesn't smell a bit like Australia. Unmistakably, it reeks of Asia. Gammy-legged village dogs, which look remarkably like dingoes, skulk among the junk. People play darts on their verandahs. Others sit and yarn beneath palm-thatched, *warung*-like stalls. Sitting pretty is a whitewashed church. Flanked by frangipanis, it's easily the loveliest building on the island.

I eventually come to a smattering of cheaper, older housing, including a number of colourful humpies near the sewage treatment plant. Dozens of children mill about, some naked, some laughing, all beautiful, but I keep my camera stowed away. Several men in dreadlocks seem less than friendly and do not return my nod. About forty Papuans are said to live here, mostly illegally, if understandably. Their mangrove villages across the water are without power, fuel and stores. Moored among the usual dinghies is a ten-metre outrigger canoe, fashioned from a massive, hollowed log. It's lashed with enough planks to comfortably seat twenty.

The Saibai Islanders aren't happy about the Papuan presence. Officially, none may linger beyond market day. After all, although some are paid cash to clip Islander gardens, short of marrying into a Saibai family (an exalted pursuit: Australian residency is gold to a Papuan), they have no access to a legal income. But there is another, easier option: the after-dark trade in PNG Gold. Saibai is an obvious, notorious and almost unpoliceable portal for the drug. Come nightfall, dinghies may steal in and out with impunity. Islanders won't betray the drug-runners for fear of retribution. There have been beatings in the past, and even the village chairman admits to having been threatened.

I walk on past the sewage plant, where the esplanade peters out into a muddy rut dipping into the mangroves. Black butcherbirds chortle from within the dense scrub. After a further five minutes the track brightens to open up to a hummock rising out of the swamp. It's the cemetery. The first dozen graves feature gazebo-like canopies festooned with plastic flowers. They lie in wait for families to come up with the money for the gravestones. There are also a number of tombstones covered in tarpaulins, awaiting their official 'opening'. The remaining tombstones are all studded with empty beer bottles. Many feature a Saibai totem alongside the pious dedications: generally a snake, a crocodile or a cassowary. One bears a goanna, but the thing suddenly jolts alive and scampers off into the surrounding murk.

Retracing my steps, I join the queue at the blue phone at the council office. It's the only public phone on the island. When I hang up, the gap-toothed Islander next in line politely points out that I have a mosquito on my leg. I glance down at the vermilion bubble on my calf and splatter it. My observer grins. He must have been watching it for some time.

I continue on down the business street to the school. School's out, but about twenty kids, boys and girls, are playing soccer. Again, I'm reminded of Asia. I join them and within a few minutes I'm drenched in sweat.

Back at the marketplace, the canteen has opened and the drinking is in full swing. At $21 a six-pack, and $70 a slab, the beer is too costly for all but the Islanders and the drug-runners. Meanwhile the traders have packed up their wares and bought their stores, mostly flour and sugar, to lug back to their aluminium boats. The tide is ebbing fast.

I buy four cans to take back to my quarters. Halfway there

I'm stopped in my tracks by an oddly familiar sound. It's the 'witchery-wheatchip' call of a willy wagtail, that most Australian of farm birds. The sound seems absurd here, like hearing a kookaburra in England. It's fluttering about behind a crisply dressed man mowing the church lawn. On seeing me, he stops his ancient machine, introduces himself as Father Enosa and asks if I'd like to look inside the church.

He opens the heavy wooden door to the sound of geckos chirping. Self-consciously I deposit my beer cans inside the door. Father Enosa pretends not to notice. He tells me the sixty-four-year-old church was paid for with 'blood, sweat and trochus'. The pews, doors and rafters were hewn from the deep-red wood of the *wongai*, traded from New Guinea. The walls are a mix of gravel, pounded from rocks by a blind man, and coral lime, canoed in from a distant reef. All up, the little church took nineteen years to build. He shows me a large *bu* (trumpet) shell, patched up with wax, with which the congregation is still called every Sunday morning. 'My assistant walks around town and blows it until everybody comes,' explains Father Enosa.

After admiring the *wongai* carvings, I pick up my cans and bid the priest goodbye. I've barely walked ten metres when a shirtless, dreadlocked man gestures me to stop. 'What do you think of this church?' he slurs, blocking my way. 'I think it's beautiful,' I say. I can smell his fetid breath, and his eyes unnerve me. They are bloodshot, livid and at less than arm's length from mine. One's underscored with a scar as long as his eyebrow.

'Yeah?' he challenges. 'I think it's FUCKED.'

The last word is spat at me. He nods at my plastic bag. 'Give me a can, brother.'

I shake my head. 'No,' I say feebly.

'Give me a can. For the road.'

'No, I won't, sorry.' I take a step sideways.

He flings an arm out to halt me. 'You give me a can, or I break your neck.'

I quickly walk around him.

He's screaming now. 'AY!'

I turn around, and wish I hadn't. Standing on the middle of the road, my tormentor drops to his knees, hands clasped around his neck, biceps bulging, thumbs on his windpipe. I can see the veins on his forehead.

'Next time I see you, I kill you!' he roars. For effect he gives his neck a sharp twist, lolls his head and lets his eyes roll back in their sockets. I stare dumbly until the sound of women yelling from a nearby verandah penetrates my shock. 'Go, go, go!' they are screaming at me, or maybe at him. I hurry back to my quarters.

The island 'guesthouse' is a demountable contractors' donga with mudflat views. My room hasn't been cleaned, but considering the state of the island, it's clean enough. My neighbour is a sewage treatment operator who thinks I'm on the run. 'There isn't nothin' to write about here,' he tells me. 'There's only one place worse than this, and that's Boigu [Saibai's sister island]. It is a shithole, mate. And I mean that literary [sic]. Sewage just bubbles up in the Wet.'

I take my cans outside, hopeful of a fine sunset. From the rock wall I watch the last of the Papuan traders pole their low boats free of the sludge. Once clear of the mudflat, several families rig up makeshift sails. Either their outboard engines are out of order, or they can't afford the fuel.

Mosquitoes float about me, only slightly fazed by my repellent. The sky is low and leaden; no sunset tonight. I gaze at the dull, grey-green disk of Papua New Guinea's mangrove coast.

Limping dogs pick over the brown rocks at my feet. Crabs scatter. I drink my beer. As the sea drops yet further, the distance to PNG seems to shrink. The mud banks merge into mudflats and the last of the boats disappears from view. The sea looks like a river mouth now, which, in effect, is all it is.

A little way down the rock ledge three boys are playing in the rubbish with a machete. I recognise the eldest one, the one with the knife, as one of the football players who ran rings around me earlier in the afternoon.

'What you looking at, Mr John?'

Papua New Guinea, I tell him. In the half-light I can no longer make out the foreign village, visible earlier in the form of a few glinting specks of tin. I imagine a rickety jetty, and a family fishing on it, gazing back at the lights blinking on in Saibai. A shithole? Hardly. How they would envy this place. How they would marvel that people so similar to them need not lift a finger to catch their fish, build their metal homes and keep their gardens trim.

Next to me the boy, whose name is Daniel, rattles the blunt edge of his knife across the rock wall.

'You ever been there?' I ask him.

Daniel shakes his head. He can't be older than ten. He tells me he's going deer hunting with his father for the weekend. Apparently the swamp teems with rusa deer, an Indonesian species running feral in Papua New Guinea. From there the animals must have swum across to Saibai. Or walked, more likely.

'Have you?' he asks.

'Have I what?'

'Been over there?' he says, waving his machete at the darkening outline.

No, I tell him.

'It's a wild place,' he tells me.

Wilder than this?

'You think this place is wild? This place isn't wild.'

Daniel turns to watch his brothers. They've found a skink and are tickling a dozing dog with it. I take a solid swig from my can.

THE WET TROPICS

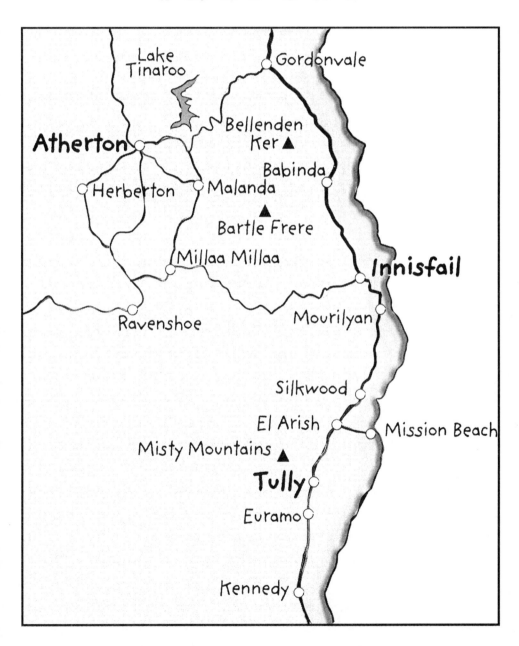

Lake Tinaroo
Gordonvale
Bellenden Ker ▲
Atherton
Babinda
Herberton
Malanda
Bartle Frere ▲
Millaa Millaa
Innisfail
Ravenshoe
Mourilyan
Silkwood
El Arish
Mission Beach
Misty Mountains ▲
Tully
Euramo
Kennedy

Travelling North V

SOME YEARS AGO, MY youngest uncle rang from Holland to say he would be arriving in Cairns the following February with a handicapped friend. Would I be able to organise a two-week itinerary for the tropical part of their Australian sojourn? All George would divulge was that his friend wished to experience reef and rainforest but had little money. She was passionate about plants, particularly orchids. She was also beautiful, he added, and he loved her. My thoughts went back to a visit of his two years earlier, also with a beautiful friend he loved. They stayed all of one weekend in Townsville and split up on the spot. She went north to find lesbian love in Cooktown. He fled west, where, inspired by *Mutant Message Down Under*, Marlo Morgan's fantasy sold as New Age fact, he hoped to divine spiritual riches by bonding with a Murri woman. His quest ran aground in a beery pub in the Territory, however, and necessitated his rescue by a passing truckie, who deposited him in Adelaide.

Yes, in many ways Uncle George, forty-six, is a tripper. He once featured nude in a full-page article in a Dutch daily. The headline, translated, was 'THE LAST OF THE POLDER INDIANS', a reference to the one-time hippie communes thriving behind the dikes in the seventies. Materialism led his contemporaries astray, but George has continued to live in the raw in a log pagoda, without electricity, atop two hectares of ponds, bush and cannabis plants.

But what about his friend? And why was he being so cryptic

as to her disability? Eventually George came clean. His friend, he said, was simply very frail. This trip was to be a final bloom of adventure before her approaching reincarnation, as he saw it, for she was eighty-eight. And yes, I knew her well. Very well. He just wanted it kept secret in case his elder siblings – all thirteen of them, plus in-laws – talked her out of it. She was Oma, his mum, my grandma. When I'd left her seaside home at the close of the previous Dutch summer, a home where every sill exulted with tropical creepers, orchids and bromeliads, I feared I would never see her again. I could have kissed him.

Of course, the family inevitably did find out – where else was George going to get the cash from? And no, not all members (descendants of Oma's fourteen children include forty grandkids and about twenty great-grandkids) were rapt. Too risky, some said. Especially with George. Even my temperate mother, who runs a farm two hours out of Melbourne, felt a foray to the tropics during the height of the wet season might be too much for an octogenarian switching directly from Holland's coldest winter in a decade.

In any event, Oma and George didn't give a damn and, one steamy evening, burst like a pair of grinning game-show hosts through the arrivals doors of Cairns Airport. She looked great in her wheelchair, a gleaming new machine borrowed for the occasion (but doomed to go back a creaking, rusty bomb after too much off-roading). We'd hardly pulled into Port Douglas when George sent Oma careening across Four Mile Beach into the warm nocturnal waters of the stinger net enclosure. Seeing Oma laughing, laughing with her dress hitched to her knees and George's bare white arse bobbing behind her, it was all I could do to resolve to keep up.

We had only a backpacker's budget to play with, but Oma was none too fussed about luxuries. She'd have slept in the back of the Kombi if we'd let her. We fished off the jetty, watched the sunset from the yacht club, drank black sapote milkshakes, plucked the season's last mangoes and split coconuts on the beach. At Rocky Point, near Daintree, some mates fried up a feast of banana prawns and barramundi, while their menagerie of orphaned fruit bats and cockatoos clambered all over Oma.

At Thornton's Beach we dropped in for coffee at Ernie's shack. Ernie runs the only crocodile cruise on nearby Coopers Creek and is probably the most laidback, good-natured ocker you could ever hope to meet. We interrupted his study of bird calls on tape, but he kept breaking into guffaws over the posh accents of the ornithological couple who narrated which species was which. He had Oma, a keen birdwatcher herself, chortling along in no time. A woman whose regal coffee-serving rituals were both the bane and glue of her family, she didn't even mind his powdered milk.

Ernie took us out on the creek to look for orchids. We found plenty, though none were flowering. No matter, Ernie regaled Oma with the ingenuous design of mangrove seeds – there were cannonballs which fell apart into wedges, mini boats complete with keels, and vine beans used as matchboxes by eighteenth-century mariners. She wanted to take them all home, but Ernie said she couldn't. It was a World Heritage National Park, after all. No sooner had he looked away, however, than the lot went straight into her handbag.

We drove on to Cape Tribulation, where we rambled through the jungle, cooled off in waterholes and spied on rat kangaroos. At one waterhole, buttressed by enormous palms and tulip oaks, we crushed soft, coloured stones and the three of us returned to the hostel daubed in red and yellow ochre. Later that afternoon we drank lemongrass tea sitting high above the Cape Trib headland, at old Willem Rijker's place.

Willem's family migrated from Holland in 1949 and walked up from the Daintree River, following what was then an overgrown timber track. Willem looked after his mother here until she died at the age of ninety-one. He picked us up in his ute from the spot where the Kombi could climb no further. Twice his ute stalled and threatened to slide back towards the coast. Bouncing around on the tray with George, our faces lashed with rain and wait-a-while vine, I watched Oma's cloud of white hair, so carefully piled into a hairnet each morning, hopelessly unravel. The fine wisps hung as wild as Willem's by the time we made it to his damp hilltop retreat, where he read Oma his poetry and showed her his rainforest seedlings.

After Cape Trib we descended south again, chewing on sugar cane, stopping at beaches, bypassing Cairns. Nights Oma would tip her handbag upside-down on her hostel bed to disgorge the day's mostly illicit harvest of rainforest fruits. Using a guide, we'd identify them one by one, and she'd note the results in her diary. We explored the wetlands north of Innisfail, dropped a hand line in an estuary and drank with bikies at the Garradunga Pub. Oma was feted everywhere we went.

One morning we pulled up at the bottom of Bellenden Ker, a mile-high dome that rises abruptly out of the cane fields near Babinda. The brooding mountain is Queensland's second highest. We were headed for the very top, but no way were we hiking. Each morning two friendly 'techies' – and the occasional guest – yo-yo up and down in a tiny cable-car to maintain a transmission tower on the summit.

Leaving the wheelchair behind, we ascended across misty chasms and jagged ridges to the wails of currawongs and catbirds. Skimming over the jungle canopy, scraping it in places, we spotted pythons coiled in treetops and a red-bellied black at a pylon's sunny base. There were milky pines, silky oaks and tassel ferns.

And orchids. Flowering orchids. White, cream and pink orchids, spilling from branches and tree forks. Oma sat agog, her face pressed against the glass until we rose into a halo of cloud and rode the remaining loops of cable in utter whiteness. At the peak, on the roof of Queensland, we burst into clear sky once again. Behind us shimmered the Coral Sea. Below us the Atherton Tablelands lay spread out like a rug. But Oma had scampered off into the stunted shrubbery. She was sure she could smell rhododendrons somewhere.

All up, we spent ten nights in the Wet Tropics. Ten humid nights of wine, cheese, gossip, laughs and George's big questions left hanging heavily in the air. For the first time I saw my grandmother cry, for George could be particularly guileless. He talked a lot about roots too. Families were like trees, he liked to say. Without roots we're dead, or may as well be. So was I looking after mine? Did I even know where they were? Or did I think I could just pack them up in the Kombi? He also went on a lot about spirituality, but Oma and I just let him.

Yet I remain awed by his devotion. He did her hair, oiled her with sunblock, shooed away the mozzies, introduced her to backpackers, teased out her stories and listened like a student. When his patience failed him, he'd meditate to soften. He wheeled her from bay to bay at Mission Beach looking for cassowaries. He steadied her binoculars so she could gasp at a jabiru stalking a cane field near Tully. He fitted her with floaties and a mask and almost taught her to snorkel off an outer-reef pontoon. And, above all, he convinced her that she had nothing to lose, and that this was a beautiful way to be.

A few weeks later, by which time the pair of them had reached Mum's farm, I got several photos of Oma in the mail. In one, she posed like a peacenik in front of the Kombi Museum in Nimbin, New South Wales. In another, she was strapped to an ultralight aircraft. On the back she'd written that she and George had buzzed like this across the Byron Bay hinterland after a hang-gliding group declined to take her because of her age. The image still makes me smile, but for a moment there, I wanted what they were having.

I thought of Willem looking after his ailing mother in the rainforest. I thought of mine running a farm by herself. And I wondered what she was doing living so far from hers. I also thought of something George had told me on their last day: that for all his journeys, for all his tripping around the world and in his head, his adventures with family were the most meaningful. It removed the element of escapism.

The next time I saw George and Oma was in Holland. I was planning a piece about trees, and George and I cycled out to a magnificent old yew not far from Grandma's village. We climbed it, sat in it and George hugged it. Prostrate on an outer branch, he began bludgeoning me with questions in his usual manner. What drove me to write about trees? In fact, what drove me to write about anything? Didn't I want to engage, to experience, to start *feeling* things for myself? But at the time I silently dismissed it all as hippie talk.

BABINDA

A Storm in a Pee Cup

ON A SUNNY DAY in the sugar town of Babinda, everyone mows. Babinda is so lush, its mango trees don't fruit. Apparently the rain washes away all the pollen, or so I'm told by the post-mistress, who empties the town's official rain gauge.

On display in the post office window, facing the street, is a man's gumboot. It's steel-capped, filled with a mix of sand and foam, sealed and gilded. Each January, meteorologists award the Golden Gumboot to the Australian town with the highest rain-fall for the year. Like the wooden spoon for the side that finishes last, the award comes without a trophy, but Babinda decided to make its own after winning a hat-trick from 1999–2001.

There the matter might have rested. After all, based on yearly averages, Babinda *is* Australia's wettest town. Its 4230 millimetres a year make it almost seven times as wet as, say, Melbourne. It once rained for eighty-nine days out of ninety-two. And it lies at the base of Australia's wettest spot, Mount Bellenden Ker, which was once at the receiving end of 1300 mm in twenty-four hours. But then things got serious. Tully, the town that also lays claim to being Australia's soggiest – on the basis of a record rainfall of 7930 mm in 1950 – decided to steal the gumboot. Well, that's how Babinda saw it. And Tully's civic leaders indeed

207

looked pleased as thieves when they announced an eight-metre Golden Gumboot would be erected to cement Tully's place as the nation's capital of rain.

For a while the towns bickered over figures. The debate even headed for the gutter: Babinda claimed Tully's rainfall occasionally possessed traces of chlorine, and Tully's mayor retorted Babinda's rain gauge had tested positive for urea. (Certainly nearby Innisfail, which decades ago was also a regular Golden Gumboot contender, showed a significant drop in annual rainfall after its gauge was moved away from the male public toilets.) But in the end Babinda took stock. It might be lush, but it was also mouldy, bedraggled and just plain depressed. The town was too wet even for hippies. So Babinda called on the 'small-town doctor', a man who criss-crosses the country to 'facilitate' small-town revival. Peter Kenyon runs the Bank of IDEAS (Initiatives for the Development of Enterprising Action and Strategies) and combines the salesmanship of Bryce Courtenay with the evangelism of Billy Graham.

Kenyon's main message is simple: an attractive place to live is an attractive place to visit. His advice, preached to over five hundred towns around the country, is to do up the main street, find a unique theme and celebrate it. Over three hundred people turned up to hear Kenyon's pep talk in Babinda. Some in town – the real estate agent, for example – had reservations about trumpeting Babinda's wettest status. Nonsense, said Kenyon. Seize the rain! The gumboot is dead, long live the – the what? the galoshes? the raincoat? the . . . Umbrella! And so it was settled. Babinda would become the Umbrella Town.

The townsfolk formed the Babinda Taskforce, run by the dynamic Carol Stroud and a posse of elderly volunteers. The taskforce's slogan is 'Sunshine in the Rain' and its symbol is a yellow umbrella. 'Tully can have its dirty old gumboot,' explains Stroud, gleefully pointing out that the newly completed Big Golden Gumboot looks bronze, not golden. 'Our "brollies" are yellow so we can carry our sunshine with us. We'll use the rain to sell our town. We can't stop it, we can't hide it and it brings great gifts, like our rainforests and our wetlands, so why not celebrate it?'

Already, Babinda has staged an Umbrella Festival and plans are afoot for a streetscape involving umbrella murals and a Big Brollie. 'The Big Umbrella will be as big as the Big Gumboot. It will feature a shower over it so that when it's not raining, people can buy tokens to turn it on,' Stroud says.

Most of the town supports the umbrella concept. 'People love the rain here, it brings relief,' says the postmistress. 'Most falls at night, in the wet season. Sometimes it rains for three or four weeks straight and we escape to Cairns for the day to refresh. But locals feel a bit protective when visitors criticise the rain. We can complain, but you can't.'

SILKWOOD

Oh When the Saints

DUSK FALLS SWIFTLY ON the cane fields around Silkwood. On the concrete porch of his presbytery, Father Tom Mullins plucks a mosquito from his cup of tea. Across the street, the town's annual Catholic climax – the whole baby-blessing, cripple-cuddling, money-bagging, tuba-booming, miracle-mad shebang – is nearly over. The women have stopped weeping, the mitred men have gone home and the Three Saints have returned to their roost in the little church, the only building in town with a fresh coat of paint.

The chianti still flows, however. Some 5000 devotees mill about the church grounds, dancing, back-slapping and talking Italian. Three ten-metre air tubes – red, green and white – roar into the night. The last souvenir pillbox is snapped up. Everything is littered with rose petals, a gift from a devout crop-duster. Having celebrated four masses and played host to the Pope's main man in Australia, His Excellency Archbishop Francesco Canalini, Father Mullins looks tired, dog-tired, but sated. He loves his whirling, tropical parish. 'Sicilians do have an exuberant way of expressing their faith, don't they?' he muses. 'But I grew up in [nearby] Tully, so they don't surprise me. Well, not as much as they used to.'

An almighty blast suddenly ignites the sky. 'That must be the fireworks,' says Father Mullins, who has spilt his tea. 'They're usually very good.'

MUCH OF THE DEEP North is deeply Italian. Encouraged by the White Australia Policy, Italian labourers began to outnumber South Sea Islanders on the cane fields early last century. Today, their descendants make up half of the sugar coast's communities and many, particularly those from Sicily and Calabria, remain devoted to their village saints and associated festivals. Tully, for example, celebrates Saint Gerardo, Babinda has Saint Rita, Ingham has Saint Antonio, Atherton has Maria della Quercia (Our Lady of the Oak Tree) and Mareeba celebrates Our Lady of the Chain.

The biggest festival by far is Silkwood's Feast of the Three Saints. Come the first Sunday in May, thousands flock to the tiny sugar town for the unveiling of Saints Alfio, Cirino and Filadelfo, a rather effeminate-looking trio stored in an alcove above the altar. The pews are packed hours in advance. Local devotees, many of them dressed in green with red trim in imitation of Alfio's toga, chant endless Ave Marias while, outside, a giant video screen captures the action for the busloads of pilgrims piling in from as far away as Brisbane.

At the parting of the curtains, accompanied by a cracking twenty-one-gun salute (provided by a mango farmer's gas cannon), the faithful gasp and rise as one. Many weep; some wail and holler for a miracle. One woman shuffles down the aisle on her knees, tears streaming down her face, to collapse on all fours at the altar.

In keeping with tradition, the saints appear festooned with last year's donated booty: gold watches, necklaces, even wedding rings. Later, the church pews are cleared away and a gilt carriage is rolled up to the altar. A ramp is attached from the alcove to the chariot and, to further clamour from the crowd, the Three Saints jolt forwards under remote control to rock down the slope like puppets.

To the cry of '*Con vera fede! Viva Sant' Alf!*' ('With true faith! Long live Saint Alfio!') the carriage bearing the saints is pushed out the front doors into a crush of followers. Officials clamber aboard to man the red velvet sacks dangling from the gilded corner posts. At once, people begin passing them money. Outstretched arms bristle with $10, $50, $100 notes. Not unlike bookies, the bagmen brandish the cash in the air, cry, '*Con Vera Fede!*' and plunge the money into the velvet sacks. Not everything is bagged, however. Necklaces of $20 notes are draped around the saints' necks, and glittering heirlooms pinned to their shields. Rousing cheers greet several disabled people as they are shouldered aboard to kiss the saints' feet. Babies, too, are hoisted aloft – '*Viva Sant' Alf!*' – and given a cheek-to-cheek with the saints before being handed back, often as not to the wrong owner.

Once the urge to donate has been quenched, the crush resolves into a joyous procession. It is said that in fifty years it has never rained on the procession and this year, too, the drizzle clears on cue. Led by the archbishop, the parade marches down the main street, past a posse of bikies, past the cane fields and dilapidated shop fronts, past handfuls of locals drinking beer on their front verandahs, and back again. All the while, the bulging money bags swing from the float like udders.

AS LEGEND HAS IT, Alfio, Filadelfo and Cirino grew up in Spain at the peak of the Roman Empire. When their parents were killed during Emperor Decius's purge of Christianity, the brothers were marched from Gascony to Sicily in the expectation they would renounce their faith. Instead, the lads' resolve and charm converted their guards en route. Alfio, the eldest, was particularly smooth, growing trees from roasted chestnuts and curing hernias by rubbing spittle on them. But, in the end, the Romans were unimpressed. At the foot of Mount Etna (marked today by the village of Sant' Alfio, where the feast lasts a fortnight), Alfio praised Jesus once too often. The Romans bled him to death by severing his tongue, tossed Cirino into a cauldron of boiling tar and roasted Filadelfo alive.

Almost 1700 years later, in 1939, the very pregnant Alfia Tornabene lay dying in a Silkwood lean-to. Or so she believed. Her husband Rosario, an emigrant of Sant' Alfio, was beside himself with grief. 'Rosario prayed for a miracle,' recalls Alfia. 'Then suddenly Saint Alfio came to him in a dream and Rosario promised he would bring the Three Saints to Australia if I lived.'

Years later, a cousin from Sicily brought out three metre-high sculptures. To Tornabene's dismay, however, the region's main churches declined his offer. 'Rosario was very hurt,' says Alfia of her late husband. 'We had to store them at home until Father Natali [from Silkwood] finally said to bring them over.'

But the clergy never assumed control. From its debut in 1950, the feast has been run by the Three Saints Committee, a band of Sicilian cane farmers so large it can organise a party just by attending. No one is quite sure how many members there are, but there are believed to be between seventy and eighty.

And every member counts. One roasts the chestnuts. One makes the *torrone* (nougat), one makes the lemon gelato – has done for thirty-five years running – and another makes the souvenir pillboxes. The oldest member of the committee is Guiseppi Parisi, ninety-two, who migrated from Sant' Alfio in 1930. His English has barely improved since. Through an interpreter, he recounts how three men shouldered a saint each in the inaugural procession. Later, the saints were paraded in the back of a ute, and people would toss money, jewellery and even plaits of hair into the tray.

According to Parisi, all jewellery donations – fifty years worth now – are stored in an Innisfail bank vault. Most cash, however, is spent on church improvements and on the following year's feast. 'Every year we improve because every year we spend more,' says Parisi. 'Every year the fireworks grow bigger, the marquee grows bigger, everything is bigger.'

Not everyone in the community appreciates the committee's efforts. The apparent largesse rankles with those of more restrained persuasion, especially following a prolonged lean period in the sugar industry. The nearest mill is broke and may not crush again. But committee president Alfio 'Fred' Maccarone is quick to dispel the perception that the committee is a bankrolling juggernaut of wealthy growers. 'The less people have, the more they give,' says Maccarone. 'Because the less people have, the more they want a miracle.'

And miracles do happen, says Sant'-Alfio-born Maria Silvestro, the proud mother of two committee men. In fifty years she has missed only one feast, the first. 'My husband had to work on the farm that day, but everything went wrong. He had engine trouble, punctures, the plough broke and he felt sick. So he said, "Maria, from now on we'll be there whatever happens."'

Silvestro is convinced Saint Alfio spared her son after a car accident. 'Charlie was in intensive care for weeks, and nobody thought he would live. Then I went to see Saint Alfio at the feast and when I came back Charlie said the pains had gone.' She also credits the saints with saving her home town. 'But don't take it from me, I get you the mayor of Sant' Alfio himself,' she says.

Sure enough, the mayor – the committee's special guest – tells me how lava was spewing straight for his village after Mount

Etna blew its top in 1928. When a procession of praying towns-folk went out to meet the flow, the lava looped around them to torch a presumably less pious town down the road.

Dina Milone, too, is a fervent believer. Wearing matching green dresses, she and her disabled daughter, twenty-eight-year-old Graziella, mount the float each year to kiss the saints and pray for a miracle. And each year Graziella flops back into the crowd as palsied as before. 'It's still a miracle,' insists Milone. 'Every year of Graziella's life is a miracle. Saint Alfio just won't let her go.'

Still, Milone won't go as far in prayer as her mother once did. In accordance with an ancient Sicilian custom, banned by bishops long ago, Milone's mother begged the saints to save her husband from what she presumed to be cancer by advancing on all fours and scraping her tongue down the length of the aisle until it bled. 'The priest here never knew about it,' says Milone. 'Mother got permission from the committee, and it was done behind closed doors.' And did it work? 'Totally. You see, doctors had spotted these shadows on his lungs and Mother was convinced he'd die. But he didn't.'

Earlier, I asked old Guiseppi Parisi how miracles came about. '*Fede* [faith], *fede, fede!*' he said. The key was to believe in them. But a belief in calamity may be a prerequisite.

FATHER MULLINS LOOKS UP sharply when I mention the tongue-scraping incident. He's sure it no longer occurs. 'I go to the committee meetings. They are a lot of fun. We have a mass before and a barbecue afterwards. But often there are things that have to be worked out between church and committee. Like when they wanted to widen the doors to get the chariot through, or when they wanted to build the ramp.'

Fireballs burst and fizzle above us. 'The way I see it, the role of the saints is to lead us to God. As long as it's a true reflection of faith, then everything is fine,' says Mullins. 'So many places are in a crisis of faith, yet the committee manages to bring in young people and build.' From the porch we watch the fireworks show's climax. Vast flaring salvos set the surrounding cane fields ablaze in reds and yellows. Mullins is right; it's quite a spectacle. It could almost be Mount Etna up there.

MISSION BEACH

How to Stuff a Cassowary

*THIRTY POUNDS (EACH) IS quite outrageous but . . . Doggett is
THE ONLY taxidermist who can do cassowaries as I want them,
and it would take any fresh man three to four years to learn how
to do it and meanwhile the chance of many fine specimens would
be permanently lost!*

Lord Rothschild, about 1900, explaining to his curator
why he was quite happy to pay to have his sixty-five live
cassowaries properly stuffed.

LATE IN 1996, WITH the Wet fast approaching, Cairns authorities
retrieved a limp-necked corpse from the edge of the city's jungle-
clad backdrop, the seventh such find in as many years. The grisly
state of the seventy-kilogram body, a female in her late twenties,
left little doubt as to the immediate cause of death. Like those
before her, she'd been mauled by dogs. An autopsy found an old
bullet from a .22 rifle lodged in her shoulder, as well as a bellyful
of chopped apple. Her scarred, knobby legs attested to a long
record of run-ins, most of them with dogs but some, no doubt,
with cars.

Annabelle Olsson, the wildlife veterinarian sent to examine the body, recognised Blue Arrow at once. She was the last of the cassowaries of Mount Whitfield, a forested range besieged by greater Cairns. When Blue Arrow was born, Cairns was a greasy sugar post, population 20 000, awakening to the clamour of tourism. Over ensuing years, the city quadrupled in size. Whole suburbs bloated up its hillslopes and herniated into surrounding valleys. By 1990 the city had cut off the Whitfield hills – then still home to seven cassowaries – from the spine of rainforest stretching from Cooktown almost to Townsville.

Blue Arrow had not gone quietly. She'd taken to terrorising the growing hordes of joggers and power walkers along the main hill track. Some she charged, many she chased. Once she kept a lunchtime jogger bailed up in a tree until nightfall. Others were kicked, sometimes dangerously. A cassowary's inner toe consists of a twelve-centimetre spike-like claw, and Blue Arrow used it to great effect. At least three walkers needed minor surgery. But just a few months after lacerating a woman's thigh and forehead for a total of eleven stitches, Blue Arrow was dead. As Olsson notes wryly, 'We don't have any problems with cassowaries any more. We don't have any left.'

The southern cassowary of north-east Queensland – another two species are endemic to Papua New Guinea – is the world's second-largest bird, after the ostrich. A female southern cassowary weighs up to eighty-five kilograms (twice as heavy as a male) and may puff herself up to a height of two metres. Her saurian legs support an enormous toupee of fine black feathers, and two wrinkled red wattles dangle from her naked blue neck like a wet scarf. The tall horny helmet, or casque, is used to plunge through scrub, and the beak is large enough to ingest mangoes whole.

Yet for all its front, the rainforest's largest denizen is on the back foot. The cassowary belongs to the ratites, an ancient flightless family which has already lost the elephant bird of Madagascar, the New Zealand moa and the Tasmanian emu. Local cassowary extinctions like the one in Mount Whitfield have occurred quite abruptly. John McKenzie, a veterinarian on the Atherton Tableland, euthanased two birds hit by cars last year. Both signified the end of their populations. One was the last cassowary in Lake Barrine National Park. The other occupied a patch of forest further east. 'She was believed to be the only hen with three males, so it looks like they're stuffed,' McKenzie says. Meanwhile, former strongholds such as Mount Spec and Moresby Range National Parks are down to half-a-dozen individuals and falling.

'It's a real problem,' says Les Moore, who has regularly surveyed numbers from Cooktown to Townsville. 'The bird lives up to forty-five years and I suspect that some of the smaller populations are made up of ageing individuals, possibly beyond breeding age. If so, biologically these communities are already dead.' Moore began surveying the birds in 1988, the year the Deep North's rainforests attained World Heritage listing. At the time he stated there were at least 2500 cassowaries left. Now he believes the figure is closer to 1500, and the cassowary is officially listed as endangered.

The Wet Tropics Management Authority points the finger squarely at habitat fragmentation. Whereas the remaining upland forests are largely protected as part of the Wet Tropics World Heritage Area, most of the bird's favoured lowland habitat, a mosaic of rainforest and wet woodlands, is not. At best, less than fifteen per cent of its lowland habitat remains, much of it in small, isolated patches under freehold title. Cane farmers and land speculators continue to clear as they like. Since 1988 the lowlands between Innisfail and Cardwell have been razed at a rate of 6700 hectares a year, or, in greenie units, a football field every forty minutes. And nowhere is the impact greater than at Mission Beach, the main tourist destination of the Cassowary Coast.

IT'S BUCKETING DOWN WHEN I arrive at Mission Beach. The Cassowary Advisory Group, a motley mix of interest groups, is meeting at the visitor's centre to assess a proposal to create a 250-kilometre corridor of cassowary habitat from Cairns to Ingham. By offering incentives such as tax and rate relief, it's hoped that farmers will preserve or revegetate crucial plots in the link-up.

Mission Beach, once best known as the launching point for Dunk Island, loosely denotes a twenty-kilometre strip of idyllic beaches halfway between Cairns and Townsville. The region markets itself as the place where the rainforest meets the reef and, as a result, this is no longer really true. Now generally sub-divisions meet the reef. The rainforest is for sale and lush stands can be whacked at will, no questions asked.

Although the new arrivals, mostly urban escapees, lay claim to greener values than their rural neighbours, both sides can sound self-seeking. Long-time locals sell their land only to complain that the blow-ins are taking over the place. Meanwhile the new-comers clear their blocks but clamour to retain the habitat next door. Tensions tend to flare over icon species. On the reef, they argue over dugongs. Along the rivers, crocodiles are in the line of fire. In Mission Beach, it's the cassowary.

In the main, the newcomers are more organised. Mary Ritchie runs the Committee for Coastal and Cassowary Conservation, known as C4. 'When I arrived here [in 1991], I was blown away by the cassowary,' says Ritchie, a pathology nurse. 'The big female is such an awesome, powerful being. She may mate with three males in one season, while the male looks after the nest and chicks. If a male is sitting on a nest and a female walks past, he will snake his head on the ground in total subservience. Often you see males with damaged casques. That the female's doing. She runs the show, she's the boss, she's just fabulous.'

Ritchie was blown away by the rout of the forest too. In her first five years at Mission Beach, the amount of rainforest on freehold land declined by almost one third. So did the region's cassowary population, now down to less than seventy birds. Last year another seven birds died on local roads and two were killed by dogs. Only a week earlier Ritchie had been called out to a beach where a cassowary had been seen swimming out to open sea. She found a trail of blood leading to the water's edge, accompanied by two sets of dog prints. Says Ritchie, 'We'll pay for this. It's the cassowary that laid the golden egg for our tourism industry.'

C4 lobbies hard against resort development, pushes for stricter dog and traffic controls and raises money to buy back vital habitat. By raising seedlings from donated cassowary dung, its nursery organises plant-outs of up to 10 000 native fruit trees a year. Recently C4 persuaded a local shire to designate 'cassowary corridors' along creeks in its town plan, and it is behind the ubiquitous, almost desperate signage urging motorists to slow down. C4 also organises forest food drops when trees aren't fruiting. In 1986 Cyclone Winifred shredded the forest and cassowaries roamed far and wide in pursuit of food.

Naturally, people fed them and doubtless many were saved from starvation. But they were run over instead. At least twenty-two died on local roads in the nine months following the cyclone. The generation that survived grew up partly dependent. Fourteen years later, many Mission Beach residents, including C4 volunteers, continue to feed the birds. So do a dozen resorts and van parks. Ritchie, who devotes most of her home and spare time to rearing orphaned wildlife, distinguishes between those that handfeed the birds – 'they're not kosher,' she says – and those that leave fruit out for cassowaries to eat. It's an important distinction, though perhaps more for humans than for cassowaries. If cassowaries come to associate humans directly with food, they may become aggressive if none is forthcoming. But a backyard feeding station presents just as many risks to the bird's survival. It still has to cross roads, brave dogs and tolerate humans. As one resort operator says, 'Cassowaries used to be naturally wary of humans. If we really care about their survival, the best thing we can do is to throw rocks at them.'

But C4's volunteers would never do that. Theirs is by and large an emotional attachment, which has done little to ease local tensions. C4 persists in blaming 'rednecks' for felling the forest and flouting speed rules. Cassowary signs have been shot at and C4's first headquarters were burnt down. One C4 volunteer tells me hick elements even bulldozed speed bumps. 'They don't give a rat's arse about the cassowary,' he says angrily.

JOAN BENTRUPPERBAUMER SPENT THREE years studying a clan of about twenty-five cassowaries at Kennedy Bay National Park, south of Mission Beach. In the tradition of Jane Goodall's famous work on chimpanzees, she followed the solitary creatures everywhere. She witnessed mating rituals, territorial clashes and the cassowary's role in seed dispersal. Even the fathers, notoriously lethal around their clutch, permitted her to stay and to see the eggs hatch.

No one has got so close to cassowaries before or since, but Bentrupperbaumer felt her biological study told just half the story. That's why she called the second half of her thesis

'Towards Understanding Humans'. 'Endangered species are endangered because of humans,' she explains. 'So we don't have to manage the species. We have to manage the humans. And to manage them, we have to learn to understand them. Even the so-called rednecks.'

Her study included an in-depth comparison of rural attitudes to the cassowary with attitudes in semiurban Mission Beach. Remarkably, she found no difference. The hinterland's old guard – including those still smarting from the World Heritage declaration which effectively killed off their timber industry – appreciated the cassowary as much as the newcomers did (though perhaps not as a feminist icon). What they didn't like was the 'upstarts' seizing control and telling them what they could and couldn't do.

Bentrupperbaumer, who founded C4 in 1990 but is no longer involved, now believes green groups like C4 risk polarising communities by claiming ownership of a species. 'When a group purports to represent a species, and raises its profile to attract support [and funding], it creates all sorts of tensions,' she says. 'The group begins to behave as if *it* is endangered. The species becomes a secondary issue.'

Bentrupperbaumer found farmers were deeply suspicious of government-funded green groups. When the owner of the property she used to access her study site heard she belonged to C4, he warned her off his land and razed the adjoining forest for fear of it being taken from him. Bentrupperbaumer, who was left to reach the study site by dinghy down the crocodile-infested Hull River, also found one of her cassowaries had been shot. The researcher feels green groups need to involve farmers, not alienate them. Otherwise, she says, 'The species becomes a symbol, even a target. You can't move conservation management along that way.'

Not surprisingly, Mary Ritchie rejects Bentrupperbaumer's

criticisms and dismisses her thesis as 'not very interesting'. She is similarly contemptuous of a report produced late last year by a senior Cairns ranger who had painstakingly collected all Australian records of attacks by cassowaries. The victims were one hundred and forty-four people, thirty-five dogs, two horses and a cow. Of the people attacked, half were chased, a quarter were charged, twenty-two were kicked, four were jumped on and three were head-butted. Most attacks amounted to hold-ups for food, and the ranger, an American, compared the situation with the black bears of Yellowstone Park. Six of the attacks resulted in serious injury, including a punctured lung, a lacerated scrotum and one death, albeit in 1926. The media, including the respected *NewScientist* magazine, loved his paper; the cassowary world hated it. The last thing the bird – *their* bird? – needed, it fumed, was bad publicity.

Says Mary Ritchie: 'Half-a-dozen birds were responsible for most of those incidents. That's why I ripped into [the author]. If you promote fear in people you will increase the expectation of risk, of adventure, and people will go looking for it. A cassowary is not such a big scary deal, providing you never turn your back on one.'

True, two birds contributed a disproportionate amount of records. One was Blue Arrow from Mount Whitfield. The other was Henry, the resident cassowary at Lake Barrine, a volcanic lake rimmed with rainforest. As at Mount Whitfield, all is quiet at Lake Barrine now. But Henry did not go quietly either.

HENRY WAS ONE OF two brothers born at Lake Eacham, another Tableland crater, in early 1989. A bout of clearing five months later isolated the lake's jungle and Henry's father deserted his offspring. The brother died, leaving just Henry and a geriatric female. Locals fed them and Henry soon began hassling visitors for food. At the age of four, having reached sexual maturity, he went walkabout. 'Henry wandered down the Gillies Highway, holding up tourist buses for food, all the way to Lake Barrine,' says ecologist Les Moore, who watched the ten-year saga unfold.

Generally Henry liked people. But not cars. One driver was stranded when a well-placed kick punctured his radiator. Hub caps formed another popular target. Says Moore, 'Being solitary by nature, Henry hated his reflection. Sometimes he'd just rage around the car park, kicking cars and chasing them.' Bill Bayne, who runs the tea-house on the lake, was fond of Henry and still maintains a shrine in his honour. No doubt Henry was great for business, but Bayne denies feeding him. 'He was like a bush-ranger the way he bailed people up, so of course they would give him stuff.' Henry was also a frustrated bachelor 'with not even an emu to look at'. No esky was safe. 'He'd sit on things like they were eggs,' recalls Bayne. 'If you left a paint tin out, he'd squat on it.'

But Henry's life as a freak couldn't last. 'One day last year a gas delivery truck came around and Henry had a go at it,' says Bayne. 'The driver heard a loud snap and Henry disappeared into the jungle for ten days. When he came out his left foot was hanging by the tendon. He was quite docile. I called the local vet and National Parks. A ranger came and jumped on him, put a bag over his head and put him in the back of a ute. Then I realised what they were going to do. I said to them, "Please, please, think about it." I offered to look after him, but no, every-thing was done with great haste. I keep hearing that this bird was already genetically dead, but that's a very cold, very scientific way of looking at it.'

Keith Smith, the cassowary project officer for the Queensland Parks and Wildlife Service, shrugs when I raise the subject of

Henry's lethal injection. The last thing anyone needed was a one-legged clown in captivity. Not only did wildlife authorities view Henry as a biological dead end and a public nuisance, but Smith freely acknowledges Henry's demise presented people with a simple message: don't feed the cassowaries. 'Our charter is to protect species, not the welfare of individuals.'

Smith is not as hard as he sounds. It's simply that he can't see the birds for the politics. In trying to coordinate a recovery plan, he's found that cassowary experts are not dissimilar to the birds themselves. That is, they are generally tough, hard-headed, solitary individuals who defend their own patch vigorously and show a tendency to crash through another's. (Interestingly, Lord Rothschild, the great animal collector who was crazy about cassowaries, was a giant of a man, naturally shy and secretive but with a booming voice and a tendency to lash out when provoked. Further, he was victimised all his life by women . . .)

'It gets weird, I'll admit,' says Smith. 'I can't even get researchers to agree how many are left, let alone how to save them.'

To add to the challenge, Queensland's Labor government has shown itself to be no greener than its conservative predecessor, under which cane expansion, tree clearing and drainage of wetlands reached unprecedented levels. Legislation to limit tree-clearing – drawn up a decade ago – remains in limbo, and each time it is rumoured to be close to passing through parliament, it sparks a spate of pre-emptive clearing.

BACK IN MISSION BEACH Mary Ritchie has arranged for me to go cassowary spotting. Her offsider, Rod Simpson, fetches me at the foot of the Big Cassowary, a tacky fibreglass construction which, at four metres tall, is barely twice life-size. Simpson hopes to show me a female called 150 Per Cent.

'She's huge,' he says. 'She's charged me a few times, because of my hat, I think. It looks like a casque. They get aggro when they start looking for a mate. By the way, your black shirt is not going to help.'

No sooner have we entered a beautiful grove of fan palms than we stumble upon a clutch of enormous green eggs. 'They're fake [part of a tourist display],' Simpson reassures me. 'If they were real, you'd run like buggery.' Further on we find a very fresh, bluish pile of seeds as big as golf balls. 'Cassowary poo's not at all smelly,' says Simpson, poking around while stealing quick glances over his shoulder. 'It's just a salad really.'

He points to a nearby footprint. 'They're a bit like Bruce Lee, they're that quick with their feet. If they charge, stand still and don't lose your nerve. If you run they think, "We've got this one beat", and they'll kick you to the shithouse.'

We emerge from the palms without spotting one. By now, I'm kind of grateful. In the car park we overhear a tour guide tell his group, 'Hope the cassowaries behave themselves.' Simpson is miffed. 'Behave themselves,' he scoffs. 'As if. Why do these people always have to beat up the danger element?'

We divert through a recently developed neighbourhood. Behind lawns cropped like velvet runs a creekside strip of jungle, a designated cassowary corridor. Suddenly Simpson spots a female cassowary huffing and lunging at a small yapping dog behind a wire fence. We stop and watch a woman in a night-gown call her dog and simultaneously toss a pawpaw across the fence. While the corrupted bird inspects the fruit, I approach to take some pictures.

'Oi, don't leave too quick,' shouts Simpson when I turn back to the car. Sure enough, the cassowary is loping towards me, head down. 'Stand still, you goose,' yells Simpson. That's fine for him to say. He's still in the car. The bird is advancing with huge, flop-footed strides. I try not to look at her claw, but her beak looks as bad. About two metres away she pulls herself up to my height and glares at me. I feel in my pocket for something, anything. She cocks her blue head expectantly. Nothing.

With a haughty shake of her crimson wattles, she stalks off across a vacant block, trailing an aura of mosquitoes. I watch her step over a low fence. She seems to be headed for the main road. In the distance, I hear the rumble of a truck.

MISTY MOUNTAINS

A Walk in the Woods

IN A TOWN WHERE the men haul cane, women brew banana wine and the mayor keeps a crocodile in his dam, Ron Hunt seems pretty much a regular Tully bloke. Big hat, big ute, big gut, big handshake, big knife. Sure, Tully's aldermen have anointed him their Citizen of the Year, but someone had to be. (And despite the rumours, the fact that he's a councillor himself apparently had nothing to do with it.) He's the farmer behind the Big Gumboot, built to cement Tully's reputation as Australia's wettest town. And he's the ex-logger behind the Misty Mountain Trails, a long-overdue network of walking tracks through some of the North's most rugged tropical jungle.

The trails are the reason for our get-together early one hot morning in front of the council chambers. As well as myself and another journalist, Hunt has invited an assortment of council employees along on a walk in the woods 'to see what he's been on about'. We're a motley crew, dressed in long pants and sleeves as advised.

'You got insect repellent?' Hunt says by way of greeting. I nod and hold up a 'tropical strength' variety of a heavy-duty brand favoured by campers.

'That's just cordial,' he says. 'Only good for mossies. Here, get some of this on you.'

He throws me a little white bottle. The label is half eaten away by a translucent clag dribbling from the spout.

'It's called "Rugged Stuff", and it's made from industrial-strength chemicals by a bloke down the road in El Arish [a nearby sugar town]. It's been approved by the right people. At least I think it has. The best part is it lasts all day. Keeps away leeches, ticks and march flies. And you're going to need if you don't want to end up with scrub itch.'

Scrub itch?

'Yeah. It's worse than ticks. It's caused by mites that bury under your skin. Drives you mad. And they're pesky little things when you want to get rid of them. I found the best thing for that is shaving cream. From tip to toe. But you don't want to get to that stage.'

I give the spout a good pump and watch the gel pool in the palm of my hand.

'Whoah!' says Hunt. 'Not too much or your arm will drop off. What you do is smear it around your ankles so the mites can't get you from below, and around your neck and shoulders so they can't get you from above. Then you do it around your waist to stop them getting near your crotch, because there's nothing worse, believe me.'

I do exactly as he says. Almost immediately a deep burning sensation sweeps around my belly, as if I've applied hot wax. When I mention this to Hunt, he says, 'Yeah, it does that. We had a lady collapse last week – nearly gave me a heart attack, she did – and I reckon it was because she just covered herself in that stuff along with sunblock. As soon as she started walking, she just overheated and keeled over.'

Once we're all safely – or lethally – girdled with Rugged Stuff, Hunt sends us to a tap in the council gardens. 'Like the original army stuff, that stuff eats plastic, so I might suggest you wash your hands well before you step into the car and start touching things. Especially when you're travelling in my car.'

'And one more thing: Don't think you're now mite-proof. This time of year you don't sit on rotten logs or fallen vegetation because it's that dry up there now that any mites or ticks will find you. One of the guys got a tick up there the other day. And even the march flies carry mites.'

His patter has made us only itchier and by now I'm scratching compulsively. Hunt doesn't miss a trick. 'That will be bird lice,' he says lightly. 'You've managed to get yourself a dose of it before you've even started.'

Excuse me?

'Well, look where you parked your car. A nice, shady spot under a fig tree, you thought. But the whole tree's shrieking with nesting [metallic] starlings. No local in his right mind would park under there.'

BUT NEVER MIND THE bugs. Nor the reports of gullies teeming with scrub pythons up to eight metres long and thick as a man's thigh. Dense, damp and steep, the Tully hinterland packs more mythology than any forest in Australia. As well as hosting the usual sightings of big cats, it has its own yowie, for instance, or bigfoot. This year alone there have been at least half-a-dozen sightings. The most famous sighting of the Maalan Man, as he is known locally, occurred in the mid seventies. It led to a furry drawing and the discovery of a footprint said to be as wide as it was long.

Claims also persist that the forest is home to a tribe of lost pygmies. Station owner Neil Alderman, for one, remains adamant that several bulldozer drivers surprised 'the little people' while clearing rainforest from his property west of Tully in the early sixties. (When I track down two of the drivers, however, one says the pygmies were simply kids from a nearby clan, while the other suspects Alderman, who'd arrived fresh from the States, fell for a prank.)

Councillor Hunt, a bushman who likes to drink from his hat and walk with a machete, doesn't believe in pygmies and yowies. But he keeps an open mind on UFOs. Heading home one night after a day in the forest, he encountered something big and bright whizzing overhead. It made the hair stand up on the back of his neck. 'I don't know what it was, and I don't want to know.'

In recent years the forest's network of gorges and waterfalls – virtually inaccessible yet close to the idyllic resorts of Mission Beach – has also made it a favourite with producers of *Survivor*-type TV shows. So far American, British and German series have been filmed here, and a French crew is expected soon.

But Hunt hopes the Misty Mountains Trails project will earn the forest a more tangible place on the world map. Budgeted at $1 million, the project links the Atherton Tablelands to the foothills of the Cassowary Coast via one hundred and fifty kilometres of walking tracks. And that's just stage one. The ultimate aim is for the trail to extend from Paluma, a mountain village north-west of Townsville, all the way to Cairns. Such a walk, traversing some of the country's wildest terrain, would doubtless rival the likes of America's world-famous Appalachian Trail.

Hunt refers to the slab of wilderness stretching north from Tully to the Atherton Tablelands as the 'Golden Square'. 'It's a piece of gold that we've got on our back door that everyone's forgotten about,' Hunt explains. But it's actually a logging term. Prior to the region being declared part of the Wet Tropics World Heritage Area in 1988, some thirteen sawmills competed for its riches. Hunt, too, made a small fortune from mining timber.

And although he quit the industry in 1972, he remained a passionate opponent of World Heritage listing during the eighties.

'Yeah, I was pretty vocal in the protests,' he acknowledges fifteen years on. 'My father was a sawmiller, and, well, put it this way, I've got sawdust running through my veins. It was all sawmill stuff we were carting out. Big stuff. Black bean, cedar, quandong and a bit of ash. But I am a greenie. So there you go. You can be both.'

Hunt is the first to admit that the clear-felling practices of the sixties and seventies left much to be desired. 'Contrary to what people believe, there were loggers there who believed that what was happening was sacrilege, and I was one of them. It was just ball and chain, slash and burn. It all had to come out and what didn't come out they'd bulldoze over and burn. I was at King Ranch Station [now the first port of call for reality TV shows] and the whole place was trashed for cattle property. Fifty square miles of stuff just came down.'

However, by the eighties he felt forestry officials were making a fairer fist of things. 'With selective logging they almost got it right. The raping and pillaging had stopped. The only thing we got wrong was the time it took the forest to regenerate. We worked on a figure of forty years, and the true figure is more like eighty to a hundred years. But aside from that, you'd be hard put to tell which of the areas I'm going to show you today have been logged.'

Still, there's no disputing that the forest looks all the better for fifteen years of no logging. While Tully eventually recovered (recent years have seen record harvests of both sugar cane and bananas), the same cannot be said for the former timber town of Ravenshoe. Located at the Golden Square's western point, it remains moribund.

Says Hunt: 'Tourism was supposed to be the panacea but as soon as World Heritage came in, the roads were closed to tourists as well as loggers. I believe in World Heritage but I don't believe in locking it up. Fortunately there's been a reversal of thought [at the Wet Tropics Management Authority] in the last eighteen months. They've come to see that if we lock away the forest too long, there will be a generation of people who won't even know what we're locking away. It's too beautiful to hide, and it's high time we recognise that.'

For the most part, the Misty Mountains Trails follow old logging tracks, which themselves trace the footsteps of the Aboriginal tribes who once migrated annually from the highlands to the lowlands and back. The trails include a number of shorter day walks, two of which Hunt is showing us today.

We pile out along a causeway across Cochable Creek, adjacent to a cool swimming hole. Hunt, who is sixty-five, assures us that the walk will be a 'fairly easy' one. 'I took a couple of seventy-year-olds up here the other day,' he says. What he doesn't say – not until we're three quarters through the walk – is that they didn't make it all the way. Nor does he mention until too late that they were 'out of sorts' for several days afterwards. In fact, in hindsight, Hunt's earlier advice to bring a 'little lunch' and a 'big lunch' was his only hint that some of us might find walking almost twenty kilometres of unfinished jungle trail a tad taxing in the summer heat.

As it is, two of the party have to retire early, one with blisters, the other from heat exhaustion. But even they agree the scenery has been well worth it. Little lunch takes place by a ten-metre-long ribbon of water tumbling into a small waterhole, though not too small for a dip. Big lunch is by a waterhole broad enough for a swimming carnival. And afternoon tea sees us high on the Cochable Plateau, gazing across a chasm at the Elizabeth

Grant Falls spilling some three hundred metres into the steamy depths below.

To be sure, the vegetation trips us, snags us, claws at us and even stings us. But no one sits on anything itchy, the pygmies keep to themselves and so, for the most part, do the insects. Our lustiest encounter is with an ant colony. Ron Hunt, walking in front with his machete, swivels round to warn us.

'Careful,' he says. 'They're jumping ants. They're aggressive and have a nasty bite. Skip past quickly or they'll jump you.'

Some of us smile. Jump us? Them and the yowies, Ron. But as each of us passes the conical nest, ants the size of paperclips leap for our lower legs. Hunt laughs as he watches us skip. 'Even Rugged Stuff won't stop them buggers biting. Them and crocodiles, I reckon.'

TULLY

There's Something Out There

CLAIRE NOBLE IS DISGUSTED that Tully should have built the Big Gumboot to celebrate its heavy rainfall. In her opinion, it should have been a Big Flying Saucer. From her balcony on the slope of Mount Tyson, Tully's deep-green backdrop, she has recorded well over two thousand sightings of UFOs in the last forty years, which amounts to about one a week. At one stage she even put her proposal for a Big UFO to Rotary, the club behind the Big Gumboot, 'but they ignored me because I'm a woman'.

Noble's not the only Tully resident to have seen unusual extra-terrestrial activity. In fact, many if not most Tully residents will, when pressed, confess to having seen 'something' sometime. The caravan park owner reveals he used to stumble upon flying saucer 'nests', or crop circles, while cutting cane by hand in the sixties. The council librarian, too, is in no doubt, and maintains a prominent display of hardback books about outer space. Even the editor of the rugged local newspaper tells me she's seen a flying saucer: 'It followed me one night as I was driving. I remember telling my mother and she said, "That's nice, dear, have another cup of tea."'

At the corner mart the shop owner tells me, somewhat

apologetically, that he hasn't seen UFOs himself, but he's happy to ask around. 'Yeah,' volunteers a woman at the counter. 'My husband's seen them. I tell him, "How many cartons did you drink?" But he swears they're out there.' A woman with a henna rinse enters the store. 'Seen any flying saucers, Lorraine?' asks the shop owner. 'Oh yes,' she says. 'But not for thirty years. I used to see them from up on the hill. They had rotating lights and hovered for a long time.' The shop owner nods and yells out to an elderly man in shorts and thongs sitting on a bench outside, examining his scratchie. 'Hey, Alfie, seen any UFOs lately?'

'Not today, mate,' replies Alfie in a thick Italian accent. 'But I hardly ever look any more.'

I join Alfie outside to read the papers. He's sitting with three other men, all with hands like hams clutching scratchies. Nearby is a small posse of backpackers waiting for a bus to take them banana picking. They're talking about a British *Survivor*-style TV show which is being filmed in the jungle behind Tully. One of the so-called celebrities involved, Uri Geller, the spoon-bending psychic, has already been evicted from the jungle camp. The day's *Australian* carries a picture of Geller. 'I am still suffering the psychological and physical effects [of my time in the jungle],' Geller is quoted as saying. 'I felt another presence . . . like there was a higher intelligence there, like a UFO.'

JUST WHY TULLY SHOULD be a hotbed of extraterrestrial reconnaissance is not immediately apparent. The pretty town lies between two jungle-clad peaks. In the dry season, when the sugar trains are chugging and the mill is humming, the air is heavy with molasses. The rest of the year it is weighed down with humidity. Asthma rates are said to be the highest in the country, but how this relates to aliens, no one is sure. Some speculate the steamy air attracts spaceships. Others worry that spaceship fumes could irritate the lungs.

Tully has been on the tongues of ufologists ever since a banana farmer discovered the world's original crop circle, the so-called Tully saucer nest, in January 1966. (When two British hoaxers confessed in 1991 to having made the famous crop circles found in English grain fields, they said they'd been inspired by the Tully discovery.)

The banana farmer was George Pedley and his eyewitness account annexed the front-page of the *Tully Times* under the headline, 'I'VE SEEN A FLYING SAUCER'. One foggy morning Pedley was making his way to his farm through a neighbour's cane farm, past a waterhole known as Horseshoe Lagoon, when he suddenly 'heard a loud ear-piercing hissing noise above the engine noise of the tractor'. At first he thought he'd had a puncture but 'then I saw it . . . twenty-five yards in front of me, a flying saucer rose at great speed from near the lagoon. My pulse quickened and my throat felt so dry and tight. My body was rigid with fright. I tried to swallow. I couldn't. But my eyes followed the huge blue-grey vapour-like saucer as it lifted from the lagoon.'

Within seconds the saucer had vanished. Pedley blinked a few times, then noticed a circle of dead reeds swirling in the swamp, some nine metres in diameter. He thought about reporting it, but was worried about the ridicule. Instead he ploughed a field for his bananas as planned. He knocked off late afternoon, told several mates about the saucer and showed them the spot. Only then did he go to the police.

Pedley, who still grows bananas in the area, didn't handle the attention well. Then twenty-seven, he fled town for a year, and no longer talks publicly about his sighting. Yet his account has never been seriously challenged. Indeed, it has become part of

UFO 'reality', as a search of the Internet makes clear. When I track down Pedley, he tells me there is nothing left to say. 'I'd just like to see some more activity to back me up.'

Fortunately Albert Pennisi, the neighbour on whose cane farm the flying saucer landed, is more forthcoming. Pennisi, now in his mid eighties, and his wife Amy are what might be termed true believers, having first observed odd goings-on from the roof of their farmhouse in 1948. Over a cup of tea at their place, Amy uses her saucer to demonstrate to me a UFO's flight. 'They tilt,' she explains, though she concedes not having seen one herself. 'If someone says it flies upright, then it's not a flying saucer. They tilt and then they swoop.'

Albert Pennisi tells me that some weeks before Pedley's discovery, Claire Noble, the UFO watcher ensconced in her house on the hill, had gone public in the *Tully Times* with a series of sightings of UFOs in the direction of Pennisi's farm. In her opinion the extraterrestrials were working in the area. Pennisi believed her. Pedley didn't.

'George thought she was crazy,' says Pennisi, sipping his tea. 'But a few nights later I had a dream about a visiting spaceship. I told George about it. I said to him, "What would I do if something landed on my property?" Well, I didn't have to wait long.

'One day I was doing some work at the beach house. When I came back George was sitting on the porch waiting for me. He said, "Don't laugh. A flying saucer landed in your lagoon."'

Pennisi immediately rushed to the site. 'When I saw the nest, I rang Father Walsh at the presbytery and said, "A flying saucer landed in my lagoon." He said, "What sort of rum have you been drinking?"'

But Pennisi didn't doubt Pedley for a second. 'George was an honest man. If he saw it, he saw it.' Pennisi places a number of photos that he took of the landing circle in front of me, as well as a number of pictures of subsequent saucer nests found on his property. 'They returned in '69, '72, '75 and '80. Then no more.'

We get in his ute and bounce down a rutted farm track towards a remnant patch of scrub at the back of his property. 'In 1969, from the farmhouse one night I saw a big glow behind the scrub,' says Pennisi. 'I thought, "Gee whiz" and I got goose-bumps. The next day I found a marking there. A saucer nest.' After that, Pennisi started walking down to the lagoon every night, often after midnight. 'My wife, Amy, didn't like it. She said, "Aren't you frightened?" But I felt I might get contact. They knew I was there. I'm sure of that. And I always took the cane knife, just in case.'

He's taken it this time too. We follow the contour of a cane field into a gully where Pennisi halts the car on the bank of the lagoon. It's bone dry and no bigger than a house block, backed by a wall of palms and rainforest. 'The machine landed right in here. Then it rose to the height of those trees [about thirty metres], turned on its side and disappeared. The water was swirling and all the tadpoles and frogs were dead.'

By the time Pennisi had arrived on the scene, the dead reeds lay matted on the surface. 'You could sit on it, like a raft,' says Pennisi. 'I sat on it with my dog.' He also dived underneath it. 'The floor of the lagoon was perfectly smooth. Afterwards I worried that maybe it was radioactive, but I'm still here, touch wood.'

A few metres away he shows me a stand of rusted star pickets overgrown with vines. 'This is where I set up a camera linked to a twelve-volt battery, with an electromagnetic trigger to photo-graph the next landing.' The camera went off one night and Pennisi sent the film off to be processed, only to be told there was no footage. The Pennisis remain convinced it was confiscated by the government.

One question remains, however. Why Tully? 'Now you're asking hard questions,' says Pennisi. He suggests I call on Claire Noble, who runs the Tully chapter of the North Queensland UFO Society. 'She's the one with the explanations. Something to do with repairing something, but all that stuff is beyond me.'

CLAIRE NOBLE GREETS ME on her balcony looking like she's off to the races. She's had her hair done and is wearing big red earrings, bright lipstick and a red and white ensemble. But she's just happy to see a journalist. 'It is tremendous, what is happening here in Tully,' says Noble, who is seventyish with a girlish smile. 'And the world must know about it for its own good.'

From her balcony she has a fine view across town, but for a row of fast-growing pines planted around the school oval below. She has requested their removal, but to no avail. Nevertheless, the frequency of UFO sightings has increased of late. In the past year alone she has recorded several hundred alien craft. In addition, she has received calls from several farmers about missing tank water. So something's up, and she suspects she knows what it is.

'Mother Earth is in terrible shape,' she explains. 'Her electromagnetic grid is out of whack and two gridlines cross over at Tully, which is why we see so much activity here. It's a powerful vortex area and they [the aliens] are trying to fix it. They have to keep checking and monitoring the Earth's grid, a bit like Telstra maintenance crews. If they don't, and we keep poisoning the planet, then Big Things will happen.'

Like what? 'I can't tell you. It is classified information,' she says, barely drawing breath. 'You might wonder where I get this information from. Well, I get it from this fellow.' She points at a framed soft-focus drawing of someone who looks like a cross between Michael Jackson and Jesus, dressed in a blue space-vest.

'Commander Ashtar is in charge of entire galactic command. He's a beautiful person who knows everything and is in charge of eighteen million spacecraft.'

It seems Noble, too, has been searching for explanations. Around the room are all manner of New Age paraphernalia, including a large dream catcher and posters of Uluru and of British crop circles. I also see she subscribes to *New Dawn*, *Nexus* and *Ufologist* magazines. She notices me leafing through them.

'What are you picking up on? Are you psychic?' she asks me.

No, I'm the analytical type, I tell her.

'Oh that's a shame. But you're not really, you know. I can tell. Ashtar likes you.'

He does?

'He does. Can you see him? He's by the door. Never mind, he can see you.'

She explains she is one of Ashtar's 'light beings', who are tasked to tell fellow earthlings to clean up their act. Ashtar's devotees are also known as Etherians, but Noble is no mere devotee: 'Ashtar and I are very close. I have seen him here, physically. Even danced with him; he was like Fred Astaire.' She giggles. 'I'm glad you understand this, otherwise you'd think I was nuts. He has spoken to me in the early hours of the morning, and it has shocked me. Once, I had tantric yoga and he activated my kundalini. It went right through me and down my spine.'

Again she giggles coyly. I stare at my feet and ask how Ashtar addresses her. 'Well, that's private,' she says. When I look up at her, I notice she is blushing. 'Actually, I can reveal I am his beloved.' I realise that there is no picture of any other man to be seen on her walls. Yet Noble was married for almost fifty years. Her husband was a soldier, whom she wed just before he left for war.

'After he came back I wondered who I was married to,' Noble tells me later. 'It was never a happy marriage but we just never separated.' While he drowned his sorrows each night at the local RSL club, she was left to look out to the skies from her balcony. By the time her husband died in 1989, she'd already 'met' her Commander.

Noble is keen to show me the house. She wants to have some work done on it, but she feels there's little point because she expects to be called away by Ashtar to join him. 'I wish he would tell me when. I could ask him, but I don't want to trouble him with my three-dimensional problems when he's got many bigger things to worry about.'

She walks me downstairs into a room featuring a large chrome pyramidal frame. Around the room are a holy cross, a star of David and a model of a flying saucer. There's also a chair under the pyramid, and a jug of water next to it. Noble motions me to sit down. 'I'll leave you here to experience the pyramid. The energy is really something. Come up when you're ready.' With a shrug I sit inside the pyramid and take down some notes. Five minutes later, when I've finished scribbling, I get up to find the door locked.

I knock on the ceiling. In reply I hear a chair scraping, then footsteps. But nothing happens. After a few minutes I knock again. Still no response. I stay put for another five minutes. An image comes to me of Noble draped in a string of garlic bulbs and sharpening a garden stake. I batter on the ceiling: again in vain. Instead I settle down to examine the glass louvres. Just as I've managed to prise loose a second pane, I hear her coming down the stairs.

From the other side of the door, she yells: 'Did you hear knocking?'

'Yes, it's me. You locked me in!'

She unlocks the door and opens it. 'Yes. I thought I might

have. Did you pick up on anything? No? Are you sure? No energy at all?'

I shake my head angrily, but she looks so crestfallen that I waver and venture: 'Well, I did feel *something*.' Immediately she perks up. We return to the pot of tea upstairs, where she tells me more about her life with Ashtar. She shows me a video of him, and several books, and yet more articles, and I variously long to laugh, to run, to scream. But I can't. Having won her trust, I'm trapped. As she blithely rabbits on, I begin to understand George Pedley's thirty-eight-year silence. Play a trick on someone like dear old Albert Pennisi, and you are going to have to live with it for the rest of your life. Of course, I could be wrong. Pedley may not have made it up.

PARADISE CENTRAL

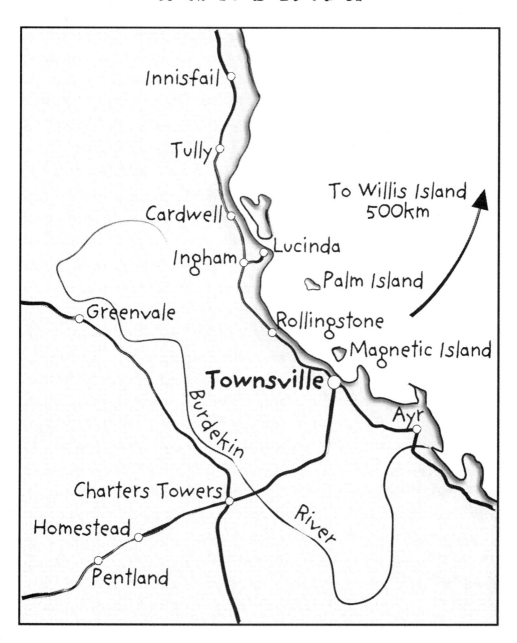

Innisfail

Tully

Cardwell

Ingham

Lucinda

To Willis Island
500km

Palm Island

Greenvale

Rollingstone

Magnetic Island

Townsville

Burdekin

Ayr

Charters Towers

River

Homestead

Pentland

Travelling North VI

YOWIES, BUNYIPS, LOST PYGMIES, jack o' lanterns, miracles, flying saucers – you name it, the people of the cassowary lowlands believe in it. Is it the terrifying tales they were told about the jungle as kids? Is it the Catholic reverence or peasant origins of the southern Italian influence? Is it the sheltered naivety of cultural enclaves, be they Spanish, Italian, Irish or Dutch? Or was it the mass enrolment in 'the school of hard knocks', the standard euphemism for so many educations truncated on cane fields and in sawmills?

The heat, I'm sure, has something to do with it. The people of the Atherton Tablelands, too, have hewn a living out of the jungle but seem an altogether more sober lot. The Tablelands' temperate climate might well attract eclectic faddists – alternative lifestylers, bio-dynamic apostles, shamanic incarnates – but it doesn't seem to generate raw eccentricity quite in the way the steamy lowlands do.

Stuck for a resident sage who might have an explanation for me, I decide to try Vivien Dickson, the editor of the *Tully Times*. Her paper is a fiercely independent thing and its look and tone have changed little since her late husband's brother covered George Pedley's UFO sighting in 1966. In news stories the *Times* refers to the mayor by his first name, which is Tip, and its views and letters regularly bristle with rants against academics, global conspiracies and homosexuals.

Dickson marches me into her unairconditioned office and resumes her seat behind a desk studded with two ashtrays, two fifty-packs of cigarettes and a large canister of salt. The interview does not go smoothly. Stumbling in vain for a journalistic connection, my 'Why Tully?' queries scratch a raw nerve. Dickson turns out to be a UFO believer herself. The problem is not Tully's gullibility, she points out sharply, after alluding to a recent letter to the editor which stated that Tully's status as a UFO capital made the town look stupid. No, the problem is my scepticism.

She lights up a cigarette.

'Have they told you about the yeti?'

'Yeah. It's nonsense, right?'

'Right. I had him to dinner the other day,' she says.

She's joking, though it's hard to tell. Her smile is hard and tight.

I put it to her that there are still locals who can't read English. Could this be a factor? Does she know of any studies of literacy rates in the region?

Dickson's eyes narrow. She asks me where I'm from.

Townsville, I tell her.

She arches her eyebrows.

'And?'

'And Melbourne before that.'

'Right,' she says, as if I'm starting to make sense.

'And Holland before that.'

'That really does explain a lot.'

Smoke chokes the room. I realise I've lost control of the interview, and wait for more. I get it.

'The Dutch are known to be arrogant. Add Melbourne to that, and there you are,' she says without flinching. 'I can see where you are coming from now. What did you say you were writing?'

A book on North Queensland, I tell her.

'How far have you got?'

I say I'm heading across the range for a week, to Greenvale, and then I'm in the home straight.

'You realise you will fail, don't you?'

'Because I'm not from here?'

'That's right. You cannot understand us.'

'But I'm writing about *my* North Queensland.'

'Yours! It's not yours!'

'I mean my impressions.'

'And what gives you the right?!'

I let this go, though Dickson seems to deem this a sign of weakness. She goes on to hammer home her advantage, goading me for a reaction with brief tirades about the inevitable Indonesian invasion, the idiocy of greenies and the economic victimisation of farmers. At one stage she asserts that toothless Aboriginal women used to throw their meat to street dogs and then 'fight them for it' once it had been tenderised. 'This is the truth,' she says, lighting up once more. 'Not your truth. *The* truth. But who listens to us? Not Canberra. Not Brisbane. Not even Townsville. The real Australia might as well roll over.'

She takes a deep drag of her cigarette.

'It's the age of the dickhead,' she says, in a last attempt to wrest a response. 'The dickhead reigns supreme.'

Shortly, driving south of Tully to scale a back road across the range, Dickson's bluster beats in my head. Ripostes queue in hindsight. My right to write about the North? What, as opposed to her right to stereotype me? And *my* arrogance? But once I leave the highway, the scenery soothes. There's no drive at once so lonely and beautiful as the crossing of the coast range. Every bend delivers a fresh glimpse of blue sea through verdant jungle. The narrow road eventually crests a rim of tall, cool rose gums before spilling into the dry interior. I skirt by an extinct volcano and enter the stunted timber of the lava plains, a rolling jumble of basalt ridges and parched dales. Over an hour and just a single cattle station later I round upon the fabled Valley of Lagoons, which so dazzled the early explorers. The lagoons, created by a lava blockage of the Upper Burdekin River, are rippling with black swans. I let the dog out for a dip, towel her off and drive on to Reedy Brook Station. By the time I unfurl my swag on a grassy bank by a meander of the Burdekin, here just an infant stream draped with soft-green paperbarks, it's too cold for a swim. I grab the hand line, thread on some meat and wait for a black bream, or maybe a sleepy cod.

What gives me the right? As the minutes pass the question seems to loll on the dark, still water, as if daring me to dive at it. What gives me the right to poke my nose into the lives of North Queenslanders? It's the wrong question, I realise. The real question, and perhaps the one Vivien Dickson meant to ask, is why?

So why am I doing this? To document the North, is my stock answer. To explore Australia in extremis. It's an outsider's prerogative.

Nothing bites and the sky turns to dusk. Above me two blue-winged kookaburras burst into their lunatics' chorus. I pull the dog close and lie back to look at them. It's a beautiful spot, yes. As close to paradise as anywhere I know. But that, in itself, is no answer either.

No, the pull of this place, and of Saibai, of Urandangi, even of Townsville, lies in its isolation. For some reason, I seem to seek it. This strikes me, suddenly, as a forlorn thing to do. Surely that's not what this trip, this book, this career is about? The homing in on others who choose isolation, the immersion in the minutiae of their lives, the seclusion of writing – might it all be an elaborate cover for loneliness?

I sit up to stare at the water. The floating question from before has sunk, leaving a deep, black abyss. I don't like the look of it. I throw a stick to splash the spell, pack up the swag and get in the car.

GREENVALE

Survivor III: The Australian Outback

GREENVALE WAS ALWAYS AN experiment, once the nickel ran out. Of course, the marketers didn't call it that. They dubbed Greenvale, three hours drive west of Townsville, the Outback Oasis. 'An excellent investment, the ultimate lifestyle opportunity,' they crowed. 'Dreams Do Come True! Secure Your Future Now!' Land and terracotta-roofed homes were going for a song and business premises were free. The town was girt by fairways and the sunshine guaranteed.

Greenvale, Australia's last purpose-built mining town, was conceived in the early seventies with an expected lifespan of twenty years. By 1993, on cue, the nickel was finished, the mine rehabilitated, the railway pulled up and the place was being shot up for army exercises. The town was to be bulldozed and buried in a vast pit, swallowed up by the North Queensland landscape like so many mining towns before it.

But in 1994 a Melbourne businessman came by and, as he told one reporter, 'thought it would be a giggle' to own a town. He snapped up the lot – eighty-five masonry homes, sixteen flats, a shopping complex, a service station, the hotel, a library, a hall, an Olympic-sized swimming pool, a nine-hole golf course, a sports ground, a school, police and fire stations, an airstrip and a rodeo ground – for a mere (rumoured) $600 000. He spent a further $3 million sprucing it up and kitting it out. He hired gardeners, repaired streetlights, gave the houses a paint job and bought an ambulance. All Greenvale lacked was an industry, but it was expected outback tourism would come to the party. Come 1996, Greenvale was open for business again.

Famously, the experiment worked. Or so it seemed. Every few months Greenvale's miraculous rebirth was toasted with media articles paying tribute to its booming businesses and happy retirees. The aroma of freshly baked bread reportedly filled the streets as the bakery battled to supply its growing clientele. By 1999 Greenvale's population had reached three hundred and fifty, two thirds that of its mining heyday.

In late 2001, however, a tiny news item mentioned the company in charge of the town, Greenvale Tourist Developments, had gone into liquidation. Apparently the population had quietly halved in the preceding year. Six months later, when I dropped in for a peek en route to elsewhere, it was down to seventy.

At the time I almost sped straight past, for Greenvale's easy to miss. The township buds off the main road (between Charters Towers and the Atherton Tablelands) across a cattle grid. Also, as signposted at a roadhouse some ninety kilometres earlier, there seemed little point in planning a stop: 'Greenvale SeVers Station CLOUSED Last fule 145km'. (Perhaps the school was struggling, too.)

I parked my car underneath a shady poinciana in front of the hotel. Inside a lone drinker stared straight ahead. He was short, fat and wheezy. After a while he glanced at me, grunted and stared back at the wall. I rang a bell. Nothing happened. 'You're gonna wait a fucking long time if you just fucking stand there,' the drunk blurted suddenly. Only his bottom lip moved. 'If you want a dur-rink, she's in the fucking kitchen.'

Outside, things were no busier. I wandered across the road into Acacia Drive, through the business centre. If this was the heart of town, it wasn't beating. The post office, library, supermarket, bakery, butcher and hairdresser's had been stripped bare. The huge swimming pool, midafternoon on a hot day, was deserted.

Beyond the pool a succession of courts peeled off Acacia Drive: Cassia, Banksia, Grevillea, Geranium. The houses were masonry bungalows roofed with red tiles. Many were empty, but a number had cars parked in their concrete driveways. There were immaculate lawns and satellite dishes. Galahs squawked overhead. The streets were kerbed and guttered. I could see *drains*. Powerlines ran underground, and street lamps stood overhead. This was no outback town, bedded in dust and sheeted with corrugated iron. This was suburban Canberra.

The first sign of life, apart from the drunk earlier, was a woman's face peering grimly out at me across a finely cropped lawn. Such was the stillness that a little further, on the corner of Eucalyptus Court, I could hear an aluminium window slide open. From behind it someone suddenly shrieked: 'PUT YOUR DOG ON THE LEASH!' The window slammed shut, a dog barked from further away, and all was eery quiet once more. Walking back with my dog now securely at heel, I paused by a noticeboard in the dead heart of town. A notice headed 'Greenvale – The Future' went on to list seven 'Potential Business Opportunities' – basically, everything was up for grabs.

But it was the announcement alongside that intrigued me. Posted by the Greenvale Progress Association, it declared that the 'Appeal against the Expulsion of Robert Palmer' would be heard seven weeks later, on a Monday. It offered no further information regarding Robert Palmer's identity or his alleged misdeeds. Neither did it set out what expulsion might involve.

But it did suggest all were welcome. All things considered, it sounded like a public lynching, at least in spirit. And that I had to see.

WHAT MAKES A TOWN implode? Chris Delios, the Melbourne businessman who became Greenvale's rebirther, says he doesn't have a clue. 'The place was humming last time I was there,' Delios tells me over the phone. 'I really don't understand what went wrong. The supermarket was making good money, land values were going up, everything was up and running. Next thing I hear, boom, it's hit a wall.'

Ill-health forced Delios to retire as a director of Greenvale Tourist Developments (GTD) in 1999. He hasn't been back since. There was also the sudden death of his dynamic right-hand man, Doug Corbett, who managed GTD and ran the pub.

'Doug and [his wife] Sue were natural leaders. They organised events, golf tournaments, cricket matches. They kept the community pumped,' recalls Delios. But he believes the sudden losses of Corbett and himself were at most minor triggers in the town's demise. 'The hard work had been done and the ball was in the community's court. It's a lovely town, with plenty of water. The only thing against it was the isolation, but I thought that the isolation would help make it more of a tight-knit community.

'Bugger me, was I wrong on that one. Everyone wanted to be a boss; I've never seen anything like it. There were at least a dozen splinter groups, including your usual committees for the golf club, the school, the SES, bushcare, the progress association. Basically, if you weren't happy with one lot, you formed your own.

'I didn't get involved. Our motto was let them do whatever they want, we'll just get on with our job. It didn't matter what we did; if we got a new office girl in, half the town would say,

"Oh, she's a nice girl," and the other half wouldn't be seen in the office with her. We'd hire a gardener and immediately there'd be a petition to have him sacked. I mean, some people were pathetic, the way they carried on. There were people who'd drive two hours to Charters Towers and two hours back rather than buy an ice cream from the local shop just because they didn't like the bloke who ran it. It was as if they had nothing better to do.'

SEVEN WEEKS AFTER MY initial visit I find the scene unchanged in the Three Rivers Hotel, a name pilfered from a Slim Dusty song to lend the pub some faux outback cred. The pudgy grump from last time is sitting on the same stool, still staring straight ahead. His name's Paddy Hansen, he's a Vietnam veteran and he's lived in Greenvale for eight years with his wife. He doesn't see much of her, however, because he spends most of his waking hours in the pub. To my surprise, he recognises me. 'Well fuck me dead! Here he is! Howya been, ya cunt?' he says with what almost sounds like affection.

I'm looking for a phone book (to track down Robert Palmer), but Hansen can't help me. 'Waddaya need a phone for? I don't ring any cunt. That's why I'm here, to get away from it, for the quiet. So wadda you doing? A feasibility study? Because the last thing this joint needs is another fucking feasibility study.'

I tell him I'm exploring the difficulties of forging a community.

'Community?' splutters Hansen. 'What community? Every cunt here's fighting on four fronts! The problem with this town is that every cunt thinks he's a local. Fuck me dead. They only have to be here two years and they reckon they run the fucking joint.'

Hansen twice makes me promise I'm not doing a feasibility study before giving me directions to Robert Palmer's place.

Palmer lives in Acacia Drive and is watering his patio plants when I walk up. He's a big man, mango-shaped, with small, hooded eyes, dark-rimmed glasses, slicked-back hair and his jeans hitched high. Three small dogs scamper about his feet and he speaks with a plummy accent. The glass door behind him rather grandiloquently proclaims him to be 'Robert Palmer, Justice of the Peace (Qual)'.

I explain my interest in Greenvale's trials without reference to his upcoming appeal and we sit on the patio. Through the glass I spy a shotgun leaning in the corner. Palmer, who calls himself a real estate agent on the basis that he manages property for absentee owners, asks me if I'm at all interested in buying a place. 'Everything's for sale, if you ask around. But if people put up signs everywhere, it would look bad.'

Palmer came to Greenvale from Tully, on the wet side of the range, to work for Chris Delios. Palmer's wife still lives in Tully and he travels back and forth, but he says he prefers the 'back country'.

After the loss of Chris Delios and Doug Corbett, Palmer stepped into the leadership void at GTD. By then the company had already sold off half the town – indiscriminately, in Palmer's view. 'Chris wanted to sell everything and get out. He wouldn't have known how hard it was to create a community, he just wanted the houses sold. I mean, he didn't have to live here, like us. Some of the people he put in the houses, well, they were unbelievable. The worst of white trash, really. If all you had on you was a hundred dollars for a deposit on a house, he'd take it. He once took a motorbike as a deposit.'

Nonetheless, for a time people made their payments and shop-keepers snapped up the rent-free premises. Lawnmowers buzzed morning and evening. People played carpet bowls, attended line-dancing classes and staged an annual rodeo. Whenever the townsfolk felt the place lacked something – a tractor for the golf course, a sit-on mower for the nature strips – they only had to ask and Delios would buy it. To stimulate community spirit and encourage people to shop locally, he came up with 'funny money', or Greenvale dollars.

But it was just a honeymoon period, says Palmer. 'Things were pleasant enough while Chris was throwing money around and people were getting their houses and gardens into gear. But then they get bored and they try new things. Like this Progress Association. All of a sudden they're forming factions and falling out and before you know it people are *hating* each other. People haven't just left. Businesses haven't just gone broke. They've been *driven* out.

'The big problem we got here is that Greenvale started with nothing. There's no core, everyone is an import. Many never owned their own home and have never been to a meeting. But everyone's on the same level because there's no natural [pecking] order, no doctors and lawyers and the like, so you get uneducated people running things with disastrous consequences. The only thing that has not happened here is a murder, and I tell you what, it ain't too far away.'

I glance again at the shotgun behind the door. Palmer notices. 'It's not there for self-protection,' he says. 'Though there's people I'd love to shoot. I keep the shotgun because there's a lot of people's dogs roaming about so I just use a bit of rat-shot to move them along.'

As I leave, he offers to show me a nearby but hard-to-get-to gorge in the coming days. 'Because if you'd come with a wad of money [to invest] I'd have told you the other story.' What story's that? 'The story of Greenvale's wonderful potential. I'm an agent for a Gold Coast developer who has bought homes and units here and is bringing Americans up for a look at tourism. If we could expand the golf course to eighteen holes, we could get the really big spenders: the Americans, the Koreans and the Japanese. Greenvale can come back. All it takes is leadership. But the people in this town wouldn't recognise leadership if it fell on them.'

PALMER WASN'T EXAGGERATING WHEN he talked of people being forced out of town. Over the coming days I hear tales of sabotage, attacks with baseball bats, burnt mail, pets sent packing and even death threats. More often, however, the spite is exercised silently. Like a schoolyard, the town seethes with wilful noncommunication, mercilessly maintained. I hear stories of cold shoulders, blacklists, shifting alliances, protracted legal wrangling and boycotts. Particularly boycotts.

Take the van park where I'm staying. The well-run park, which abounds with wildlife and comes with a hardware store, a freight business and a nursery, is for sale. But the couple running it tell me they are fleeing, not leaving. 'I've just dropped $100 000 off the price,' says the owner, an amiable workaholic who's writing a novel based on his experience. 'We can't take it any more. The normal people have already been driven out and it feels like we're survivors, the last ones standing.'

His wife adds: 'We've had weeks without a single sale in the hardware store. One time we had a woman come in who'd been boycotting us. You know what she said? She said, "I hate you, but that doesn't mean I can't shop here."'

Although the boycotts appear to have brought the town to its knees, the boycotters seem unrepentant. 'The people running the supermarket had to go,' one grim-lipped woman tells me. 'So do the people at the caravan park.' In her opinion the town needs to get rid of 'just' six more people. She even names them – they include the school principal, a sculptor, the local handyman and Palmer. Says she: 'Either we get rid of these people or we attract more so they are pushed back into their little corner. At the moment they can make too much noise.'

IF THE TOWN WERE a sporting team, then the Greenvale Progress Association is both its players' union and cheer squad. The association receives a small sum of money from the shire council, based in Charters Towers, and the town, if you look intently enough, looks the prettier for it. There are roadside plantings, for instance, and a small park. But progress is another matter. Particularly now that GTD's receivership means the players have been left to run the team.

Gavin Nash is the Progress Association's president. In his opinion, much of the animosity about town is 'projected anger'. Nash points out that for many the move to Greenvale has proved to be financially disastrous. Most bought their homes for about $70 000. Now they are hardly worth half that. Many mortgagees have simply stopped making payments to GTD's administrator on the basis that they were duped, a tussle which will likely be played out in the courts. Those who have stayed are either financially trapped or stubbornly determined to tough it out on their terms.

It's the stubborn who hold sway in the Progress Association and appear to have it in for Robert Palmer. For a time Palmer, as GTD's senior representative, was the association's acting president. But his bombast won him few friends. GTD and Palmer parted ways and the association asked him to step aside. He refused. There was a vote of no confidence, followed by further motions, angry slurs and legal posturing, with

Palmer at one stage threatening to sue the association for defamation. 'In the end we voted to exclude him from membership altogether,' says Nash. 'Our fear was that he was out to destroy us.'

Nash, who has worked in town for two years as a potter, pub cook and spiritual counsellor, says his past year at the helm has been utter hell. He plans to resign at the association's upcoming general meeting, the week after the Robert Palmer appeal. 'It's an illusion there's power in the president's position,' says Nash, whose close allies, the vice-president and the treasurer, will resign with him. 'The boot's going to be on the other foot from now on. We've got the numbers and we'll control [opponents] from the floor. We'll give them the time they gave us.'

The Palmer appeal, set for Monday afternoon, is to be Nash's last hurrah as president. With unrestrained glee he predicts it will be 'a ripper'. Nash concedes Palmer has support: 'Most of Rob's supporters don't show up at our meetings and vote by proxy. My guess is he would carry up to thirty votes and we've got sixty-seven members.' But he has a surprise in store: 'Proxies don't count at *appeals*. No one seems to be aware of this and I'm not telling Rob. It's in the constitution and he should know the constitution.' He grins triumphantly. 'I'm going to hold the floor very tight. Rob will put his case first, the management committee will reply, and there will be a vote. If anyone else talks, I'm going to eject them from the meeting.'

ALCOHOL ASIDE, THE TOWNSFOLK seem to be afflicted with two main vices. The first is Schadenfreude – one person's cow-trampled lawn is another's happy day. The second is sarcasm. In one of Gavin Nash's final flourishes as president, he handed out presidential nominations to nine 'white ants' he felt had been undermining him, including Robert Palmer. One of them, Aleks Dragicevic, called his bluff and accepted the challenge.

Dragicevic is a skinny, bearded man with earnest eyes who runs an optimistic little business called Handz on Massage, specialising in 'healing reflexology and deep tissue massage'. He also helps his partner Joy run Mother Earth's Treasures, a rock and teaspoon gallery at the entrance to town. I find him there cementing amethyst crystals into a concrete pyramid the size of a large tent. Dragicevic explains his interest in rocks occurred relatively recently. 'Before, whenever someone gave me a crystal, it would disappear. I just couldn't keep them,' he explains. 'But it turned out I'd had a curse put on me in a past life. A friend of mine released me from the curse and since then the crystals haven't disappeared.' Which is just as well, for there are thousands of them. I note that the last entry in the gallery's visitor's book is seven months old, though Dragicevic assures me people have dropped in since. 'I even had Bob Katter in here the other week.'

It is Dragicevic's fervent hope that his crystal pyramid will help heal the town, either spiritually or by attracting tourists. Meanwhile he does what he can: 'I try to clean up the bad energy around the place every night. But it doesn't seem to do much good.' When I ask him how, he explains: 'I try to follow Jesus Christ's path of unconditional love. Every night I give everyone in town a dose of healing, consciously. The whole town gets all of my love. So much love that people have moved because they can't handle it.'

He asks me if I'm 'also a psychic'. I say no, but ask him if, being a psychic himself, he fancies his chances against the one other candidate for president of the Progress Association. He smiles slyly and says, 'These town people think I'm a wuss.' A wuss? 'Yeah, a wuss. A pushover. They don't realise what they'll get if they vote me in. I'll use my psychics to the max. I can be very, very powerful. They may come to fear me, to see how dangerous I am.'

AT THE PUB I'M comforted to find Paddy Hansen on his usual perch and in his usual state. He wants to know how my feasibility study is going and what I think of Greenvale's potential. A little too frankly I suggest that Greenvale should be fenced off and turned into a reality TV show, along the lines of *Survivor Two: The Australian Outback*. At the end of each week the Progress Association could meet to vote someone out of town. Hansen gasps a wheezy laugh. 'Fuck me dead,' he says. 'That's feasible. And I'd put me money on Bert to win it.'

Bert Cussens is an ex-miner who graces Greenvale's funny money as the town's 'honorary life governor'. Hansen suggests I talk to him. 'He's our one wise man. You'll recognise him. He's got Santa's beard and he's minus an arm, the silly bugger. He broke it and it got infected. Hurt like hell, apparently. He'd be sitting here next to me at the bar butting out cigarettes in that arm to kill the pain. I could smell it going bad. One day I said, "The old cunt's got gangrene." Turned out he did. The doctors had to cut the cunt off.'

But Cussens has no wish to discuss the state of the town when I find him the next morning at Robert Palmer's place. 'I'm not getting involved,' he says wisely. Palmer's seated officiously behind a large desk in the middle of the room abutting the patio. The shotgun's still in the corner, but an extra rifle leans against a bookcase. From his desk, which is adorned with a little Australian flag, Palmer has a good view of the street. The wall behind him bears a number of real estate flyers promoting lush properties near the coast. I assume

Palmer is selling them, but no, he explains he just likes the pictures.

I ask Palmer what he's working on. He shows me: it's a legal letter concerning the local historian. Palmer's taking him to court. It will be the ninth time in two years, by Palmer's count. Palmer's the agent for the man's absentee landlord, and Palmer wants him out, allegedly for neglect. Palmer maintains it has nothing to do with the fact that the man is one of those agitating against him.

We talk about his appeal, which is scheduled for the following afternoon. Palmer says he knows he won't have the numbers, but claims he's not in it to win it. 'I want to be rejected,' he says. Why? 'Because I want to take them to court.' For what? 'For defamation.' So he wishes to bankrupt the association? 'No, just those who vote to reject me.' He looks at me as if it all makes perfect sense.

DESPITE ALEKSANDER DRAGICEVIC'S PSYCHIC powers, there's only one candidate left in the presidential race, and it isn't him. The Progress Association's management committee, sometimes known as the Gang of Four, has decided to reject his nomination on the basis that he handed in his signed form twenty-five minutes after the specified deadline. 'He knows the rules,' an unbending Gavin Nash explains later.

I find the president-in-waiting, Dennis MacAulay, at home watching television, bare-bellied, chain-smoking and snacking on chips. It's three in the afternoon. MacAulay's wife is out, at the hotel, where she's meeting with her three colleagues on the Progress Association's management committee to finetune tactics for the Palmer appeal.

MacAulay, a former earthmover from Mackay, does odd jobs around town, such as mowing the pub lawns, looking after the pool and coordinating burn-offs. He also sits on a number of committees and is the nonplaying president of the golf club. (No one plays golf these days; with its ant-bed greens and cracked fairways, the course is essentially a dog run.)

The MacAulays have been in town for two years, having bought their house with a $1000 deposit. Like several others, however, they've ceased paying their mortgage. 'The house isn't worth now what it was, so we're not paying that,' MacAulay says bluntly. 'The powers that be will have to sort something else out.'

But MacAulay swears the town is 'in its turnaround year'. 'People say there's fifty in town, I say there's ninety. Greenvale will go ahead definitely.' His plans, as president, include the establishment of a fossicking field and 'a museum of old machinery to keep the tourists occupied for a bit longer'. Despite the resistance of local station owners to the notion of people fossicking, fishing or camping on their land, dreams of tourism persist. (Pipe dreams, literally. One former resident famously applied to build the Big Bong in town, but his plans to make Greenvale the hemp capital of Australia foundered on state legislation.)

MacAulay also predicts fresh mines and a new national park, centred on Broken River Gorge, a limestone-walled waterhole which is nice enough but muddied by cattle. 'I've been there. I'm not into nature but I've sat there for three quarters of an hour and there was no one there and I reckon some blokes would love it. We got some rare bird here, too, they reckon.'

ON THE MORNING OF my last day in Greenvale, I'm greeted by a fiftysomething woman likewise walking her dog on the golf course. I haven't seen her before, but she knows who I am. 'I'd just like to tell you that this is a lovely community. I've been here since 1998 and I would never move. Everyone knows everyone here. Oh, it's wonderful.'

I elect to spend the rest of the morning holed up in my camp, reading. After lunch I stop in at Patz Bazaar, a breezy craft shop, for a cup of tea. Pat Hayward, who spoke to me frankly but off the record at the start of my stay, asks me for my thoughts. After I've finished, Hayward looks somewhat taken aback. 'Oh dear,' she says. 'We haven't given you a bad impression, have we? There's really nothing wrong with Greenvale. There's a few personality clashes, but you get those in every town.'

I head across to the pub to wile away the hour before the appeal, which is to be held diagonally across the road, next to the community hall. Paddy Hansen's in position. Four empty stools away is a rodeo rider, in town on a spree. He's picked the wrong town. He rings a bell a second time for service and Hansen ticks him off: 'You know what will happen to that bell? It will ring every time you sit, because if you keep pulling the cunt, someone's gonna jam it right up your arse.'

The bull rider laughs and begins telling Hansen about the thrills and spills of his bull-riding career. Mostly spills. 'I've broken me knees, me wrist, me elbow, me lower back, me neck, me right arm, me left shin, three of me fingers. But I reckon I'm lucky so I always buy the [rodeo] clowns a beer after each ride because they've saved my hide that many times.'

Hansen looks at him. 'Yeah? Well you're a fucking amateur. I've copped worse injuries falling off this fucking stool, and no matter how much I pay the clown behind the bar, it doesn't help any.' I can't help but smile. Hansen may be an alcoholic, and the bull rider may well harbour a death wish, but at least they're only out to hurt themselves.

I leave them and join those gathering opposite. Plastic chairs from the hall have been set in a circle under a tree laden with enormous brown fruit shaped like giant zucchinis. I realise this must be the exotic sausage tree that I'd read about in a town brochure. I weigh one of the colossal fruits in my hand. It's hard and heavy as a brick.

About twenty-five people take their place. Palmer is seated plum underneath one of the dangling sausages, flanked by his supporters. The managing committee is arraigned to his left. Nash calls upon Palmer to speak first. Palmer refuses, asking that the allegations against him be read out first. But Nash won't budge. As Nash spouts regulations and constitutional overtures, Palmer's supporters clack their tongues and shake their heads. When Palmer pipes up, the management committee's supporters mutter and shake theirs. And so it goes, the volume steadily rising. Within five minutes Nash has lost all control and the meeting degenerates into a chaotic exchange. A chair is knocked over as, in ones and twos, people stalk off in disgust, including, eventually, Palmer himself. There will be no vote. The plotting will continue. Greenvale will die. I return to the pub to join Paddy Hansen in getting wisely drunk.

WILLIS ISLAND

Under the Weather

HANN WAS MY OFFSIDER. We travelled from Sydney to Willis by steamer and on board was a New Guinea magistrate [who] kept Hann sozzled all the time. Arriving at Willis, Hann was incapable of descending the gangway to the surfboat, so he was put in the cargo sling together with the beer supplies given to him by the magistrate . . . There I was, full of inexperience, a big heap of stores scattered on the beach amongst which sat the inebriated Hann. I sort of felt alone . . .

Weatherman Eric Riethmuller, writing about his 1927 arrival
on Willis Island.

THE FIRST THING TO strike the visitor to tiny Willis Island, Australia's loneliest and most cyclone-prone outpost, is the smell. It's as acrid and sudden as falling face first in a platter of goat's cheese. The second thing to hit the unwitting is, well, nine times out of ten, the guano itself.

Birds are everywhere, it seems. Dusky noddies adorn the roofs, while the surrounding shrubbery, half-a-dozen palms and a long-suffering casuarina tree are studded with brazen boobies. As well, the coral cay is overrun by rails and pockmarked by mutton-birds, which nightly attempt to undermine the foundations of the Bureau of Meteorology station and its various components: the radar, tanks, huts, masts, monitoring boxes and cyclone shelter.

And yet, of all the things that the supply ship MV *Pacific Conquest* brings the 'voluntary marooned' weather watchers of Willis Island – beer, soap, a politician, a passage home and human contact – it is the arrival of four more birds that evokes the warmest welcome.

Perhaps, given that cats and dogs are banned on this shiny button in the Coral Sea, chickens are as good a companion animal as any. Perhaps the white leghorns symbolise a niche of domestic order in the midst of thousands upon thousands of wheeling, screeching, excreting seabirds. Or perhaps the islanders have been dreaming of drumsticks.

Whatever. After six months of being able to walk no further than two hundred metres in any direction, Robert McFarlane, the officer-in-charge, and Robin Paton, one of the outgoing watchers, seem more concerned with liberating the chickens than themselves. They dispense quickly with introductions and lug the cardboard boxes of poultry to the chook shed.

The pen is bristling with hundreds of orange hermit crabs, their shells the size of golf balls, scrapping over a pile of food refuse. Dried guano drips like candlewax from the chicken wire, where fifty-odd red-footed boobies roost every night. McFarlane and Paton pick up the hens one by one, inspect them for health and vigour and ask that they be nice to Old Bob, the geriatric rooster whose virility was blown to bashfulness in the last cyclone. 'Welcome to paradise, ladies,' says McFarlane, before setting them free to meet and compete with the hermit crabs.

LIFE ON WILLIS ISLAND, notionally a tropical idyll on an unspoilt coral reef, has its moments. Unlimited snorkelling, for example. Magical sunsets. And you get used to the smell, if not the noise.

But the only shade comes courtesy of a few scraggly palms under which, if the guano doesn't get you, the ticks surely will. And they're as big as pine nuts. In addition, except for what little water decants off the generator shed roof – too noisy even for the boobies – the collected rainwater is horribly thick, muddy and oily. The islanders call it guano juice.

That there is human habitation at all is, paradoxically, due to the isle's uncanny knack for cyclonic encounters. Cyclone Katrina recently sideswiped it with winds of a hundred and twenty kilometres per hour, while hundreds of booby and noddy corpses, picked over by crabs and pickled by sun and salt, still litter the foreshore where Cyclone Justin loved and left them a year ago.

Though mostly unsung, the Bureau of Meteorology's intrepid staff at Willis Island have been a crucial cog in North Queensland's warning system against cyclones for the past seventy-six years. With the help of the island's radar and weather data, official cyclone warnings have become more targeted over the years, limiting the shutdown of schools, tourism, military exercises, ports and industry. Cyclone casualties, too, have declined steadily since the station was established in the wake of two deadly storms within weeks of each other in 1918.

The first (unnamed, as cyclones weren't christened until 1959) destroyed a thousand homes in Mackay and killed thirty people. The second took almost a hundred lives in flattening Innisfail and drowning a nearby Aboriginal community (now Mission Beach).

At the time there was a widely held belief that Willis Island lay

smack in the path of any tropical cyclone aiming for the inhabited coastline. There was a certain geographical logic to this: the
island lies five hundred kilometres due east of Cape Tribulation
and about seven hundred and fifty kilometres north of
Rockhampton, which makes it kind of hard to get around, even
for a tempest.

In 1922 no one was sure whether it was safe to inhabit a tiny
cyclone-prone coral cay protruding barely six metres above the
high-tide mark. Only one way to find out, said the government
navigator of the day. Six months later, he'd proved it was possible
to perch on the island in total isolation and remain both alive
and sane. And that was before airconditioning.

THE TRIP TO WILLIS Island takes thirty hours one way from
Townsville. Every six months, in mid-June and mid-December,
the Bureau of Meteorology dispatches a ship to restock and
service the station and exchange weather crews.

The MV *Pacific Conquest*'s live cargo is four chickens and
twenty men, comprising the ship's crew, half-a-dozen contracted
tradesmen, bureau engineers, the new station crew, the bureau's
Queensland director, Rex Falls, and his three guests: Senator Ian
McDonald from the sugar town of Ayr, his press secretary and me.

The new station crew is unusual in that there are only three of
them: the usual one technician who maintains everything from
the radar to the lawnmower, and two – instead of three –
observers, who maintain a twenty-four-hour weather watch
between them.

Across Australia, robots are gradually replacing the bureau's
three hundred plus observers, and a number of the bureau's
fifty-nine observing stations have already been fully automated.
However, Falls does not envisage Willis Island being deserted

once more. 'The isolation and harsh conditions make security and maintenance a problem. We'll always need someone there and it would seem cruel to leave just one.'

Observers like to say theirs is not a job but a lifestyle. In the days when the greying bureau (the average age has climbed to forty-seven) still recruited staff, stations from Arnhem Land to Antarctica were potent lures. There were no obligations to fashion or family. The work was routine and communal, consisting as much of general housekeeping as weather monitoring. As one Willis Island veteran, Jeff Smith, puts it: 'My generation joined for life. You couldn't leave, you'd be too maladjusted to go anywhere else.'

So when all's been recorded, monitored, entered and predicted, what do Willis Islanders do to ward off cabin fever? 'Dreenk,' says Freddy Blanc, the *Pacific Conquest*'s Swiss-born cook and a veteran of these biannual trips. 'Many brew zeir own beer, you see. But eet's horreeble!' he says, clutching his head with both hands. 'Guano Lager, zey call eet. Or Booby Bitter. Ugh!'

The ship coasts smoothly through the day and night. Pods of dolphins occasionally hitch a ride on the bow wave. Terns prowl the ship's wake. Rex Falls regularly dangles a thermometer over the side. After thirty-eight years with the bureau, the weatherman-turned-administrator can't help himself. Any excuse for a spot of fieldwork.

The water temperature is over twenty-nine degrees. Falls says cyclones require just twenty-six to form. Which sounds ominous, until Falls explains that during El Niño phenomena, when the waters of the South Pacific are even warmer, tropical cyclones tend to occur further east. Hence, with the present El Niño being the biggest on record, the east coast may well be spared a big blow this cyclone season. Which it has been, thus far.

The island finally shimmers into view. 'There's more trees than I thought,' says thirty-two-year-old observer Brendan McMahon. 'Though I reckon we might plant a few more. A shady mango wouldn't hurt.' At this, Falls almost has a fit. 'You can't do that, you might change the climate record!' he splutters.

McMahon's housemates-to-be are a fifty-year-old fellow Tasmanian and a techie from Melbourne. Previous crews have been known to spend their entire tour of duty stark naked. Not this lot. 'Uh-uh,' says McMahon. 'I'm not a water person,' says the techie.

The ship anchors on the reef's edge, about three hundred metres from shore. An amphibious barge is winched off the back deck. It looks like a bad prop from an old war movie. As we file aboard, Falls checks his watch. 'Eight am. Should be a balloon launch any minute,' he says. Sure enough, a balloon about 1.5 metres in diameter shoots up out of what looks like the island's outdoor dunny.

Falls explains these are released every six hours and ascend up to thirty kilometres – about three times as high as a jumbo jet's flight path – before bursting. An attached radiosonde measures humidity, temperature and air pressure at different levels, while the observers track it by radar to calculate wind speeds. 'It's the upper winds that steer cyclones,' says Falls. 'These data are obtained from all over the world to give us a global forecasting model.'

Our ugly grey barge rears up onto the beach and rumbles up a short track to the station. Twenty men stand on its back, some pointing cameras. In hindsight, it probably looked like an invasion. The welcoming party, three hirsute men and one woman, certainly aren't overly welcoming. Overwhelmed, more like it. Their reaction hints at how well they got on. Not like the previous lot, who were practically leaping up and down to be rescued apparently. Upon their return to the mainland, several needed counselling.

'Those guys were tired and cranky because they had three cyclones on tour. It was batten down the hatches most of the time and then clear sand and clean up for the remaining months,' the red-bearded Robert McFarlane explains later.

The only thing to faze McFarlane's mob through the dry, non-cyclone season is the human whirlwind whipping around them at present. The mechanics and engineers have already fanned out across the island, fixing fridges, mending motors, rewiring, repairing, refuelling and restocking, pausing only to tut-tut at the state of the water filters or the size of the weevils in the pasta jars.

Then there's the new crew wanting to be taught the tricks of the trade, a senator seeking small talk, a boss trying to debrief them, a journalist asking questions and a cook with a Swiss-French accent having kittens in the kitchen. McFarlane and Robin Paton escape to tend to the chickens, and Chris Hughes, the twenty-four-year-old techie, heads off to walk a lap of the island. Commotion really isn't for him. After Willis, he's off to an Antarctic posting for fourteen months. As Jeff Smith, the fur-riest observer, explains, 'When we first got here, we each told our life stories three times in the first day. Things get a little quiet after that.'

Robin Paton, forty-two, only the fifth woman to stay at Willis, hopes to be stationed next at Giles, which is the inverse of Willis Island in a sense, being a watering hole surrounded by the Gibson Desert. 'This is a wonderful lifestyle,' she says. 'No distraction, no shops, no fashion. It's a bit escapist, I suppose. But I get to read so many good books.'

So how long will it take to get used to mainland living? McFarlane shrugs. 'I've seen people do stints like this and come away permanently affected. As it is, I can't remember my phone number.'

'Yes, you forget things,' says Paton. 'You're so used to grabbing things you need out of the storeroom that you walk out of super-markets without paying.'

Many observers return to the island, in one case thirteen times. Both McFarlane, forty-four, and Jeff Smith, forty-seven, are on their second tour. Smith says he found it harder going this time because he misses his wife so much, whereas his 1983 tour was 'the best six months of my previous marriage'.

For entertainment, crews have a TV, videos, a pool table and a library. The islanders also get a mail drop midtour, courtesy of the RAAF. The package includes mail, medical supplies and, if the pilots are obliging, takeaway food. Once islanders also had a fishing dinghy at their disposal. But it was confiscated after an observer cracked and struck out for the mainland on one tank of fuel. The bureau has never replaced it, arguing that fishing should be discouraged for fear of ciguatera poisoning, caused by eating the flesh of certain fish. Seeing the fish may beat eating them anyway. In 1994, a weather crew documented the island's natural history and recorded one hundred and seventy-seven species of fish.

McFarlane and Paton take us on a tour of the huts and grounds. First stop is the storeroom. McFarlane holds up a bottle of grape juice. 'You stick in some yeast, let it ferment, and it comes out as a rough rosé,' he enthuses. 'Not a bad drop at all.' On the way out, we spot an old electricity bill stuck to the fridge. 'To give it a homely touch,' grins Paton.

The bar looks quite homely too. The numbers on the clock on the wall have each been replaced with the word 'beer'. Posters for Booby Bitter and Guano Lager adorn the walls and a visitor board reveals that during the past tour, just two ships called in to say hello – a dive boat and the navy. 'The navy drank all the rosé on us,' McFarlane says ruefully.

The business – and airconditioned – end of the station is on the other side of a thriving vegetable patch. It consists of three rooms packed with computers and communications equipment. We traipse to the hydrogen generation shed, where the H (hydrogen) is split from H_2O to inflate the weather balloons, and to the radars, the water tanks, the desalination plant, the generators, the pumphouse, the incinerator, the weather gauges and the chicken pen. Yes, there's a lot of work to do too.

EVENINGS ARE PARADISE ON Willis Island. The scraggly palms become picture perfect when silhouetted. The vista is of a honey-coloured sea, smooth as glass, rippled only by the odd turtle head. It's egg-laying time, and soon, come nightfall, they'll be heaving themselves ashore to reshape the beaches. But the scene is sullied for McFarlane and co. For six months this was theirs alone. Smith grabs a beer and seats himself under the satellite dish, well away from the invaders, staring out to sea. Chris Hughes, the techie, is off on another lap of the island. McFarlane is biding his time for a last moonlit encounter with the turtles. Only Paton, a one-time activist, is in form, grilling the press secretary about the need to balance conservatism with compassion. Six months of pent-up frustration over daily news broadcasts finally gets an outlet.

The Guano Lager flows a little more freely the second evening. Oddly enough, the talk in the tropical twilight centres on Antarctica, what with most observers having completed a tour or two there. They are unanimous that Willis Island is lonelier than Antarctic bases such as Mawson, Davis and Macquarie Island. 'Here we get no visitors, no medical staff and, when visitors do come, they do so in such large numbers that it is traumatising,' says Jeff Smith.

'Isolation is relative anyway,' says McMahon. 'In Antarctica, going to the toilet, you'd sit there three abreast and afterwards you'd gas and ignite what you'd produced. It was quite a ritual. Back home, I'd go to this poky room with just a button to push and no one to talk to. Now that was lonely.'

Suddenly the senator spits out a mouthful of beer. Apparently he sensed a fat insect bobbing against his lips. But Smith is laughing his head off. He has given the senator a stubby of Garlic Bitter, a special home-brew in which the guano flavour is disguised with garlic – about ten crushed cloves per stubby, no less. Says Smith, 'Willis doesn't do much for your social skills. My mother recently told me: "If you come back from this trip the way you did last time, don't bother!"'

So does he feel that the observer's lifestyle – the vegie garden, the wildlife, the sharing, the skinny-dipping, the steady rather than stressful workload, the crop that no one talks about because there is a senator present – is a refuge of sorts for those who declined to leave the seventies behind them? 'Yes,' nods Smith, grinning wildly. 'There are a few characters among us like that.' As an afterthought he adds, 'But if you think I'm hairy now, you should have seen me then.'

THE AMPHIBIOUS BARGE IS parked out the front and everyone is ready to go, but for the techie. He's lapping the island one last time. Smith squats opposite me brandishing two stubbies. 'Oh no,' I say, 'not the Garlic Bitter,' and thrust it back at him. 'Oh yes,' says Smith, and unscrews the top. The thick stench envelops us. Some passing mechanics hold their noses.

'You can't deny a man his last farewell drink,' he says. I take a sip. It's disgusting. Still, I have an inkling I could get used to this. I ask him if he'll ever be back. 'You never know. I'll miss it for sure. Especially the lifestyle. If only I could have all this,' he says, waving his stinking stubby all around, 'and my wife here with me, I'd be perfectly happy.'

We skol to that and, reeking as all get-out, clamber aboard the barge for the crowded trip back to Townsville. There, at 2 am on the wharf, is Smith's wife in a short red dress. 'Hello, my love,' she says as Smith prepares to leap across. 'Gosh, do you look feral!' Just wait till she gets a whiff of him.

TOWNSVILLE

King Billy Goes Off

AT NOON ON A brilliant Townsville Sunday, the stumpy figure of Louis Beers makes his way unrecognised from the public bar around to Room 6 of the Dalrymple Hotel Motel, a squat, garish blue cornerstone of the city's industrial west. Skirting fans arriving in the car park, Beers, toting his stage persona in a bag, trudges through the drive-in for a six-pack of his sponsor's product.

'I like to relax while I get ready before the show,' he says, patting his great tropical gut with some affection. 'There's an element of nerves here today because it's a live recording.'

Within the dull-blue decor of the motel room, Beers quickly strips to where his waist might once have been. 'I'll get stage one on,' he says, retreating to the bathroom with a small sponge, a tin of black theatre make-up and a stubby. He paints his face, his neck, his arms, his hands. He gets in under the nostrils, dabs his crow's-feet and doesn't miss the double-chin fold. He swivels around to urinate loudly in the bowl and breaks into a wheezy laugh as he pulls up his tracksuit pants. 'Stage two. Now I've got a black dick as well.'

It's warm, he's perspiring, and the paste needs to dry. Beers sits on a corner of the dull-blue bed and uncaps another beer. He looks like a very pregnant penguin. 'I'm so disappointed,' he announces in mock seriousness. 'I heard down at the TAB yesterday that the Murris were having their NAIDOC [National Aboriginal and Islander Day of Observance Committee] dinner here last night, in the same showroom, so I went for a look. You should have seen it, ay. The tables were all decked out in red and yellow and black, the napkins the same; it looked a picture. Such a pity they've taken the lot away. They could have at least left the flags up for me.'

He dons a dull-blue shirt over the remaining pale flesh. Sweat is running down his temples and pooling under his eyes, but the make-up seems safe. He daubs some white face markings on his cheeks, lathers his jaw with glue, straps on a beard and pats it into place. The hat goes on next, then the microphone. Lastly he wipes the paste off his nails to leave them pink. He stares levelly into the motel mirror. 'G'day, King Billy,' he says in a thick Murri accent. 'You seen 'im Louis Beers?'

BEERS IS A COMEDIAN. And for a white man who paints himself black and tells Aboriginal jokes, he's had a rather charmed run really. Having started out on breakfast radio the year Gough Whitlam came to power, his King Billy Cokebottle character is now well into its thirtieth year. *The Dirty Dozen*, released last month on cassette – 'for the truckies' – and on CD, is his twelfth recording in as many years. Sony, it seems, can't get enough of him. Tape sales are fast approaching a quarter of a million.

Cokebottle's success and longevity defy his ever-shrinking mainstream exposure. Once heard on radio across the north from Perth to Brisbane, these days he's shunned by all but one Darwin program director. Even Mount Isa has dropped him. In his home town of Townsville, too, he feels misunderstood. A television advertisement for a local 4WD hire company was pulled after viewers complained. ('What brings you here, King Billy?' a fisherman asked. 'This car here,' Cokebottle replied.) A second try at TV work, in the form of a live cross on Channel Nine's *Today Show,* was shot down by the ABC's *Media Watch.* ('How about this little effort from Townsville,' said the caustic host as he introduced a clip of King Billy atop the city's Castle Hill, claiming the surrounding country as his.) He gets no local press and his public profile has been relegated to an irregular five-minute slot on an obscure community radio station. Which is fine by Townsville's sizeable Aboriginal community. 'It's best to ignore him,' says Shorty O'Neill, a local black activist. 'The more publicity, the bigger he gets with the rednecks.'

Yet Beers continues to course along the nation's soft white underbelly, touring the regions, tiptoeing around the capitals. If anything, his popularity is growing. Sell-out crowds during a recent ten-stop tour of regional New South Wales have sparked plans for his first tour of Victoria.

Jenny Pryor, North Queensland's ATSIC commissioner, hopes the Victorians will run him out of the state. Having heard him on radio, she's adamant the character, if not Beers, is racist. 'Murris have their own sense of humour, but it is his use of broken English that really offends me. It stereotypes us as stupid. The fact is that for many Murris, English is their second or third language.' And as for painting himself black on stage: 'He hasn't got the right. He's just making money off the backs of blacks.'

Federal Race Discrimination Commissioner Bill Jonas knows of no complaints that have been brought against King Billy Cokebottle. In fact, Jonas has never heard of him. But he warns there's a very fine line between humour and vilification. According to Jonas, it's one thing for an ethnic group to poke fun at itself, and quite another for a different race to do it for them, particularly if the latter has historically oppressed the former. You'd be hard put to find a German in Hasidic dress telling Jewish jokes for a living, for example.

'Aborigines have been the butt of much more than jokes in this country,' says Jonas. 'If these jokes come as part and parcel of a wider context of historical put-downs, then they may be seen to be perpetuating a notion of racial inferiority and thus be in breach of racial vilification laws.' Which, perhaps, is why in this country it is tolerably funny for a TV comedian to mimic, say, a Pakistani cricketer or a Greek grocer, but not (as TV sports identity Sam Newman found out) an Aboriginal football player.

'You have to look at it from the point of view of the person who is the butt of the joke,' says Jonas. 'It has to be the kind of joke that the subject can joke along with.' And there's the rub. Jenny Pryor might not be amused, but she concedes that Aborigines have mixed feelings about Beers. Some think he's funny, others call him a mate. One even calls him family. And the police think he's hilarious.

LOUIS BEERS DRINKS AT the Herbert Hotel, a working-class pub popular with blacks in Townsville's feeble city heart. Most days he's there by noon. He has his own corner, with a little plaque, promotional posters and a cordon of big-bellied types. Beers is still on a high, having just got back from his tour of New South Wales. 'The crowd at Armidale was the biggest they'd had since Slim Dusty came through about five years ago,' he says. 'We closed the door at five hundred in most places.'

Of his albums' six hundred-odd recorded gags, the majority feature Morton, King Billy's hapless brother. Morton Cokebottle is a drinking, thieving, womanising yet well-meaning fool, a lovable loser forever in trouble with the police.

He has a wife, Giddigan, and an endless array of cousins, such as Gibbit, Goddit, Lookout (the blind one) and Willy Bin. But there's no narrative. In fact, Beers has written only twenty gags from scratch. The other five hundred and eighty are pinched adaptations, in that as often as not Morton is a reincarnated Irishman, or a blonde, or a Kiwi. 'I don't play instruments, I don't sing,' says Beers. 'I just do straight-out stand-up with an accent.'

Beers says he's only once had racial vilification laws raised in relation to him, when an insurance agent rang up offering to cover him against it. 'I told him to piss off.' Beers insists he's on the right side of the law. He must be, he says, because police number among his biggest fans as well as his closest friends. 'In their working life, cops tend to see a lot of Morton,' Beers explains. 'My humour is very close to home for them.'

Just how close to home was famously revealed in a video of a fancy-dress party held in 1992 in the outback town of Bourke. Several members of the local constabulary arrived daubed with black shoe polish. One sported a noose around his neck and grinned as he explained he'd come as Lloyd Boney, a young Aborigine who'd hanged himself in the nearby Brewarrina watch-house five years before. The video, which surfaced at the height of concern over police treatment of Aborigines following the Royal Commission into Black Deaths in Custody, sparked outrage nationwide. Not from Beers, however. 'It was a private "bad taste" party and as far as I'm concerned the cops should have won first prize. That footage was never meant for national television.'

Over the years Beers has performed at a number of private police functions, both in Western Australia and Queensland. His daughter later tells me that 'Dad was always joking around with his copper mates' while she was growing up. And not only joking, says Beers. 'When I was in Perth, I used to drink in the police canteen all the time. The blokes always reckoned I should run for parliament and get the job as Minister for Police and Aboriginal Affairs.'

THE BEERS FAMILY MIGRATED to Perth from Holland when Louis was three. 'Dad was a brickie who told tons of stories and jokes, but they'd be lost in the interpretation from Dutch to English.' The task fell to Louis to improve them. As the youngest and short-est of five brothers, he wielded his wit to get even. 'I was telling gags all through primary school. Mimicking Aborigines came later, when I was tied up with football. There were half-a-dozen Aboriginal footballers in the team and we were all good mates. That's when I got my name Cokebottle, because we became blood brothers using a broken coke bottle. They reckoned I was more Aboriginal than they were.'

At twenty, Beers was running a city menswear store when he befriended a regular customer who gave him his break on radio. King Billy Cokebottle appeared daily on air for the next fifteen years. By the late eighties, however, times had changed. Following a rash of complaints from listeners, Aborigines and academics, his station dropped him. King Billy seemed finished. Beers also lost his day job. Embittered by a lack of further opportunities, he moved to Gove, in Arnhem Land, to work as an electrician's assis-tant. 'I did six months there, long enough to get my Aboriginality back,' he deadpans. 'As well as my sense of humour.'

Meanwhile his former Perth boss had moved to a Townsville radio station and coaxed Beers to rejoin him in 1990. King Billy's resurrection in the Deep North led to performances at sports clubs and private parties, further recordings and even a video. 'Suddenly you've got this alter ego making money, so I thought I may as well run with it. There's nothing else out there for me at my age,' says Beers, who is fifty-two.

'If I'd been a one-hit wonder, selling 100 000 overnight, I would have been hit, bang, finished by now. Comedians don't last. But my success has been happening slowly, through word of mouth, which means that my use-by date has been extended.'

To Beers, Melbourne is the last frontier, a bastion of political correctness. So far he has only cracked the city for a private show. He's hoping to make bigger inroads soon. 'Once people have seen the act they know there's no racism or animosity towards Aboriginal people. I'm an Aboriginal mimic. I paint myself up because it's funnier to look at. So what?'

Curiously, Ernie Dingo, the Aboriginal comedian and TV presenter, is a King Billy fan. 'Louis has always been a larrikin,' comments Dingo. He first bumped into Beers in a Perth mall more than twenty-five years ago. 'I heard this fella have a dig at me and when I looked around here was this short white bloke, carrying on. Then I twigged, "You're the bloke from the radio!"' Within days, Dingo began working for Beers in his menswear shop. 'He's been a good mate ever since, and I'm very picky,' says Dingo.

'There is no harm and no malice in what he does,' he insists. 'The only reason people object is because he is white. If he were black, he'd be fine. I tell Aboriginal jokes on stage and people laugh. So does Mary from the Kimberley [an Aboriginal drag act from Broome]. But we don't have a mortgage on being black. This little fat white man, he knows what he's doing when he comes out of his dressing-room. He's just doing it for a laugh.'

THE SHOWROOM OF THE Dalrymple Hotel Motel fills up fast. The $10 cover charge includes a pot of beer from the sponsor. Beers prefers his live recordings to be Sunday lunchtime gigs as the audience is likely to be better behaved and not at the track. Besides, by evening Beers is usually half gone himself.

The woman on the door is petite, softly spoken and slightly bashful. You'd never guess it was Mrs Cokebottle. 'This is me missus,' grunts Beers in character. 'People always askin' me, "How does a blackfella git someone like her?"' Christine Beers manages a tired smile. She works full-time for the city council, handling nuisance complaints about barking dogs and the like. The pair have been married for twenty-nine years and she schedules her holidays so that she can join her husband on tour. She says she likes to work on the door because she gets a lot of feedback after the show. 'Quite a few people wonder if he's really Aboriginal,' she says. 'Last time I had someone say, "I hear he's really ugly underneath." I had to watch myself there.' I linger to pick over the CD stand. Christine Beers recommends the six-pack special. 'It's a very mixed crowd today,' she tells me. 'Anyone from eighteen to eighty is here.'

Actually, the scene seems rather homogenous in the gloomy hall. About two hundred and thirty people are spread around tables bedecked with stubbies and packs of Winfield Red. Two in three are middle-aged men, mostly in rugby jumpers or short-sleeved shirts. About half-a-dozen have brought their Filipina wives along. Meanwhile the warm-up music being played is by Ladysmith Black Mambazo, the ever-so-suave Zulu a cappella group. Someone apparently has a sense of humour.

A blond year-old baby in the corner turns out to be Beers's grandchild, Richard. He's part Aborigine. I'd heard previously that Richard had been a 'twenty-four-hour pregnancy'. That is, Beers's twenty-six-year-old daughter Louise found out she was pregnant the day before the birth. As Beers told it to me: 'Doctors called her in and said, "You're pregnant and we'd better do the ultrasound." She had the baby next morning. Saved a heap on maternity wear.' Louise, who, all things considered, is surprisingly slim, later confirms the tale.

As Beers takes the stage, Hayden Butler, Louise's Aboriginal partner, takes Richard in his arms and points at his sooty grand-dad. Whether the child recognises him or not is unclear. But he seems to think he's funny. As does Butler. And the rest of the crowd is laughing too. Every thirty seconds or so there's a great rollicking guffaw. Brother Morton, as usual, takes the brunt of the material, but there's something crass for everyone: jokes about mothers-in-law, priests, men on Viagra, ugly women, dementia, Slim Dusty, even police. At the end of the show Beers steps outside to sign autographs in the glare of the hotel car park. A young couple approaches him for a joint photo. Beers happily obliges, and helps himself to a handful of backside while he's at it. 'You dirty bugger,' yelps the girl, who is of South Sea Islander descent. But she's laughing. As they walk away, she says to her partner, 'He doesn't look quite as good in the light, does he?'

Staying North

LOOKING BACK, MAYBE THE North hooked me on that very first trip, the one where our mango-orange family wagon made it to the banks of the Daintree but no further. We'd taken the inland route north instead of the coast road. But to a thirteen-year-old birdwatching tragic it was no less impressive. Somewhere beyond the crossing of the Tropic of Capricorn there was an explosion of new species. We'd break by riverbeds so I could scan the fringing gums and paperbarks for parrots. We'd slow down near dams in case I missed a duck. And I'd make Dad stop the wagon whenever I spotted an unfamiliar silhouette on the powerlines. It drove my sisters nuts. But my favourite spots were the small towns where we'd overnight en route. By first light I'd be out prowling the streets of Clermont, Charters Towers and Ravenshoe, pointing my binoculars into people's backyards to see what honeyeaters might be tonguing their bottlebrushes. My travel diary consisted of each day's new species, complete with a description of their terrain, the company they kept and their behaviour at the time.

Our destination was Yorkeys Knob, north of Cairns, where we stayed ten summer days. The Knob, as locals called it, was a bird nerd's wet dream. It was here I saw my first sunbird, the exotic cover-bird of my guide. The motel backed onto a gully of rain-forest scrub (it's gone now), which chimed with friar-birds, orioles, coucals, koels and black butcherbirds. There was also a spooky low booming sound coming from a dark copse of banyan trees. It took me days to discover its source, a magnificent Torres Strait imperial pigeon.

Just weeks later we moved back to Holland, to a grim new town in the grip of winter. This was, in effect, our third migration, and I was a starkly different kid to the gregarious, soccer-mad tearaway that had left Holland five years before. The migration to Australia was strange enough. But the real shock came a couple of years later when we moved from inner Melbourne, where we'd initially settled, to a farm two hours east. At school, half an hour away by bus, cricketers and footballers ruled. Suddenly soccer was for poofs.

One day some kids my age visited the farm on bicycles. They asked Mum if they could go rabbiting. She said sure, and would they take me along? But this wasn't play. Each kid carried a ferret in a small cage. Upon finding a warren, they'd net off every burrow, release a ferret within and wait for the terrified bunnies to erupt into the nets. Then they'd slit their throats and skin them. I wasn't shocked. Just fascinated. It was as if I'd landed among aliens. Of course, I was the alien. It took fully two years to feel at home. I learnt to cart hay, play tennis, follow horseracing. I built a bird hide on the dam. Then we emigrated again.

Uproot a kid enough times and he learns to sprout fewer roots. Friendships become shallower and home bonds more strained. After we moved to Vught, I sought out little company but my own. Before or after school, and on weekends, I'd cycle out to various nature reserves within a twenty-kilometre radius. There were grasslands, fens, dunes, oak groves, pine forests and an arm of the Rhine delta within easy reach. I'd surprise owls before dawn, watch grey harriers court at dusk, and stake out nesting black woodpeckers. I also took up photography.

But my forays weren't only about birds. Wherever I went I would seek out the spot that gave me the most sense of space – the top of a dune, the crown of a tree or the midpoint of a disused railway bridge across a swamp. What I was really after was a haunt where the landscape would stretch to the horizon in every direction without any indication of human impact – no powerlines, no roads, no other humans. This was a big ask in Holland. My favourite hangout became a vast heathland. The horizon was occluded by pine forest behind which were farms, but at least I could pretend.

I wasn't unhappy. At least, it didn't occur to me that I might be. But the whole family had trouble finding their place in Holland. We all desperately missed the farm and the adjacent bush. And so, within three years, we emigrated back. By now I was sixteen. During my final year at the local high school, ornithology didn't seem a serious proposition to anyone I knew. 'What do you want to study insects for?' asked the careers teacher. At the eleventh hour I followed my father into medicine. My mother's response was blunt: 'Medicine? You are more interested in animals than in people.'

I ignored her, as you do. But she was right, of course. I was half a doctor before I came to my senses, fled to Cape Tribulation and eventually gave up jungle tours for journalism. Really, it was a natural progression: I went from watching birds to observing people. Like birdwatching, freelancing gave me the excuse to roam. And, like birdwatching, the subject matter seemed richer, wilder and more colourful in the Deep North.

Now, almost a decade on, friends ask me what I'm still doing here. I ask myself the same question. I've tried to leave a number of times, yet I keep coming back.

In large part, or so I tell myself, it's still about the stories. Sometimes I feel like I'm still peering into people's backyards, setting off dogs, upsetting the inhabitants. I guess I've come to prefer my reality harsh. It's the first thing I miss when I return to Melbourne. People down south invariably ask me how I can live among rednecks. 'What do you do for intellectual stimulation?' they ask. 'Don't you find it limiting? How do you handle the small-mindedness?' But these are the same inner-city types who – sheltered by privilege and spoilt for opportunity – reduce reconciliation to a walk across a bridge or the signing of sorry-books.

Yes, northerners are parochial. A recent newspaper survey found that North Queenslanders' fourth-most admired person *in the world* was a local TV weatherman and breakfast radio jock who wears monstrously loud 'Tropical Friday' shirts all week round. Also finishing ahead of Nelson Mandela were anti-immigration campaigner Pauline Hanson, Australian-made entrepreneur Dick Smith, Bob Katter (of course) and the Mayor of Townsville. (Readers voted Slim Dusty the world's best entertainer, followed by Farnsey, Kylie, Barnesey and, coming in at number five this time, the TV weatherman again.) And yes, many are reactionary. Take Magnetic Island's *Community News*. Its weekly sprays of ill-grammared vitriol at anyone without a 'real job' – greenies, students, academics, bureaucrats – are beyond parody.

But then the North *is* Australia in extremis – geographically, culturally and politically. As a southerner, you can rail against the North as much as the North's editors rant at the South, but what is the point? There's a wild side to living in a place that suffers fools gladly. In recent years North Queenslanders have elected to parliament a shopping centre Santa, a twenty-five-year-old soldier, several cowboys and a pint-sized Italian with a penchant for wearing kilts. It's a cast to match the Village People.

But that's the problem, too, isn't it? The more seriously the North takes itself, the easier it is for an outsider not to. There's a fine line between smiling and sneering, between irreverence and cynicism, if there's a line at all.

After returning from the Torres Strait, I sought out Ray Crooke, the artist, in his unit on the Cairns Esplanade. Crooke has been painting the North for over half a century, having shown a fondness for the small-town landscapes of Chillagoe, Normanton, TI and Laura in particular. His work bears a measured benevolence that stands in stark contrast to the frothy cassowary-on-a-beach pap that passes for art in the boutiques of Port Douglas, Cairns and Airlie Beach.

Hailing from Melbourne, Crooke fell for the tropical landscape while travelling inland up Cape York with an army convoy during World War II. Later he decided the North afforded him more space and time in which to paint, and for many years he and his wife June lived in Yorkeys Knob, then a place of layabout revelry which Crooke likened to Steinbeck's Cannery Row.

Now in their eighties, the Crookes deplore the development that has since encrusted Cairns, including the Knob. 'It is no longer the paintable place it once was,' says Crooke, whose more recent work focuses on Fiji.

Yet the Crookes are staying put. They like where they live, at palm-tree height. Each morning they wake to familiar birdsong and can see Torres Strait pigeons right outside their window. 'It's a connection that I wouldn't like to lose at this stage in our lives,' says Crooke. 'I suppose we call ourselves North Queenslanders. I don't feel at home in Melbourne any more, put it that way.'

Crooke is no longer just an observer. He's become engaged. It's quite a transition, and one I've yet to make. But perhaps my feeling for the North is no longer about the stories, after all. Maybe it's still about the birds. I like it here. Frangipanis poke through the French windows of the enclosed verandah. Geckos stalk moths on the ceiling. I like sleeping beneath a mosquito net, writing in a sarong, raiding the neighbour's mango tree and being able to see the sea from the back porch. In the back of the car I keep a bucket of hand lines. As for sprouting roots, well, I've started a vege garden. The Thai herbs are doing really well.

You've got to stop someplace. Occasionally I think back to that suicidal ride west with Asterix and Obelix, the drunk carpet layers. It could have ended horribly, but whose fault would that have been? I should have got off earlier. The quest for space, for adventure, for isolation – and with it, the run from responsibility, family and, ultimately, self – is all very well, but eventually, if taken to the very end, it may well finish up in a caravan on blocks in Urandangi.

ACKNOWLEDGMENTS

THE MANUSCRIPT BENEFITTED FROM Jordan Baker's warm support, Julia Stiles' deft editing touch, her daughter Indigo's criticism (she vomited on it), Karla Pincott's dog's literary mauling (she ate it), publisher Bernadette Foley's tolerance, my sisters' kindness and my mother's love.

Thanks also to the three photographer friends who have had a distinct influence on my work, and beyond. They are Glenn Campbell, Ian Kenins and, in the early days, Simon O'Dwyer.

I must acknowledge Steve Mullins's fine research on the Jardines and the Torres Strait. I'd also like to thank the Barramundi Brothers, Seaman Dan and the Mills Sisters for the music: whenever my faith in the North's finer points began to flag, a few choice songs soon set me straight. Glenn's compilation of *Mango Country*, the cassette, is worth a listen, though the Slim Dusty tracks are a bit much.

This book is based on a four-month trip in 2002, but includes some earlier forays. Versions of the chapters on Alva Beach, Drinkastubbie Downs, Urandangi, Chillagoe, Cape Keerweer, Oma, Silkwood, Mission Beach, Misty Mountains, Townsville and Willis Island have appeared in *Good Weekend*, the weekend magazine of the *Age* and the *Sydney Morning Herald*, and my gratitude goes out to Fenella Souter's fine team of subeditors.

A FEW
POSTSCRIPTS

Urandangi Ray never did get his car going but Canadian Linda stayed three months regardless. They remain affectionately in touch. Murrandoo Yanner has been jailed. It's a terrible waste of talent, and I hope he's out soon. Mission Beach's cassowaries are down to forty-five in number. So is the population of Greenvale. And Oma is sadly missed.